THE EMOTION AMPLIFIER THESAURUS:

A Writer's Guide to Character Stress and Volatility

SECOND EDITION

**ANGELA ACKERMAN
& BECCA PUGLISI**

THE EMOTION AMPLIFIER THESAURUS: A WRITER'S GUIDE TO CHARAC-
TER STRESS AND VOLATILITY

First edition published in 2014
Second edition published in 2024

ISBN: 978-1-7361523-3-1 (Second Edition)

Visit the authors at their Writers Helping Writers˚ site (http://writershelpingwriters.net/).

Edited by Lisa Poisso and Michael Dunne
Book cover design by JD Smith Design
Book formatting by JD Smith Design

THE WRITERS HELPING WRITERS® DESCRIPTION THESAURUS SERIES

 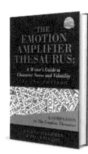   

Over 1.2 Million Copies Sold Worldwide

Available in nine languages, sourced by universities, and recommended by editors and agents all over the world, this best-selling series is a writer's favorite for brainstorming fresh description and powering up storytelling.

The Emotion Thesaurus: A Writer's Guide to Character Expression (Second Edition)

The Positive Trait Thesaurus: A Writer's Guide to Character Attributes

The Negative Trait Thesaurus: A Writer's Guide to Character Flaws

The Urban Setting Thesaurus: A Writer's Guide to City Spaces

The Rural Setting Thesaurus: A Writer's Guide to Personal and Natural Places

The Emotional Wound Thesaurus: A Writer's Guide to Psychological Trauma

The Occupation Thesaurus: A Writer's Guide to Jobs, Vocations, and Careers

The Conflict Thesaurus:
A Writer's Guide to Obstacles, Adversaries, and Inner Struggles (Vol. 1)

The Conflict Thesaurus:
A Writer's Guide to Obstacles, Adversaries, and Inner Struggles (Vol. 2)

TABLE OF CONTENTS

INTRODUCTION TO THE SECOND EDITION OF THE EMOTION AMPLIFIER THESAURUS

Prior to the 2012 release of our flagship book, *The Emotion Thesaurus: A Writer's Guide to Character Expression*, it lived on our blog as a collection of lists that helped writers describe different feelings a character might have. Each week, we would choose an emotion and dive into showing it through body language, thoughts, visceral sensations and the like. Because show-don't-tell is a struggle for many, especially when portraying a character's feelings, this thesaurus became something of a cult favorite. Our blog visitors began asking for specific emotions, and we were only too happy to comply.

But over time, we noticed a pattern with these requests: not all of them were emotions. Some were better classified as a state or condition that could influence what a character felt or steer them to bigger reactions.

Instead of dismissing the suggestions, we leaned into them, examining how these emotional tuning forks could unbalance characters and lead them down a path of poor judgment, bad decisions, and mistakes. We gave them a name—**emotion amplifiers**—and created an e-booklet covering fifteen states (*pain*, *exhaustion*, and *boredom*, to name a few), along with information on how they could be used to nudge characters toward outbursts and missteps.

The popularity of this minicompanion to *The Emotion Thesaurus* told us there might be more amplifiers capable of disrupting a character's control over their feelings. Spoiler alert: there were! In fact, the more we studied them, the more we saw their multifaceted nature and scope, which extended far beyond what we originally imagined amplifiers could do. As well as altering a character's emotional state, amplifiers serve as catalysts for conflict and tension, magnify internal dissonance and psychological distress, and even support story structure.

Now, many years later, we're excited to share this information through an expanded edition of *The Emotion Amplifier Thesaurus*.

Inside this second edition, you'll find fifty-two states and conditions with the power to amplify a character's feelings. You'll learn how to deploy them to create friction and conflict. You'll explore how to showcase the physical, cognitive, and psychological strain they cause. You'll also discover how emotion amplifiers can destabilize a character's equilibrium during important story moments.

Readers relate to and connect with characters in psychological distress because personal vulnerability is part of the human experience. This guide shows you new ways to bring readers in close as you cause trouble for your characters, pushing them onto shaky emotional ground when it most benefits your story.

WHY DO STORIES NEED EMOTION?

Imagine if, in the real world, your experiences were missing an essential ingredient that rendered them unmemorable. You'd hike to a lookout over a pristine glacial lake, yet gazing down at its mirrored surface, you'd feel nothing. Or on a whim, you'd cruise through your old neighborhood past your childhood home, but it would seem unremarkable—no different from any other house. Even on your son's wedding day, his happy tears wouldn't affect you at all.

Envisioning special moments without the emotions associated with them isn't just disturbing, it's terrifying. Emotion is central to who we are. It gives meaning, good and bad, to our experiences and shapes our desires, actions, and values as we move through our world. Emotion helps us evolve and grow and keeps us connected to others even as we navigate our individual paths.

As people, we love new experiences because they make us feel like we're living life to the fullest. But work, family, and community commitments along with other constraints (like physical limitations, financial barriers, and too little time) impair our ability to do everything we want. This is why stories are so appealing and addictive; through them, we can live many lives, encounter untold realities, and walk in the footsteps of others who think, act, and believe differently than we do.

But for a story to work, it needs emotion—and lots of it. Emotion is the bridge that helps readers slip from their reality into a fictional one, because when characters have needs and desires and feel things as people do, readers can relate. Even when a character's goals and challenges are unfamiliar, their emotions offer common ground. Readers know the pain of loss, the devastation of letting someone down, and the sting of betrayal. They recognize the rush of satisfaction that comes from hard work and achievement. So when a beloved character faces situations like these, readers empathize.

Because emotion is central to the human experience, it should be easy to write, yes? Oh, if only. In truth, the more realistically a character is portrayed, the trickier it is to get their feelings onto the page. Authentic characters think and behave like real people—people who lock up their bigger emotions and want to avoid the discomfort of being judged and exposed, as we all do.

Characters who bottle up their feelings create two challenges for writers. First, readers may have trouble connecting with them and what they're going through. It's hard to empathize with a character who's hiding their feelings; without that rapport, sooner or later, readers will close the book and move on. Writers must find ways to convey what characters are really feeling, even when the characters themselves are afraid to embrace those emotions.

The second challenge is that characters who repress their emotions tend to struggle to examine their deeper feelings and do the internal work needed to evolve. Without personal growth, their emotional blocks may continue to hold them back, preventing them from achieving what they want most, be it close relationships, meaningful goals, or self-acceptance. It's no easy task to get a character to examine their own vulnerabilities, but this is what has to happen for their internal journey to unfold.

To create a compelling story, writers must know how to open a character's emotional vault and let the ghosts out. We need to push our characters to face personal truths, even when it hurts, and crack their defenses so they can no longer hide from what they feel.

One effective strategy is to deploy an **emotion amplifier**, a specific state or condition that influences what the character feels by disrupting their equilibrium and reducing their ability to think critically. *Distraction, bereavement,* and *exhaustion* are examples of amplifiers that create friction. Emotionally speaking, they become the wooden blocks that destabilize the entire Jenga tower.

Consider Jake, a character who awakens to hot fingers of *illness* creeping through his body. On the cusp of a long-overdue promotion, he doesn't dare call in sick, so he showers and heads to work. At the warehouse, he climbs into a forklift and begins his day of moving pallets and loading trucks in the pickup bay. Two guys on his crew haven't shown up, making the shift even rougher. Everything requires more effort. Jake's head buzzes. Noises bug him. He feels like he's moving through molasses, but he's got to work at double speed. As he rushes back and forth across the floor, he's growing lightheaded. Where the hell is his foreman, who promised to pitch in?

Can you feel the strain Jake is under and how close his emotions are to the surface? How long until the weight of sickness causes him to snap at a coworker, make a rash decision, or become so flustered he injures someone?

Amplifiers are an added condition or situational burden that must be coped with on top of everything else. They're a challenge, conflict, and emotional destabilizer rolled into one, capable of causing physical, cognitive, and psychological discomfort. The presence of an amplifier makes it harder for a character to think things through and stay in control of their emotions. And if characters become more volatile or lower their guard because they're distracted, they're more likely to miss something important and make a mistake.

Let's say Jake's dulled reflexes cause him to drop a pallet of product, ruining the inventory and creating a safety hazard. He's reprimanded by his foreman, who never did come to help but has plenty of criticism to hand out. Hot with fever and frustration, Jake goes off about how he's always the one who shows up, even when he's sick, but never gets any appreciation. One outburst and a few ill-advised words later, Jake's hopes for a promotion lie in ruins among the crushed cargo.

Although amplifiers can wreak havoc by disrupting the status quo, that doesn't make them inherently negative.

This is true for Yara, single and forty, who has spent her life being perfect—the perfect daughter who chose the major her parents wanted, endured law school, and became a top trial lawyer like her dad. She's the considerate neighbor who keeps her lawn mowed and retrieves her garbage bin as soon as the truck goes by. At her firm, she's the partner willing to take the difficult cases. She's the aunt who gets her nephew exactly what he wants for his birthday. And Yara's the one who shuttles her elderly parents to appointments because her siblings always have other things to do.

Sounds exhausting, doesn't it? Being all things to everyone, never disappointing. In fact, some days Yara can barely force herself out of bed into another day of exceeding expectations. But she hides her exhaustion well because she's learned that not being perfect means being less loved.

Then one day, smiling her way through a routine follow-up with her doctor, Yara gets the shock of her life: She's pregnant.

She sits there, breathless, hands clasped on her knees. She was careful. Used protection. It was a one-time thing, a rare invite home after that charity dinner! Her chest squeezes, and her lower lip starts to tremble. Not only is her perfect, boxed-in life falling apart, but the wall holding back her emotions is also crumbling. The doctor struggles to handle this new Yara, who is bent over and spilling out questions between sobs.

Pregnancy itself is not negative. But for Yara, it will drastically disrupt her life, bringing increased exhaustion, morning sickness, and more. How will she fare, considering the responsibilities already on her plate? Will she freak out at work and embarrass a senior partner in front of a client? How long until her resentment at always sacrificing for Mom and Dad becomes full-on rage toward her siblings, who never share the load?

Emotion amplifiers, both large and small, are ideal for pushing a character over the edge—because sometimes, that's exactly what writers need to happen. Smart, savvy characters who always make the right choices aren't very interesting. But characters who blunder, lose control, or forget their filter? Now we're talking! We relate to those characters because we all own the *I overreacted* T-shirt.

These challenges can also generate a much-needed change of perspective for the character. Yara's pregnancy could be the catalyst that nudges her into rejecting unreasonable expectations and, through her own child, discovering unconditional love.

EMOTION AMPLIFIERS AND INTERNAL DISSONANCE

Amplifiers are useful for introducing friction and making a character more reactive, which puts their true feelings on display. But they have an additional superpower: shining a light on contradictions within a character that create significant mental distress.

So, what are internal contradictions? The best way to explain is by posing a question: Have you ever experienced internal tension from an unsettling situation, like a neighbor who keeps his dog chained up day after day? Or maybe you're doing something you don't feel one hundred percent good about, like pulling into McDonald's when you've been trying to make better choices and eat healthier.

This tension is called **cognitive dissonance**, the psychological discomfort caused by contradicting thoughts, perceptions, values, or beliefs, and it's quite common. It may present as a small niggle in your everyday decision-making or a haunting problem that keeps you up at night.

When dissonance bubbles to the surface, people experience anything from confusion and indecision to worry, guilt, regret, or shame. For example, maybe you've talked yourself into getting McDonald's because it's been a hellish week, but you still feel guilty as you order. When the food arrives, you indulge—it's so good! But your Big Mac euphoria lasts only as long as the burger does, and now you're regretting the decision to cave to your craving. Worse, you're mentally beating yourself up for not having the willpower to resist. Cognitive dissonance is powering this discord, because you (a) like eating Big Macs but (b) want to lose weight and be healthy.

What triggered this inner tug of war? *Stress.* Had your work week been a breeze, this amplifier would not have intensified your longing for a delicious fast-food reward and overpowered your commitment to healthier eating.

Another form of internal contradiction is **emotional dissonance**, where you find yourself pretending to feel an emotion that doesn't align with what you're experiencing—for instance, faking enthusiasm about your boss's terrible marketing strategy. You're a team player, and you know from experience that he won't listen to contrary opinions, so you put on your *rah-rah* face like everyone else. In this case, the dissonance is mild because you've weathered his bad ideas before and you aren't invested enough to state how you really feel.

But emotional dissonance isn't always minor. Sometimes the emotion you'd have to fake is so far from what you feel that it clashes with your values or personal identity. Acting in alignment with an untrue emotion can mean sacrificing your belief system and going against who you are.

Let's say your boss's marketing strategy is driven by a closely guarded secret: the company needs to dump a supply of expired baby formula that's been repackaged with fresh dates. The sales manager explains that the product is fine and this happens all the time, so just keep quiet and get out there and sell, sell, sell.

But can you, knowing the formula could be contaminated? Will you be able to feign confidence as you hit up those neonatal units and pharmacies to convince people to buy your product? Or is this something you can't do because it crosses a line and violates your core values, regardless of how badly you need the bonus for meeting your sales quota?

Here, the divide between your true feelings (contempt and shock) and the emotion you'd need to fake (confidence) is much wider. Whichever you express reveals your identity: Are you the sort of person who does what's right or what makes money?

Everyone protects their self-perceptions—things they believe to be true about themselves. Characters are no different. Emotional dissonance raises the stakes by challenging their view of themselves, creating confusion, uncertainty, or regret.

Ongoing emotional dissonance that threatens someone's identity can do a lot of damage. A character enduring domestic abuse but who pretends to others that everything's fine risks eroding her own self-worth. A protagonist repressing who he is because he feels unsafe may become disconnected from his authentic self. The longer identity-focused tension persists, the more harm it does. If this struggle is central to your character's arc, be sure to explore how emotional dissonance is powering it.

Thoughts and feelings often intertwine, so a character's internal dissonance may include both cognitive and emotional forms, especially when they're making decisions, creating a prickly knot to untie . . . if they can.

FORCING CHARACTERS TO DEAL WITH THEIR DISSONANCE

Internal conflict is fed by cognitive or emotional dissonance. A character who wrestles with incompatible wants and goals or discovers information that challenges their views of the world, themselves, or others will experience psychological distress. Try as they might to ignore or suppress it, this distress typically grows to the point that they feel compelled to resolve it.

But inner conflict is called conflict for a reason: the character is pulled in different directions and doesn't know what to do. When the right or best decision means a harder road, the choice becomes even more difficult.

Introducing an amplifier at an emotional crossroads applies the additional strain needed to force a character to deal with their discomfort rather than hide from it.

Imagine Silva, who is shocked to learn that her best friend Claire is cheating on her husband, Rick. Claire begs Silva to keep the information secret, and normally, she wouldn't share something told in confidence. But this? Staying silent doesn't sit right. Silva has strong beliefs about fidelity and views an affair as the worst type of betrayal. She hates the whole situation and wishes she could go back in time to when she was blissfully ignorant. Instead, she has an agonizing decision to make—say nothing out of loyalty to Claire or stay true to her moral code and tell Rick.

Dissonance caused by a clash of core beliefs and high stakes is hard to resolve. After all, if Silva tells Rick, she's nuking her friendship with Claire. But if she says nothing, she'll struggle to be around her friend, not to mention look herself in the mirror, because keeping the secret makes her feel complicit. To figure out what to do, she applies **emotional reasoning**, weighing and measuring the various factors in the hope of gaining clarity about her path forward.

For example, it might be easier for Silva to keep this information to herself if Claire's husband isn't a nice guy—say, if he's verbally abusive or controlling. Silva might resolve her dissonance by telling Claire that his behavior is further proof it's time to leave the marriage.

But what if Rick is a good guy, maybe even someone Silva considers a friend? In this case, keeping the secret means protecting one person by betraying the other. Another factor is whether the two have children. What if revealing the truth triggers a divorce and turns the family inside out?

As she grapples with what to do, Silva considers other factors, like how good a friend Claire is. She tries to think back to a time when she kept the truth from someone, or if she's ever felt as Claire does (needing love in a way her partner doesn't provide). And if Silva herself has ever experienced betrayal, especially the sort that would put her in Rick's shoes, this too plays into her reasoning.

As Silva weighs each factor on her mental scale, she may come to any number of conclusions.

1. She's lost respect for Claire and their friendship might not survive, but despite believing the affair is wrong, she agrees not to tell Rick. Silence comes at the cost of her integrity, but she refuses to be responsible for unraveling their family.

2. Her morals won't let her keep Rick in the dark, and she's upset Claire has put her in this situation. She decides Claire should bear the brunt of the emotional discomfort and delivers an ultimatum: *Either you tell Rick, or I will.*

3. She doesn't want to keep this secret, but she also doesn't feel right delivering news that could break a family apart. If she continues to run into Rick, she'll have to say something, so she removes herself from her friends' lives.

Difficult decisions usually carry a price tag—in this case, pain for either Silva or her friends. She doesn't want to hurt anyone, but there's no way to avoid it. And one way or the other, she's being forced to sacrifice friendship, integrity, or both.

So what emotion amplifier created dissonance for Silva? It was the *pressure* of being asked to keep Claire's secret. That pressure made Silva deeply uncomfortable, pushing her to sort through her conflicted feelings and values for a solution to end her discomfort.

However, amplifiers are a double-edged sword. As they squeeze a character, forcing them to address their situation and the dissonance it's caused, amplifiers simultaneously charge the character's emotions, making rational thought a challenge. This complicates the weighing-and-measuring process. As the strain increases, the character may start looking for an easy way out. A reflexive choice—cutting corners, compromising, surrendering the decision-making duty to someone else—creates a bigger mess down the road that must eventually be dealt with.

But hey, conflict is good for the story, right?

The truth is, there's no easy fix for problems that create dissonance. That's what makes internal conflict so agonizing. Even if a character takes their time and works through their situation carefully, they may still end up regretting or second-guessing their choice. But through the process itself, they'll come to understand themselves better, and this is necessary for growth. Their struggle also invites readers to a private viewing of their inner struggle and vulnerability, strengthening the reader-character bond and encouraging engagement, because readers empathize with the pain of having to make hard decisions.

For help figuring out your character's personal weigh-and-measure process and how cognitive dissonance will impact their decision-making, see **Appendices B** and **C**.

THE UPSIDE TO EMOTIONAL STRESS

I t might seem evil to intentionally cause internal discomfort for our characters, but there's a good reason to do it—a lot of good reasons, actually—and they're all related to character development.

FACILITATING SELF-AWARENESS

Most of us find it difficult to look within ourselves at our areas of struggle, and characters are no different. They may be in denial about many things, including how fear is holding them back—the fear of disappointing others, of stepping out of their comfort zone, or letting go of the past to become who they were always meant to be. When we force characters to endure emotional stress, they have no choice but to examine themselves and the inconsistencies they live with. It also gives them a chance to set aside false beliefs and discover their own strength.

Let's imagine your story has a character with self-esteem issues, either because they lack self-belief or others doubt them. Day-to-day, they take a back seat to other people and avoid situations that would call attention to their perceived weaknesses. But when something meaningful is on the line, an amplifier like *competition* or *scrutiny* can produce additional stress and help build resiliency, allowing them to see what they're capable of. And down the road, if they face a situation that normally would have made them afraid to act, their newfound confidence can give them the courage to step up. This type of growth becomes possible because of the emotional stress they endured.

ENCOURAGING SELF-ADVOCACY

Another potential positive of emotional stress is when it pushes an overloaded character to advocate for themselves. Consider a teacher who oversees an after-school program for teens that provides a safe space for them to come together and socialize. She started the group with a handful of kids, but it quickly grew, and with it, the work of organizing activities, providing snacks, and managing a range of personalities. The school's administration is quick to promote the program and brag about it in the media, but when funding or volunteers are requested . . . crickets. Because this teacher loves her kids and she knows how much the program is needed, she soldiers on.

But if we add an amplifier such as *burnout* in the classroom, an emerging *mental health condition*, or *chronic pain* from an injury, the teacher could reach a point where she must find her voice and demand help. Emotional stress often has to reach a critical level before characters will extricate themselves from an unsustainable situation and stand up for themselves.

UNDERSCORING THE NEED FOR CAUTION

Amplifiers sometimes act as false flags, lowering a character's guard and lulling them into thinking they're safe and everything is fine. When a character experiences *attraction* or *arousal*, for instance, their emotions are activated as they focus on the other person, engaging in playful conversations, becoming more intimate, and pursuing pleasurable sensations. But as their attention is diverted, they may fail to notice an enemy closing in or an ally being compromised. During a private moment with their partner, they might let slip a weakness or vulnerability, something that can be used against them.

The repercussions of being caught up in the moment generate emotional stress one of two ways, producing complications the character must address or alerting them to a close call they've narrowly escaped. Regardless, the experience teaches them to be more aware and may help them avoid disaster later in the story.

PROMPTING CHARACTERS TO HONE THEIR SKILLS

Emotional stress from a challenge or problem can force a character to shake the rust off old skills or, out of necessity, learn new ones. Consider *mortal peril*, when life hangs in the balance. In this situation, the need to act and save themselves may cause a character to snap back into who they were in their combat days—a lethal killer. Or imagine an urban youth who is the sole survivor of a plane crash in the wilderness. To overcome *hunger*, *thirst*, and *danger*, they'll have to develop survival skills on the go.

In circumstances like these, the emotional stress arising from an amplifier drives characters to take the steps required to successfully navigate their situation.

INDICATING A NEED TO SEEK HELP

Emotional stress often helps a character recognize when they've lost control. For example, the psychological strain of an extreme amplifier like *possession* could understandably cause a character to break. They might become hysterical or disassociate, shutting down completely. These acute responses demonstrate the presence of a true crisis, and when the character comes back to themselves, they'll realize the situation is beyond their control and seek help.

While high emotional stress can feel unbearable, the body's automatic response comes with a safety feature: it stimulates the part of the brain that feels empathy. This means that characters undergoing intense strain are more likely to feel a kinship with others who are suffering. Internal stress, especially when it's shared, brings people together in a way that external pressures do not. They commiserate, pool information, and become more open to offering and receiving help. This is why, when the chips are down, characters who don't normally see eye to eye often come together.

USING AMPLIFIERS TO REVEAL PERSONAL GROWTH

Although amplifiers activate emotions, increasing the chance of a bigger response from the character, they don't always result in missteps or mishaps. Instead, over the course of a story, they could show how the character is growing.

Amir is a recent university graduate with great job prospects. Three companies have offered him positions that would kick-start his career in biometrics—exciting but nerve-racking, because it's such a big decision. It doesn't help that one of his classmates is a few weeks into her first job and already regrets her choice.

With each passing day, Amir grows more conflicted, unable to choose. He has trouble sleeping, and his temper flares at the smallest thing. His girlfriend, tired of getting her head bitten off, has had enough and calls it quits. Then, after weeks of waffling, the most promising offer is rescinded, leaving Amir with the two least favorable options.

Fast forward six months and Amir is facing *indecision* again—this time, regarding his living situation. A big rent increase is coming, so he must choose to remain in a cramped, expensive apartment near his friends or relocate to a more affordable place closer to work. The hold on the new apartment expires in a few days; as the deadline looms, his old insecurities and panic rise.

Once more, everything seems to set Amir off. He becomes aware of how often he's apologizing for being a jerk, and he remembers what that cost him last time. His decision paralysis is familiar, too; it cheated him out of a great job opportunity before, and he doesn't want that to happen again. He realizes he must change the way he responds to indecision, so he sits down and creates a list of pros and cons for moving. An obvious choice emerges, and he informs his current landlord that he'll be gone at the end of the month.

Hitting Amir with the same amplifier—indecision, in this case—is a way to showcase his growth. The first time around, he flounders and flails. But the second time, armed with hindsight and a new sense of self-awareness, he rises to the occasion.

Personal growth is especially important for characters traversing a change arc, and it doesn't happen all at once. The path to internal examination and maturity is lined with many milestones indicating progress. Let's look at a few of the incremental benchmarks you can build into your character's journey.

Recognizing Landmines: In the past, the character failed to spot danger until it was too late, and they suffered terribly. The upside of this experience is that they've learned to be attentive and prepare more thoroughly. If something happens now, they can react from a place of strength, better positioned to save themselves from preventable fallout.

Setting Boundaries: The character sees how their inability to say no in the past resulted in *stress*, *exhaustion*, *pressure*, or even *danger*. Setting reasonable boundaries now to protect themselves and minimize the effects of new amplifiers is a sign that they're moving in the right direction.

Asking for Help: Some trials are too difficult to navigate solo, a lesson that a stubborn, independent, or untrusting character may need to learn the hard way. Once they do, however, the desire to avoid needless suffering teaches them to better recognize situations where they need help, and by asking for it, they demonstrate maturity.

Choosing Positivity: If a character tends to be negative, show growth by shifting their mindset. This could mean they focus on strengths instead of weaknesses, engage in positive self-talk, see the good side of trials and troubles, or practice gratitude. Transformation typically begins in the mind, so even a small change like finding the silver lining in a single bad situation shows readers that change is underway.

Regulating Emotions: Self-control is a major aspect of emotional maturity. Things are simple when life is peachy but become harder when an amplifier like *pressure*, *illness*, or *pain* is in play. Recalling the problems that were caused by a past loss of emotional control may encourage the character to restrain themselves this time around.

Using Self-Distracting Techniques: Unpleasant circumstances aren't always avoidable. Sometimes characters simply must get through them. Self-distraction strategies like entertaining themselves when they're *bored*, focusing on something else when they're *hungry*, or noticing the good when they're *stuck* in a crappy situation are all healthy responses. Using these techniques after failing to do so in the past shows readers how far they've come.

Not Giving Up: A character's transformation journey isn't linear; there will be ups and downs. In the beginning, when facing difficulty, they often revert to their previous dysfunctional ways, which doesn't work—but hey, there's comfort in familiarity. As they mature and grow, returning to old habits stops being their go-to response, and instead of giving up, they try again or try something new.

Emotion amplifiers are perfect for testing a character's growth because their response highlights their progress (or lack thereof). But when in their journey should growth markers occur?

Luckily, that's already been mapped out; we simply need to take a closer look at story structure to see where these important moments should fall.

USING AMPLIFIERS TO SUPPORT STORY STRUCTURE

Earlier, we talked about how important emotion is to the success of a story. But there's another element that must be in place for readers to get the most out of their emotional ride with your character: structure.

If you've researched this subject, you know there are many story models out there, and they're all slightly different. The most popular forms tend to follow the three-act structure, which resonates with many readers, regardless of genre or format.

> **Act 1** sets things up for readers by establishing the protagonist, their story goal, the setting, and all the basics.

> **Act 2** builds on that information, introducing escalating conflicts (both internal and external) that block the character from their objective.

> **Act 3** resolves the story conflict in a showdown that determines whether the protagonist succeeds or fails at achieving their goal.

Within this simple framework, certain events need to happen not only to progress the plot, but also to encourage the character to become more self-aware, make positive internal progress, overcome setbacks, and so on. This journey is essential if your character is to progress realistically from *Once upon a time* to *The End*. It's not an easy path, though, and sometimes characters balk; they'd rather stay where it's comfortable and safe, thank you very much. The status quo may be stagnant or even unhealthy, but it's what they know.

But a stalled character means a stalled story—which is death for reader engagement. At times like these, your protagonist needs a nudge (or a full-fledged shove) to reach the next important story event.

This is where amplifiers come in.

To illustrate how emotion amplifiers get a character moving while also supporting story structure, let's examine our favorite model, Michael Hauge's Six-Stage Plot Structure, which is beautifully explained in his book *Writing Screenplays that Sell*. This model divides a story into three acts and shows the key points in each. In the right order and at the right places, these points move the character through the story in a logical fashion without sacrificing pace.

SIX-STAGE PLOT STRUCTURE MODEL

0%	10%	25%	50%	75%	90-99%	100%

Stage I	Stage II	Stage III	Stage IV	Stage V	Stage VI
SETUP Fully in identity	**NEW SITUATION** Glimpses essense	**PROGRESS** Vacillates between identity and essence	**COMPLICATIONS & HIGHER STAKES** Moves steadily into essence	**FINAL PUSH** Retreats to identity then fully essence	**AFTERMATH** Transformed existence

OPPORTUNITY Turning Point #1	**CHANGE OF PLANS** Turning Point #2	**POINT OF NO RETURN** Turning Point #3	**MAJOR SETBACK** Turning Point #4	**CLIMAX** Turning Point #5

ACT I	ACT II	ACT III

Setup: The protagonist is living in their everyday world, but they're emotionally stuck or dissatisfied in some way.

Opportunity (Turning Point 1): Called the catalyst in other models, this point consists of a challenge, crisis, or opportunity that pushes the protagonist into pursuing a certain story goal. That decision sets them on a journey that sweeps them out of their ordinary world and into a new one.

New Situation: The protagonist is adjusting to their new world, figuring out the rules and their role while dealing with obstacles that crop up. At this point, the character is largely unaware of their own faults and how they contribute to a lack of fulfillment.

Change of Plans (Turning Point 2): Something happens that creates an awakening for the protagonist, clarifying what they need to do to achieve their goal. They begin moving purpose-fully in that direction.

Progress: Fully conscious of their goal and their new plan, the protagonist takes steps toward success by gaining knowledge, honing skills, or gathering resources and allies. Although they may be growing in self-awareness, they're not yet able to fully comprehend the depth of internal change that needs to occur.

Point of No Return (Turning Point 3): The protagonist's situation becomes more difficult than ever as a death or significant loss pushes their goal seemingly out of reach. Forced to face what's holding them back (their flaws, fears, lies they've embraced, and so on), they commit to changing their dysfunctional methods and evolving in the pursuit of their goal.

Complications and Higher Stakes: Though dedicated to personal change and healthier methods, the protagonist is assailed by escalating conflicts and increased stakes that make it more important than ever to reach their objective.

Major Setback (Turning Point 4): The protagonist experiences a devastating setback or failure that makes them doubt everything. Their plan forward will no longer work, and all seems lost.

Finally rejecting any beliefs, biases, or doubts that were holding them back, they adapt their plan.

Final Push: The protagonist pushes forward with everything they've got, proving through their choices and actions that they've fully embraced the internal changes necessary to succeed.

Climax (Turning Point 5): This is the final challenge, the big showdown between the protagonist and the force(s) opposing them, that definitively establishes the victor in the story.

Aftermath: Readers glimpse the protagonist's life in the aftermath of the climax. If they've succeeded in achieving their goal, they're evolved and emotionally fulfilled; if they've failed, they're back to where they started (or worse).

It's clear from this progression how each point leads logically into the next. This structure creates a balanced story with a complete beginning, middle, and end.

AMPLIFIERS IN STORY STRUCTURE

The flow of a story seems logical when seen through the lens of plot structure, but guess who really dictates this fun little road trip? Your characters—who don't always cooperate.

Characters tend to resist change, especially the internal kind. An emotion amplifier nudges them from one point to the next with opportunities for decisions that add volatility, increase vulnerability, and make the situation worse. As the story progresses, particularly in the second half, amplifiers can also begin revealing growth, as the characters adapt to new challenges and make better choices.

Let's see how amplifiers have been used to this effect in some popular movies and books.

Inebriation: In *Sweet Home Alabama*, Melanie, who has spent years creating a new life for herself in Manhattan, returns to her hometown to get a divorce, which her estranged husband is reluctant to grant. Frustrated by her lack of success, she gets drunk during the **Progress** stage, turns nasty, and outs her best friend. This leads directly to the **Point of No Return**, when she awakens in a hungover stupor and realizes that her horrible behavior has caused her husband to finally sign the divorce papers. She should be excited to be able to put her past behind her and fully recreate herself, but she realizes she's been pursuing the wrong goal all along.

Mental Health Condition: In *As Good as It Gets*, Melvin is isolated and miserable due to his untreated obsessive-compulsive disorder. In the **Progress** stage, he learns that his preferred waitress Carol isn't working at his usual diner anymore because she must care for her chronically ill son. His desperate desire to regain his comfortable routine (and pursue Carol romantically) prompts him to hire a doctor and pay for her son's medical treatment. It's an extreme and strange thing to do, and Carol questions his motives. She lets him know that while she's grateful, she's not grateful enough to sleep with him. While this wasn't the motivation for his actions, he realizes that in his current state, he'll never find love. This is his **Point of No Return.**

Instability: The Nostromo vessel is floating in outer space, light years away from help, when an alien makes its way onboard (*Alien*). In the **Complications and Higher Stakes** phase of this classic movie, as crew members are picked off one by one, the captain is forced to pursue the alien into the air ducts to try to kill it. He fails, leaving protagonist Ripley as the senior officer with an enhanced security level that enables her to discover the Nostromo's true mission, which has rendered her and her crew expendable (**Major Setback**).

Hunger: In Cormac McCarthy's *The Road*, a father and son travel to the coast in a hard, post-apocalyptic world. During the **Progress** stage of the story, the father's hunger drives him to enter a building he otherwise would have avoided. What they find there sends them running for their lives, questioning humanity's right to survive. They stick to the woods, wet, cold, and hungrier than ever. A quote explains the father's mindset at this point: "He was beginning to think that death was finally upon them." Their foray into the house of horrors, driven by extreme hunger, has propelled them to their **Point of No Return**.

Each of these examples uses an amplifier to drive the character from one turning point to the next, a technique that could work just as effectively for you. Once you've created a basic outline for your project, explore amplifiers that could be placed strategically to propel the character into the various stages of their story.

Sometimes you might even find that a single amplifier ties into the entire story, enabling you to use it repeatedly as a driver.

Isolation is a recurring theme for Lucy Moderatz in the movie *While You Were Sleeping*. The **Setup** reveals that her parents have died, and she has no other surviving family. She lives alone with her cat and works in a lonely toll booth in Chicago. She's stuck there on Christmas Day when her longtime crush Peter (who she's never actually met) is mugged, after which she saves his life. When she's introduced to his family at the hospital (with Peter in a coma) someone mistakes her for his fiancée (**Opportunity**), and Lucy doesn't correct them.

In the **New Situation**, Peter's family invites her to a belated Christmas celebration, and she initially declines. But back at home with a microwave dinner and only her cat for company, she changes her mind, a decision that leads directly to the **Change of Plans**.

Dinner with the family introduces Lucy to Peter's brother Jack. During the **Complications** stage, she and Jack spend time together and she develops feelings for him, which is relatively simple until Peter wakes up from his coma. . .

There's much more, but this is enough to show that isolation is Lucy's motivator. The loneliness borne from her isolation is the primary driver influencing her decisions and pushing the story from one point to the next.

In this way, the theme can deliver the perfect amplifier for repeatedly informing a character's choices and actions. If you know the theme for your story, consider options that reinforce it while also steering the plot events. Finding a perfect recurring amplifier for a story is rare, however, so this shouldn't be forced.

Genre can also provide ideas for a repeat amplifier. A bleak post-apocalyptic story like *The Road* is a natural setting for *hunger, cold*, and *exhaustion*. Likewise, *attraction* and *arousal* are common amplifiers in romance plots and subplots. Thrillers and action stories often include multiple instances of *danger, stress*, and *mortal peril*.

Another way to identify suitable amplifiers is to scan the entry portion of this thesaurus for ideas. Doing this ahead of time while planning can save a lot of frustration during the revision stage.

USING AMPLIFIERS TO CREATE DRAMATIC TENSION

Emotion and tension often go hand in hand. If character emotion is low, story tension is also probably waning. On the flip side, when emotion is high and it's written effectively, tension is likely on the rise.

Dramatic tension is the feeling of anticipation surrounding what happens next. It's the golden ticket for reader interest, because when a character is in trouble and the outlook is grim, readers worry. This worry translates into empathy and a need to read on to see if the character will be okay. For this reason, it's important to keep the tension in each scene at an engaging level.

Consider the first book in *The Hunger Games* trilogy by Suzanne Collins. Tension is high throughout the story because of the primal stakes: death is constantly on the line. But Collins ramps it up even more by adding stressors in the form of amplifiers. At the start of the games, she removes fresh water from the arena, threatening *dehydration* and adding another life-threatening factor to worry about. She introduces the tracker jackers and their *psychosis*-inducing stings, increasing reader suspense and fear for Katniss's safety while she's incapacitated. After Rue's death, Katniss slips into a period of *bereavement* that's almost as worrying to readers as her delusions, because anything could happen to her in such a vulnerable state.

Like a sadistic head gamemaker, Collins never lets the heroine off the hook. She continues to throw Katniss new and more alarming problems that make it more difficult to survive an already impossible situation. And the agony pays off. With each new amplifier, two important things are accomplished for the character and the reader.

First, Katniss experiences elevated stress. We've already covered the impact of emotional stress on a character, and this example clearly demonstrates how stress makes it difficult for Katniss to think clearly and make the best decisions. Poor choices lead to bigger problems, which causes more stress . . . It's a continuing cycle that keeps readers riveted as the tension rises from page to page.

Second, these amplifiers heighten Katniss's emotions to the point that they can't be ignored. With each new stressor, she grows more afraid, paranoid, angry, or depressed. As readers, we feel those emotions right along with her. We're drawn into her story and root for her in a way that guarantees we'll keep reading to the very end.

WHEN DOES A STORY NEED MORE TENSION?

Because tension is such a crucial element, you want to make sure you've got enough of it. How can you tell? There are a few things you can do in the planning and revision stages to check your story's tension level and see if it needs a little extra juice.

Map It Out: Once you've plotted the structure for your story, you may be able to see where tension is lacking. For each scene in your story map, ask yourself two questions:

1. **What is the character after?** Protagonists need a goal in every scene, a stepping stone toward the main story objective. Can you identify that scene-level goal, and does it

meet this criterion? If it doesn't, readers will subconsciously recognize that the story is wandering, and the tension will atrophy. In this case, you may need some surgery to cut the scene and make the whole story stronger. If the scene goal is otherwise sound, you might be able to salvage it by revising with the character's goal in mind. Gaining clarity yourself on the scene-level objective often revitalizes a lackluster scene, adding the zip that was missing.

2. **What's standing in the way of the character getting what they want?** Once you've defined the scene goal, make sure someone or something is blocking the protagonist from achieving it. Because if the character gets what they want without opposition, where's the fun (or tension) in that? Too many pages without conflict result in a story that drags (and readers who start daydreaming about what's in the fridge). Keep success uncertain by adding appropriate conflict, which increases dramatic tension and gets readers wondering how things will turn out.

Include Meaningful Stakes: Unfortunately, conflict alone doesn't always generate tension, and conflict without tension doesn't engage readers. To unsettle readers and get them worrying about the character's future, something significant must be at stake—a cost incurred if the protagonist fails to navigate the situation successfully. Each conflict in a scene needs a serious *or else* attached to it.

For stakes that effectively motivate the character, make sure they fall into one of the following categories:

Personal stakes negatively and directly affect the character (and possibly someone they care about) if they fail.

Far-reaching stakes result in a loss or consequence for many people.

Moral stakes threaten the character's foundational ideals and beliefs.

Primal stakes (also called death stakes) involve the potential loss of something major, such as innocence, a relationship, a career, dream, idea, belief, reputation, or a physical life.

Stakes, even far-reaching ones, should touch characters on some personal level. This is why a blend is often a good idea. Personalizing the stakes gives the protagonist skin in the game by endangering something or someone important to them. When readers see how high the stakes are for a character they care about, the compulsion to read on becomes even stronger.

If you're unable to identify what's at stake in a given scene or you haven't conveyed it adequately to readers, the dramatic tension will likely flatline, leaving them dissatisfied.

USING AMPLIFIERS TO ENHANCE TENSION
When you've examined the scene goal and stakes but tension is still flagging, it could be time to add an amplifier. Like salt in a stew, emotion amplifiers enhance the ingredients that are already there, improving the overall blend.

These examples show how amplifiers add intensity to a scene.

Using Amplifiers to Introduce Temptation

Mandy's a smart kid, but in her financial situation, the only way she's getting into college is with a sports scholarship. Rumors are swirling about scouts coming to the next game, so she needs to outdo herself on the field.

Unfortunately, daily practices, community service hours, and homework make it hard for her to prepare, and her stupid-busy schedule has left her exhausted. She can't possibly do her best in this game. But then she remembers that guy in AP Chemistry, the one who sells Adderall to kids looking for a pick-me-up. Mandy has never stooped to that level—she doesn't use drugs—but she's so tired and has worked so hard. Maybe a little boost would be okay, just this once . . .

Here, the temptation to use a stimulant to overcome *exhaustion* tips the balance of Mandy's internal weighing-and-measuring process as her desire for short-term relief threatens to override her morals. Readers have much more to worry about now than whether Mandy will perform well at the game; we all know the danger of *just this once*. If she gives in, this moment could morph into a secret she'll have to hide or an addiction that could put all her goals in jeopardy.

Using Amplifiers to Force Difficult Decisions

Since his wife's death, Juan has raised their three young kids by himself in a rural, impoverished village. Relocating to a better area with more opportunities would require an arduous trek through the jungle, and for that, they'd need to be strong and healthy, a challenge considering the lack of resources and clean water.

Then one day, food supplies to the village are cut off. As hunger sets in, Juan is faced with an impossible decision: leave now, knowing not all his children will survive the trip, or stay and hope against hope that things turn around.

In this heartbreaking scenario, things start out bad enough as Juan struggles to manage his family's unstable circumstances on his own. The addition of *hunger* not only exacerbates the situation, but it also creates a horrible Sophie's choice dilemma. It's a no-win scenario, because whatever he chooses, pain and regret will follow.

Using Amplifiers to Reveal Insecurities or Secrets

Zuri has finally met the perfect guy, one she could see herself marrying. Meeting his family is the next logical step, but they're all brainiacs with unpronounceable degrees and prestigious careers—and Zuri teaches preschool. What will they possibly talk about, proper nose-wiping techniques? Who's better, Dr. Seuss or Eric Carle?

She shakes away her doubts and smiles at Dean as they walk up his parents' front steps. It's going to be fine. She's going to be fine.

But when they're welcomed inside, she's hit with a wall of noise—loud music, dozens of people talking and laughing in a jarring cacophony, a TV blaring in the next room. Dean says something, but she misses it, her mind full of broken glass. How will she be able to carry on any sort of conversation in all this?

She makes her way across the room, edging toward the walls and trying to act cool.

Her hand in Dean's is sticky and she's feeling lightheaded. So far, she's been able to hide her noise sensitivity from him, but she had no idea his academic family were such party animals. She grabs a drink but can't swallow past the panic clawing its way up her throat. Everything is definitely not fine.

Poor Zuri. She's so close to having everything she wants. But to get there, she'll have to perform under an overwhelming state of *sensory overload* while maintaining her well-guarded secret.

Using Amplifiers to Increase Vulnerability

The number seven bus squeals to a stop and the doors wheeze open. Ed gingerly exits, favoring his bad hip. Eager to get home, he shuffles along a cracked sidewalk bordering a row of buildings with torn awnings and graffiti-scrawled walls. Wait. This isn't right. Where's the park entrance and tall pines lining his route home?

The bus pulls back into traffic, and Ed's heartbeat stutters. He'd gotten off at the fourth stop. That was the way home. Or was that to get to the doctor's office?

A group of young people slouch nearby, smoking something pungent and eyeing him. One peels away from the building he's leaning against. "Hey, old man. You lost?"

"I . . . I don't know." Where is he? And where's he supposed to be going?

This senior is far from home in a not-so-safe area, and our uncertainty about the intentions of the local boys increases the dramatic tension. When it becomes clear that Ed is also dealing with *cognitive decline,* our worry escalates because his mental fog pushes the situation from unsettling to dangerous.

Vulnerability always enhances an already tense situation, and it's a natural offshoot of many amplifiers, so keep it in mind when you need to up the ante.

Exhaustion. Hunger. Sensory Overload. Cognitive Decline. These are only a handful of amplifiers that increase tension for readers and characters. Just make sure the amplifier you choose fits naturally into the story moment and with the existing conflict.

AMPLIFIERS AND SECONDARY CHARACTERS

Emotion amplifiers don't have to happen directly to the protagonist to affect them. They can be just as effective when used peripherally via a secondary character.

In *The Fellowship of the Ring*, the company is stuck outside the mines of Moria while Gandalf tries to open its magical gates. Boromir, frustrated and impatient, throws a rock into the nearby pool of water and wakes the Watcher who lives beneath. The whole company is nearly killed before escaping into the mines. Boromir's rock, thrown in stress and frustration, results in them getting trapped inside the mines, overrun by orcs, and eventually losing Gandalf.

As the hero of the story, Frodo does nothing to cause these events. But the ripple effect of his sidekick's *stress* directly impacts him, heightening tension and both reader and character emotion.

It should also be noted that an amplifier doesn't need to be extreme to incur big results. Sometimes, like the tightening of a screw, it simply increases tension for the main character, which leads to poor decision-making. In *It's a Wonderful Life*, George Bailey comes home from the worst day to end all worst days to find his daughter sick with a cold. Though her *illness* is nothing to worry about, it's the final straw for George, causing him to fly off the handle and act in a way he never would under normal circumstances. Soon, he's standing on a bridge in a snowstorm, contemplating suicide.

One of the interesting things about amplifiers is that not every person responds to them the same way. When different characters are hit with the same amplifier, their unique reactions reflect the differences in their personalities, their ability to function in the moment, and how quickly they rebound.

In the movie *Sleepers*, four childhood friends in Hell's Kitchen, known for causing trouble, are sent to a juvenile detention center where they are sexually and physically abused by the guards. Thirteen years later, the boys are free adults whose lives have taken starkly different paths. Michael and Shakes, while struggling with their *trauma*, are managing. They've graduated from high school, navigated college, and are doing their best to move on with their lives. But John and Tommy haven't fared as well. They're now career criminals, in and out of jail and working for the Irish mob. They've become so hardened by their trauma that when they encounter one of their abusers, they don't hesitate; they shoot him in cold blood, in full sight of a roomful of witnesses.

This story illustrates the contrasting responses people have to the same amplifier. Two of the characters were able to move forward despite their trauma. The other two couldn't, and at a critical time, their rage rose up in a costly mistake.

Clearly, amplifiers are incredibly useful for increasing tension and heightening emotion. Whether inflicted upon the supporting cast or the main character, they're a strong option when authors want to mix things up and keep complications fresh.

USING AMPLIFIERS AS WEAPONS

Many emotion amplifiers are internal, manifesting within the characters themselves. We see this in the case of *hyperactivity, arousal, intoxication, malnutrition,* and *pregnancy.* Other amplifiers—*cold, confinement, instability*—are triggered by an external factor. But some of the most damaging amplifiers are the ones generated by other people, because they're purposeful and targeted.

Authors aren't the only ones who know how volatile an emotion amplifier can be; other characters are aware, too. Villains, rivals, frenemies, antiheroes, and other morally flexible characters recognize the advantage of a strategically used amplifier in sidelining an opponent or furthering their own agendas. Using an adversary to destabilize your protagonist heightens friction between the two, strengthens tension, and reminds readers that the opponent is a force to be reckoned with.

When an adversary has the following purposes in mind, an amplifier might be just the ticket to bring them about.

MANIPULATING MOOD

Mood is a temporary state of mind often influenced by external stimuli. Moods tend to lean toward negative or positive. They affect a character's perception of themselves, other people, and their situation and influence their decision-making.

This means someone with a vested interest in changing the character's mood can easily do so with an amplifier. Maybe they purposefully put the protagonist into a state of *exhaustion* by disrupting their sleep, or they force them to endure the hardship of *cold* temperatures by killing their heater in winter. As their mood swings, the protagonist goes right where the adversary wants them: emotionally elevated, irritable, and distracted from what really matters.

ENSURING COMPLIANCE

Antagonists tend to crave compliance; after all, it's a lot easier to dominate people when they're not actively fighting against you. If the protagonist hasn't yet recognized their enemy, all the adversary has to do is quietly manipulate their situation to weaken them. Then they can step in and lead the character in the wrong direction, offer self-serving advice, or magnify any cognitive or emotional dissonances already in play.

In the movie *Ghost*, Molly's husband Sam is dead and she's in the throes of *bereavement*. Her good friend Carl (who, unbeknownst to Molly, was responsible for Sam's death) is now subtly putting romantic moves on her. His attempts are unsuccessful, so he takes a different tack by pushing her deeper into grief, deliberately using her situation to make her more vulnerable and open to suggestion—a despicable but frequently successful way to gain control and influence over someone's decisions.

Another way a character can ensure compliance is by introducing an amplifier to create an undesirable situation, then using that situation to "rescue" the victim.

Consider a greedy land baron who wants to take over a town that's ripe for the picking, if he can just depose the matriarch. So he uses his considerable resources to create a local famine. Crops fail, people and animals go hungry, and the coming winter promises even greater suffering and death. Fear becomes as abundant as food once was. The matriarch, unable to identify the cause of the famine, is powerless to resolve the problem.

Then a stranger comes to town. He expresses sympathy for the villagers and reverses the famine using his wealth to provide food until the next harvest. The indebted villagers begin to view him as more capable and resourceful than their own matriarch. Voilà! Through a fabricated disaster fueled by *hunger* and fear, the antagonist has earned the trust of the people and is on his way to claiming the village for himself.

CAUSING A PSYCHOLOGICAL DERAILMENT
But what if it's not enough to simply win people over? In extreme cases, an antagonist may need to break down their opponent mentally and emotionally before building them back up in their own image. Leveraging the following amplifiers can help accomplish this.

Isolation: Separating a character from other people and even the wider world creates an unmet need in the area of social connection (love and belonging on Maslow's hierarchy). Isolated characters make easier targets because of their emotional vulnerability and their longing to be accepted by others.

Confinement: Trapping or restricting a character in some way makes them emotionally volatile and reliant, forcing them to depend upon their captor for release, information, or whatever they need to survive.

Forced addiction: Creating a dependency on drugs, medicine, or other substances alters the character's mental state, tempting them to sacrifice their moral code and reconstruct their priorities as the substance becomes the most important thing.

Torture and **trauma:** These potent tools, applied directly to the character or indirectly to loved ones, make the protagonist more fragile and easier to break.

Brainwashing. Thought reform through altering the character's beliefs, attitudes, and behaviors is the tool of a morally destitute antagonist. This subtle process twists fear and hope in a perverse way to rewire the subject's brain to align with the adversary's own ideas.

These are difficult notions to consider, particularly as we know these amplifiers are used in the real world for heinous purposes. As such, writers shouldn't deploy them casually. But they are legitimate options for a corrupt character who's motivated enough to use them.

NOT JUST FOR VILLAINS
The use of amplifiers to achieve an unethical goal isn't limited to the bad guys. Your detective protagonist might employ one to gain the trust of a suspect or coerce someone into telling the truth—say, by *confining* the perp to a jail cell or physically turning up the *heat* in an interview room. A therapist may gently use a client's *trauma* to facilitate self-awareness and healing, and desperate parents could use *pressure* to pull information from a child keeping a dangerous secret.

In extreme situations, good people can be pushed to do appalling things, too. In the movie *Prisoners*, Keller Dover is a law-abiding man and loving father. But when his daughter is abducted and the police are ineffective at questioning the person he believes is responsible, he does something wildly out of character: he kidnaps the suspect and tortures him for information on his daughter's whereabouts. The moral ambiguity of this movie makes it difficult to watch, because we recognize that Keller is a good guy and we relate to him. We all associate ourselves with good, not bad, and if Keller can lose his moorings and turn so easily from right to wrong, it could happen to any of us.

As authors, we can be neutral in our use of emotion amplifiers to shape the story the way we want. But when our characters are the ones wielding the power, don't make the mistake of assuming that only monsters are capable of dark deeds.

OPTIMAL TIMES TO USE AN AMPLIFIER

By this point, you should be aware of the multifunctional nature of amplifiers. There's no end to the ways they can be used, and when you're working with certain character types or story elements, they're especially beneficial.

EMOTIONALLY INTELLIGENT CHARACTERS

Empathetic characters with strong self-regulation, self-awareness, and social skills have a high EQ (emotional quotient). This makes them skilled at reading other people, managing their own feelings, and carefully controlling their emotions.

But sometimes a big response is needed to provoke a mistake or lapse in judgment. Amplifiers can destabilize an emotionally intelligent character at crucial points in the story. Not only does this create problems for them to solve and an opportunity for self-reflection, it also lets others know they're struggling. Characters who are in control of their emotions are often viewed as strong, capable, and having it all together. A poor reaction or mistake reveals that they're not okay and still need help.

SOCIOPATHS AND PSYCHOPATHS

Another group of people who are less likely to lose emotional control are those who lack empathy. It takes a bit more work to trigger a blowup in a psychopath or sociopath, but an amplifier like *confinement*, *danger*, or *compulsion* can strong-arm them into an explosive reaction.

EMOTIONALLY NUMB CHARACTERS

Characters with circumstances that create distance between them and their emotions may appear to readers as if they don't feel anything. A character with alexithymia, for example, has difficulty identifying, experiencing, or expressing emotion. Mental health conditions such as schizophrenia that include emotional numbness as a component also fall into this category. Forging connections between readers and these characters is especially challenging; using an amplifier often nudges them toward volatility, producing emotions readers can recognize and relate to.

Another reason amplifiers work well for emotionally numb characters is because of their commonality. If the character is unable to express what they feel in the wake of an amplifier, the writer can make the cause and effect clear, helping readers fill in the emotional blanks. This works even for amplifiers the reader hasn't experienced but has heard or read about, such as *psychosis* or *possession*.

HIGHLY TRAUMATIZED CHARACTERS

Past trauma is another universal element of the human experience. It can upend a character's life, sowing dysfunction in key ways.

Painful experiences force characters to emotionally protect themselves, and not always in a good way. They become skilled at keeping people and hurtful situations at a distance, but their methods often cause isolation and difficulty connecting with others. When negative feelings break through, unhealthy coping mechanisms like detachment, disassociation, or avoidance keep the character from experiencing them. If repeatedly buffering themselves from negative emotions prevents them from working through the past and moving forward in a healthier way, the damage from trauma remains ongoing.

Unresolved trauma can also lead characters to believe they'll be hurt again if they let their guard down. This outlook erodes one or more of their basic human needs, and the emotional shielding they've adopted to protect themselves keeps them from achieving the goals that would bring their needs back into alignment.

A highly traumatized character who isn't open to healing won't be able to tackle their past head on, all at once. Instead, their confidence and self-worth must be built up a bit at a time. This can be done by introducing amplifiers the character can successfully navigate.

Mikhail paces a path in his living room carpet, sweating and aching while *substance withdrawal* sinks its claws into him. As his anguish increases, his determination to get clean weakens. He scrolls through his mental list of places to get what he needs to take away the pain. Those names, those faces, those places . . . all are waiting beyond his apartment door.

He takes a step toward it.

"Daddy?" A sleep-heavy voice cuts through his thoughts. Abel, in his duck-print onesie, stands in the bedroom doorway. "Can I have a drink?"

"Of course." Mikhail's voice cracks and he hurries to the kitchen faucet before Abel sees his tears. *Remember why you're doing this.*

While putting the three-year-old back to bed, he notices one of Abel's stuffed animals on the floor. He carries it to the living room, wedges a chair against the front door, and places the bedraggled giraffe on it. All night, through shakes and fever, he stares at the stuffed toy, an unlikely guardian against the darkness on the other side, until the sun rises and the shadows disperse.

The trauma that created Mikhail's addiction is still there, and he may not be ready to work through it yet. But this successful navigation of a difficult part of his recovery gives him strength and purpose, both of which set him up for more growth in the future.

STORY AND SUBPLOT FODDER

Amplifiers sometimes provide inspiration for a main story line or subplot by reinforcing the consequences of emotionally charged choices. Many writers have used amplifiers in this way to weave incredible stories.

One example is the movie *Fatal Attraction*. Dan is a married man who lets his *attraction* for Alex override his judgment, resulting in an affair. She becomes obsessed with him, and when Dan tries to end things, Alex becomes unhinged. She stalks him, invades his private life, kills his daughter's pet bunny, and initiates an attack at his home that ends with Alex dead in the bathtub.

In *The Matrix*, Neo faces *indecision* over a symbolic choice that will shape his reality: blue pill or red pill? Blue will return him to the programmed dreamworld of the Matrix, where his experiences with Morpheus will dissipate and be forgotten. Red will awaken him to the real world, hardship, and the truth of his existence. Indecision is a recurring amplifier as Neo learns he is an instrument of fate, where every choice carries weight not only for him but for all humankind.

Gerald's Game, a novel by Stephen King, utilizes different amplifiers to tell the story of a romantic getaway gone wrong. Jessie, the protagonist, is assaulted by her husband and handcuffed to the bed. But things worsen dramatically when he dies of a heart attack, leaving her confined. As she suffers from *dehydration*, *fatigue*, and *hunger*, Jessie hallucinates, reliving repressed trauma involving childhood sexual abuse. Her memories of not being protected set her determination on fire, and she draws up the strength and courage to save herself.

The versatility of emotion amplifiers can save you when you've written yourself into a corner or a character isn't cooperating. If you're looking for somewhere to start, consider the amplifier that can be utilized for any character in almost any situation: *pain*.

PAIN: A POWERFUL AMPLIFIER

Pain is an unfortunate part of life. As characters go about their days working, building relationships, pursuing goals, and blowing off steam, things don't always go as planned, and they get hurt. How quickly and fully they heal depends on their individual responses to pain and the type of suffering they're dealing with.

Most of us are familiar with physical and emotional pain, but other kinds may amplify specific emotions and lead to unique shades of dissonance (and therefore, unique ways to resolve inner stress). Here are some of the broader types of pain to explore as amplifiers.

PHYSICAL PAIN
Physical pain is the neurological response to bodily harm caused by illness or injury, and its severity depends on its source. The quality, intensity, and duration of pain from stepping on a Lego is less than what will result from a catastrophic train crash. A character stepping on those little bricks of torture finds the pain short-lived, and the emotions amplified are relatively minor: frustration or annoyance. But the pain after waking up in the debris from a train crash could emanate from a crushed limb, broken ribs, or something much worse, and the intensity scales much higher: agony, panic, or hysteria.

EMOTIONAL PAIN
Emotional pain is caused by an intense, uncomfortable emotion in the wake of a difficult experience. It runs along a broad spectrum from minor to severe, short-lived to long-term, and it varies in intensity. The embarrassment of a public wardrobe malfunction doesn't last long, but the discomfort is still powerful. Profound distress arises from more serious sources of pain: the death of a spouse, the triggering of an old trauma, or certain mental health conditions.

Regardless of its quality or intensity, emotional pain is as unpleasant as physical discomfort and prompts the character to pull away from the source to make it stop. Emotions that can be amplified here will vary depending on the situation, but frustration, anger, guilt, fear, insecurity, and confusion aren't uncommon.

PSYCHOLOGICAL PAIN
A close cousin to emotional discomfort, psychological pain arises when a character's emotional pain lingers and metastasizes. It burrows deep, a constant ache, warping their view on life. Everyday challenges and difficulties become harder to handle, and the character may question themselves or wrestle with meaning and purpose. Deep down, they can't help but feel their life is not what they expected it to be.

Unresolved trauma is a frequent source of psychological pain. Parental abandonment, sexual abuse, and wrongful imprisonment are common examples, but any wounding event that's not dealt with can trigger it. The same is true of certain mental health conditions that are difficult to treat or come to terms with, such as PTSD.

Psychological pain wears characters down. It's always there, touching and entangling multiple areas of their life. It creates unmet needs and impacts self-esteem, autonomy, and control. Amplified emotions for psychological pain always tie into the root cause. When they plunge into the deeper end of the spectrum, feelings like hopelessness, powerlessness, depression, anguish, despair, shame, or worthlessness could develop.

SOCIAL PAIN

Social pain is caused by negative interactions with other people. It often results from relational conflict, bullying, rejection, exclusion, breakups, or loss. People are social creatures, so suffering in this way really leaves a mark, shaking a character's self-esteem and sense of worth. It may cause them to feel disconnected, devalued, or aggrieved. Anger, betrayal, confusion, sadness, humiliation, shame, loneliness, and worthlessness are emotions that could be heightened via social pain.

SPIRITUAL PAIN

When a character believes they have a spiritual side that connects them to something larger than themselves, situations that threaten their faith or cause them to doubt their purpose in life can lead to spiritual distress. Emotions commonly amplified by spiritual pain include confusion, disillusionment, uncertainty, and doubt.

CHRONIC PAIN

This specific form of physical pain is associated with chronic illness or injury. It's defined by its persistence, lasting many months or years despite treatment. Chronic pain is especially detrimental and eventually leaches into other areas of a character's life, spawning emotional, psychological, social, and/or spiritual distress on top of the prolonged physical pain. A character suffering in this way may experience heightened feelings of depression, despair, frustration, powerlessness, resignation, or torment.

HANDLING PAIN: A DEEPER LOOK

Pain is universal—every character experiences it. Their ability to control and deal with pain, however, is individualized and depends on several factors, some baked in and others external. To write it well, it's important to know what these are.

Pain Tolerance: Every character has a maximum amount of physical suffering they can handle. The higher a character's tolerance, the more discomfort they can withstand. This limit depends on genetics, age, experience with pain, and how much mental, emotional, and physical stress they're already under when the amplifier is introduced.

Personality and Values: A character's dominant traits and values play a crucial role in how they respond to pain. A stoic character handles physical suffering differently than someone who is melodramatic, needy, insecure, or morbid. A character with strong values like determination and courage will use these resources to fortify themselves against discomfort. Take the character's personality and core values into consideration when planning how they'll react to pain.

Being on Display: A tumble down a staircase is painful and may possibly sour a character's mood, but if no one is there to see it, they're free to focus on the pain, process what happened, and take time to recover. However, if someone witnesses their fall, the character may become self-conscious and minimize their injuries to avoid being viewed as weak. This may cause them to become emotionally reactive as they struggle to do two things at once: escaping scrutiny while repressing their pain.

Responsibility: Another factor in a character's ability to manage pain is whether they're responsible for someone or something else. When suffering strikes, if they have an important duty to uphold, they may see the pain as secondary. Characters adopting a mind-over-matter approach often ignore or minimize pain until they've accomplished what needs doing. Of course, becoming incapacitated while others are in danger can escalate matters by adding emotional or psychological pain to the character's physical discomfort, so this can be a double-edged sword.

Pharmacological Factors: Self-medication also influences a character's pain response. Alcohol, illegal drugs, and some medicines dull the senses and influence a person's reactions, but they don't necessarily make people less emotionally volatile. Mood-altering substances often lower a character's guard, causing them to become more talkative and open to speaking uncomfortable truths. With so many possible outcomes when pharmaceuticals are involved, consider them carefully when crafting a painful scene.

Special Outliers: When it comes to pain, there will always be exceptions: characters with conditions or abilities that dull their discomfort or render them exempt from certain forms of pain. A psychopath has a higher pain tolerance than other people, and while they do experience emotional pain (especially regarding disappointment and dissatisfaction), the range of causes is narrower.

Another example would be someone with congenital insensitivity, a rare condition in which they cannot feel physical pain. While this might seem like an asset for an action hero or uber villain, it makes the world a more dangerous place; if they get severely hurt, they may not realize it until serious damage has been done.

There are many other conditions that influence how someone experiences pain. Careful research into a character's physiology and emotional background will alert you to factors that play into their responses and make them truly unique.

WHEN TO AVOID AMPLIFIERS

We've discussed at length all the good things that can result from a well-placed amplifier. But as with all narrative devices, they work best when they're used effectively. It's crucial to recognize when an amplifier *isn't* the best tool for the job, so let's talk about when to avoid their use.

THE RESOLUTION PHASE OF A SCENE OR PLOT LINE

It's common knowledge that a successful story has a clearly defined beginning, middle, and end. The same formula applies to strong scenes.

The beginning of a scene is an opportunity to show the scene goal, the thing the character is hoping to do that moves them toward their overall objective.

But then conflict arrives in the form of obstacles, adversaries, or dilemmas; the middle of the scene is dedicated to the wrestling match with that conflict. This is the perfect place for amplifiers to augment tension and complications.

The end of the scene shows whether the character is successful in reaching their goal. (Hint: most of the time, they aren't.)

A visual image of the tension in a scene might look something like this:

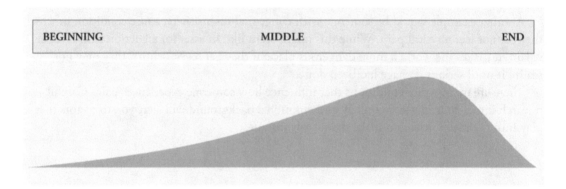

Tension rises during the scene as the protagonist encounters conflict and amplifiers that make it more difficult to get what they want. After a prolonged climb, the tension reaches a peak before dropping off as the scene is resolved and comes to an end.

An amplifier applied during the end stage would ramp things up again, delaying the resolution—but this is the time to de-escalate the situation, not fan the flames. Once you reach this point in the scene, it's best to hold off on introducing a new amplifier.

But what about cliffhangers? you ask. *Half the chapters in the books I read end with serious conflict, high tension, and a character smack dab in the middle of an amplifier situation.*

Ah, but in this case, you're talking about *chapters*, not *scenes*. While the two terms are often used interchangeably, they're not the same.

Scenes are the basic building blocks of a story. Every scene should follow a defined structure, and the scene is not complete until all the elements have been included. The arc above is a visual representation of that structure. Amplifiers should be avoided during the resolution portion.

Chapters, on the other hand, are used to divide the story into manageable chunks for readers. Rather than adhering to a certain structure, the end of each chapter is arbitrarily determined by the author, a choice that depends largely on style.

A chapter might encompass a complete scene, or it might end in the middle of one. In the latter case, the chapter could end with high tension and amplifiers galore because it hasn't yet reached the end of the scene. Ending a chapter at this point often results in a cliffhanger, and there are good reasons to do that. But amplifiers should be avoided at the completion of a scene, whether it coincides with the end of a chapter or not.

REVELATORY MOMENTS

As characters trudge along in their growth journey, you'll be throwing every difficult thing imaginable at them. In the beginning, they won't respond well because they're stuck in their old dysfunctional, ineffective habits. But as the story progresses, they'll experience periods of introspection (often following a big event) that lead to a light-bulb revelation. They'll realize they've been believing a lie, or the shielding behavior they thought was a strength is their greatest weakness and is holding them back. These moments of clarity push the protagonist to rethink their methods and make much-needed changes that help them succeed.

At times like these, characters need to be thinking clearly. If their thoughts are fogged by *exhaustion*, *burnout*, a *hangover*, or *cognitive decline*, the likelihood that they'll come to a logical conclusion is low. Save amplifiers for the events that lead to these introspective interludes, and you'll put your characters in the strongest position to become self-aware and embrace change.

ZEN TIMES

If you're doing your job as the author, the protagonist will spend a lot of time frustrated, angry, afraid, or uncertain. Amplifiers are great for creating situations that escalate to those emotions.

But a story in which the protagonist is always emotionally activated can grow tiresome for readers. It will also lessen the character's authenticity because they're unable to experience a complete range of feelings.

Since amplifiers influence a character's emotions and make them more volatile, they're not so effective at eliciting relaxation and inner peace. At the point in a scene or story when the protagonist needs to be composed and conflict-free, hold the amplifiers for another time.

WHEN A CHARACTER CAN'T TAKE ANY MORE

Authenticity is crucial when writing realistic characters. In every way possible—their motivations, fears, flaws, strengths, quirks, and so on—characters should imitate real people. Just as we each have our own breaking points, your characters have theirs, too.

So how far is too far? This often becomes obvious during drafting. As you continue abusing the protagonist, you'll realize you've crossed a line or are close to doing so. Critique partners will also let you know when things have gone on long enough. Either way, that's the time to stop. Drive the protagonist right to their breaking point, but stop short of pushing them past it.

Conflict and tension are vital pieces to a successful story puzzle, so it's necessary to keep turning up the heat on our characters. The moments discussed above are good examples of times when an emotion amplifier can work against the story. Leave them in the toolbox until the right moments, so they can do what they need to at the right time in the story.

A WORD ON MENTAL AND PHYSICAL HEALTH CONDITIONS

Amid so much discussion of states and conditions that amplify emotions or make a person more reactive, we feel the need to clarify that mental and physical health conditions shouldn't be temporary affectations, randomly assigned, sensationalized, or used as a device to suit the story's purposes.

In the real world, these conditions can represent a struggle for some, an accepted part of identity for others, or both. No matter what the condition is, however, one important fact is set in stone: people are people, not conditions. They are individuals with vibrancy and depth and should be treated as such.

Words have power, and the way we handle sensitive topics in our stories shapes how readers view those topics in the real world. When writing about mental or physical health conditions (or even identity, for that matter) we have an obligation to research the facts and portray them accurately. And when we use a condition as an amplifier, we must do so respectfully to avoid harming the very people we're writing about.

As an example of how a mental health condition may amplify emotion, consider Lisa, a character who has lived with agoraphobia most of her adult life. This anxiety disorder causes her to fear leaving her fourth-floor apartment. It doesn't define Lisa; she's happy and safe in her space, has necessities delivered, works from home, and uses chat rooms and online gaming for social interaction.

Life is good, until she notices a small bug emerging from the wall outlet—and then a few more on her bedsheets. Realizing she's looking at bedbugs, Lisa gets to work eradicating them. She orders traps and mattress cases. She tapes all the outlets closed, washes her clothes and bedding on the hottest setting, and puts her cushions and pillows on the balcony so the sun can kill the little buggers.

By the end of the week, Lisa is exhausted. She's barely slept and has fallen behind on work, but it will all be worthwhile once the bugs are gone. Unfortunately, they refuse to be evicted. After all the scrubbing, cleaning, and vacuuming, she's still finding them.

Now imagine Lisa's landlord stopping by to let her know she'll have to temporarily vacate the premises so the building can be fumigated.

The idea of leaving her apartment, going down the elevator, and stepping into the street makes Lisa's stomach fish-jump into her throat. No, absolutely not. She can't do it. Her thoughts run a mile a minute, and she can't pull in breaths fast enough. She tells the landlord in no uncertain terms that she won't leave, and the treatment company will have to figure something out.

Aware of her condition, the landlord is sympathetic. Perhaps he reserves a hotel room for her across the street to minimize her exposure to the outdoors. He may gently show her the tenant agreement with her signature, acknowledging that she must allow bonded workers into her apartment for necessary maintenance.

In a state of near-panic and denial, Lisa doesn't see these well-meaning actions as anything but a threat. She feels cornered and overwhelmed, knowing she can't leave but will be forced to do so. As pressure builds, she yells at her landlord, telling him that this is her apartment and he can't make her go. She slams the door and collapses against it, shaking, with no idea what to do.

In a situation like this, Lisa's agoraphobia becomes the final straw that throws her ability to manage the bedbugs out the window. It's not her mental condition that stifles her; on the contrary, she's learned to live with that. The story itself isn't about agoraphobia—that's only one aspect of who Lisa is. It's only this predicament that amplifies the challenges associated with her condition, bringing it to the forefront in this scene.

Unfortunately, fiction is filled with hurtful stereotypes regarding health conditions and identity, and as writers of today, we must hold ourselves accountable and do better. Representation is important, and we want readers to be exposed to different lived experiences. To do this, we must research to understand the people we're writing about. When characterization choices are made with purpose and handled respectfully, readers see a character's true authenticity and will connect to them based on their strengths and individuality.

If you choose to write a character with a condition, give them depth beyond their diagnosis. Invest as much characterization into them as you do every cast member, and unless the story is specifically about their mental or physical health journey, don't put their condition front and center.

Use these amplifiers with purpose and care. Above all else, remember that people are more than their health profile, and our characters should be, too.

FINAL WORDS FROM THE AUTHORS

As you browse the thesaurus entries that follow, we encourage you to think about how amplifiers blend emotions and conflict to provide added punch. The entries provide behaviors, thoughts, visceral sensations, and other cues in response to an amplifier, just as *The Emotion Thesaurus* entries do for emotions. We've also compiled scenarios for building conflict and tension, to help trigger ideas about when and where each amplifier might best be used.

With so many potential amplifiers to choose from, it's tempting to use them every time we need to build up conflict and elicit emotional reactions. But like conflict, too many amplifiers can make the writing feel episodic. When a character is *stressed, malnourished, aroused, exhausted,* or in *pain* scene after scene, their suffering feels overdone. To avoid weakening the plausibility of the character's experiences for readers, use amplifiers strategically to enhance the story moments that need them most.

Because amplifiers inherently destabilize or direct a character's emotions, overuse will lead to melodrama. Just as an emotional response should match the intensity level of the event triggering it, the intensity of an amplifier should appropriately fit the situation.

Know your reasons and purpose for every emotion amplifier you choose. If you're considering one that burdens the character and influences their feelings at a crucial moment, you're probably on the right track.

As a true companion to *The Emotion Thesaurus*, this book includes a list of emotions in each entry that are most likely to be magnified, allowing you to decide which amplifier works best for the feelings you wish to generate. We hope this makes it even easier to get more emotion on the page.

Happy writing,

Angela Ackerman & Becca Puglisi

THE
EMOTION
AMPLIFIER
THESAURUS

ADDICTION

DESCRIPTION: This compulsive need for a substance is marked by acute physiological symptoms when the substance is withdrawn. Though people can be addicted to any number of things, this entry is limited to cues associated with substance addictions. For related information, see HANGOVER and SUBSTANCE WITHDRAWAL.

PHYSICAL SIGNALS AND BEHAVIORS
Being under the influence a lot of the time
Denying they have a problem
Poor hygiene (unkempt hair, yellowing teeth, chipped nails, etc.)
Sallow skin
Bloodshot, glassy, dull, or red eyes
Dilated or contracted pupils
Impaired coordination and slow reaction times
Manic activity
Suspicious odors on the breath, clothing, or skin
Tremors and sweating
Twitchy movements
Slurred speech
Having trouble staying focused on a conversation (going off on tangents)
Forgetting to eat
Sleeping a lot (or having difficulty sleeping)
Not showing up to appointments or social engagements
Financial difficulties, such as not making rent or having a car repossessed
Asking others for money (using a plethora of excuses)
Stealing money (or valuables to liquidate into cash)
Neglecting responsibilities at work or school
Difficulty maintaining healthy relationships
Leaving old friends and clinging to new groups of people who also use
Difficulty keeping a job
A spaced-out appearance
Decreased eye contact
Delinquent or criminal activity
Driving under the influence
Risk-taking behaviors
Emotional volatility and outbursts
Manipulating others to get what the character wants
A life categorized by high drama
Co-dependent behaviors
Dishonesty and deception
Fluctuating moral lines
Becoming reclusive
Being irrational

Making promises and not keeping them
Becoming irresponsible and unreliable

INTERNAL SENSATIONS
Feeling hyper or jumpy
Lethargy or fatigue
Impaired vision
Dry mouth
A warm, floating sensation or, alternatively, a heaviness in the limbs and head
Twitchy nerves and muscles
Increased sensitivity to sound, texture, taste, and smells
A "crawling skin" sensation
Craving the substance when they're not using it (anxiety, pain, aching, etc.)

MENTAL RESPONSES
Fixating on the source of the addiction
A sense of euphoria upon using
Counting the minutes until the next hit
Needing to use more to get the same experience that used to come with a lesser amount
A lack of motivation
Mood swings or aggression
Memory loss, and an inability to account for large chunks of time
Time distortions (believing time has slowed or sped up)
Impaired judgment
Blaming others; evading responsibility for their actions
Guilt or regret
Self-pity and self-loathing
Suicidal thoughts

EFFORTS TO HIDE THE ADDICTION
Denial about having a problem
Making excuses for absences, forgetfulness, or tardiness
Lying about using, or admitting to past use but saying they've since quit
Avoiding socializing with friends and coworkers (to hide the habit)
Misdirection; deploying guilt tactics with loved ones to avoid blame
Hiding track marks by wearing long sleeves
Explaining away any "off" behavior as being due to work stress, being sick, etc.
Using eye drops, mints, or mouthwash to mask odors and other telltale signs
Demanding more privacy
Evasive behavior (sneaking out, hiding substances around the house, etc.)
Withdrawal symptoms

ASSOCIATED POWER VERBS: Sweat, twitch, shake, tremor, fidget, jerk, flick, snap, argue, lie, deflect, manipulate, mumble, slur, shutter, obsess, desire, yearn, crave, beg, itch, hide, conceal, stow, sneak, cover, clutch, trade, buy, steal, take, shoot, swallow, smoke, pop, cook, heat, inject, plunge, tremble

EMOTIONS GENERATED BY THIS AMPLIFIER: Anguish, Anxiety, Bitterness, Conflicted, Defiance, Denial, Desperation, Determination, Devastation, Discouragement, Doubt, Eagerness, Powerlessness, Remorse, Satisfaction, Self-Loathing, Shame, Worthlessness

DUTIES OR DESIRES THAT MAY BE MORE DIFFICULT TO FULFILL
Staying sober
Getting a job that requires drug and alcohol screenings
Keeping a job (due to frequent absences, unreliability, etc.)
Self-forgiveness
Embracing healthy coping mechanisms for stress, trauma, and triggers
Regaining someone's trust
Achieving a lifelong dream
Gaining custody of a child
Saving money for the future
Being honest about their addiction
Caregiving responsibilities

SCENARIOS FOR BUILDING CONFLICT AND TENSION
Travel delays that make it difficult for the character to get their fix
Family events where there is little privacy, such as a funeral or baby shower
Being in a new location and not knowing how to access the drug of choice
Being pulled over by police for a routine stop with drugs in their vehicle
Getting caught in a lie (or forgetting what lies they've told to whom)
Being blamed for money going missing
Getting fired or kicked out of school
Being subjected to an intervention
Being pressured to attend rehab when the character isn't ready
The character waking up in a dangerous place with no memory of how they got there
The character losing their driver's license and having to take public transportation
The character's financial situation changing, making it difficult to use
Being arrested (for driving while impaired, public indecency, etc.)
Being given an ultimatum relating to the addiction (a spouse threatening to leave, possibly being kicked out by parents, losing custody, etc.)
Overdosing

> **WRITER'S TIP:** *Some characters are high-functioning and may be better able to weather the fallout of addiction. Consider the supports around your character that may mask symptoms or prop them up. For example, financial means will make the expense of a habit less noticeable, and the presence of handlers (family, aides, etc.) will help the character remain presentable and functional.*

AROUSAL

DESCRIPTION: Heightened emotions and (oftentimes) sexual activation arise when a new source of interest appears. Because arousal can look different for men and women, this entry focuses mostly on generalized aspects that are common for both. For more ideas, see the related ATTRACTION entry.

PHYSICAL SIGNALS AND BEHAVIORS

A head lift and strong eye contact
Eyebrows pulling down and in as the character visually seeks to read the situation
Focusing their gaze on the subject and holding it there
Forgetting what they were doing (their interest now being consumed by the person activating their desire)
A straightening of the body, especially if the source is returning interest
Eyes that appear focused
A smoldering gaze
The character touching their own face or neck (skating fingers along the jaw, rubbing at an eyebrow, tapping the lip, etc.)
Abandoning what they're doing or the people they're talking to
Leaning in toward the source
The lips parting slightly
A visible flush to the cheeks
The character pulling at the neckline of their shirt, touching the exposed skin
Lifting the head to expose the neck
Glancing around to see if anyone has noticed their reaction (especially if it's not the right place to feel arousal or there's an element of danger)
A gaze that travels, taking in every aspect of the other person
Plucking at clothing to adjust it as the character's temperature rises
Becoming unresponsive to others (not answering a question, taking a step away, etc.)
Playing with jewelry (spinning a ring, touching a charm on a necklace, etc.)
Self-soothing gestures (stroking their own arm, playing with their hair, etc.) if the character is unable to engage with the other person
Moving toward the person they're attracted to
Becoming fidgety if the character is unable to act on what they feel (due to other people being present, other responsibilities in the moment, etc.)
Ignoring other duties or people
Entering the source's personal space (or welcoming them into their own)
Playful friendliness that becomes physical (such as taking the other person's arm) or more intimate (if the other party indicates it is appropriate and welcome)
Pressing closer, using the body to erase as much distance as possible
The voice softening or becoming huskier
Speaking suggestively or flirtatiously
Seeking an opportunity to be alone with the other person

INTERNAL SENSATIONS
Body heat rising; the character feeling warmer
An increase in heart rate (the pulse beginning to pound)
Physical sensitivity
A tingling sensation in the chest, hands, or erogenous zones
Certain areas swelling in response to the arousal (the lips, groin, etc.)
A fluttery sensation in the chest or stomach
A feeling of looseness as tension dissipates
Increased saliva causing more reflexive swallowing
A sensation of heat in the face
Breaths that quicken

MENTAL RESPONSES
Hyper-attention on the other's voice, movement, and cues as the character seeks to read their interest
The source of arousal becoming more important in the character's mind
Being drawn to the other party's attributes that magnify the character's emotions
Sexual thoughts
The character becoming self-aware of how their body is responding
Picking up on details regarding the source that they didn't notice before
Finding it hard to focus on other things
Becoming flustered in a positive way
Being present and in the moment, with other thoughts and concerns falling away
Losing track of time
An increased sense of urgency
Feeling out of control but being excited by the feeling
Emotions activating
The character playing out possible scenarios or fantasizing about the other person
Relying on intuition more than logic or prolonged thought
Becoming biased in favor of the source
Playing hard-to-get (feigning disinterest)
Trying to rein in emotions through self-talk (if the time or place is not right)
Rationalizing why it's okay to give into temptation

EFFORTS TO HIDE THE AROUSAL
Turning slightly so they can use side glances to monitor the person
Repositioning or covering themselves to hide engorgement (if the arousal is sexual)
Fixing their gaze on a distant point; actively avoiding eye contact with the person
Speaking slowly; choosing words carefully
Focusing on their breathing to force a state of calm
Giving the body a shake (as if to throw off the effects of arousal)
The character mentally coaching themselves to appear nonchalant
Asking questions to divert attention from their arousal response
Changing the topic of conversation or deploying tactics to try to regain control (getting up to pour drinks for guests, attending to a task that will allow time to refocus, etc.)
Making an excuse to leave (to avoid the danger of temptation)

Avoiding the source of their arousal

Pretending to be turned on by someone else for whom the arousal is acceptable (a date, significant other, etc.)

ASSOCIATED POWER VERBS: Arouse, excite, interest, stir, whet, rush, draw, pull, provoke, boost, bolster, entice, ignite, incite, trigger, prompt, evoke, build, raise, inflame, stimulate, urge, drive, fuel, soothe, infuse, awaken, reawaken, rekindle, hinder, wake, wind up, brace, spark, attract, rouse, summon, warm, heat, need, tease, lust

EMOTIONS GENERATED BY THIS AMPLIFIER: Annoyance, Anticipation, Confidence, Desire, Determination, Disappointment, Dissatisfaction, Eagerness, Elation, Emasculation, Embarrassment, Excitement, Frustration, Impatience, Longing, Lust, Nervousness, Obsession

DUTIES OR DESIRES THAT MAY BE MORE DIFFICULT TO FULFILL

Focusing their full attention on a job or task while the source of arousal is around

Staying committed to a spouse or significant other

Keeping the arousal a secret (if the source is someone the character shouldn't engage with)

Concentrating on a mundane activity—such as participating in a meeting or chatting with a neighbor—while aroused

Keeping promises that conflict with what the character really wants to do

Responsibilities that will take the character away from the person of interest

Being present mentally and emotionally for other people when the person causing arousal is close

Masking the effects of their arousal (being distracted, acting with bias, physical symptoms, etc.) around people who know them well

Putting logic before emotion

Denying what they feel with any level of conviction

Being honest about their feelings (if the arousal must be kept secret)

SCENARIOS FOR BUILDING CONFLICT AND TENSION

An obligation trapping the character, making it impossible to pursue their arousal

Others being aroused by the same person, creating competition

Experiencing arousal when the character is being scrutinized in some way

Being so emotionally aroused that the character misses a clear danger or threat

Working closely with a flirty coworker

Being taken advantage of because the character's judgment has been compromised

Being aroused by someone who isn't typical for the character, causing internal struggles and soul-searching to understand why

The character's interest going unreciprocated by the other person

Attending an event with an ex (such as a child's wedding) where old feelings rekindle

> **WRITER'S TIP:** *With arousal, keep in mind that the viewpoint character's attention and thoughts will be fixated on the person who has heightened their awareness. This person will become the center point of all their thoughts, actions, and reactions, so describe these things accordingly.*

ATTRACTION

DESCRIPTION: Attraction is a compelling sense of curiosity and pleasure regarding a specific person. While a milder level of interest may arise when the character desires an object (such as a coveted vintage car), true attraction is usually between people, so this entry focuses on human interactions. For more intense responses associated with attraction, see the AROUSAL entry.

PHYSICAL SIGNALS AND BEHAVIORS

The character stopping what they're doing and staring
Freezing up mid-sentence
Rapid blinking as they process the sudden attraction
Dropping their gaze when it's met by the other for the first time
Tilting the head down and smiling
Touching the mouth and drawing attention to the lips
Mirroring the other person's movements, gestures, and posture
Stealing furtive glances
Asking others about the person of interest; gathering information about them
Angling the body toward the other person
Giving a little wave and smile if the character is caught looking
Sweaty hands
Finding opportunities to talk to or get closer to this special person
The character touching their own hair or smoothing their clothes
Giving the person a compliment to connect with them
Thrusting out the chest and lifting the chin
Wetting the lips
Asking the other person questions that grow more personal in nature
Sharing memes and saying things to try to get a laugh
Sitting side-by-side so the legs or shoulders touch
The character giving this person their undivided attention
Studying the person carefully, looking for clues as to who they are, what they like, and possible areas of common interest
Paying attention to what they do and say to learn more about them
Seizing an opportunity to talk to them and asking questions out of fascination and a desire to know more
Perking up (straightening, smiling, etc.) when the other party enters the room
An open gaze; directly meeting their gaze
Constantly talking to friends about this special person
Losing interest in other things when the source of attraction enters the room
Becoming tongue-tied; fumbling for words
Watching the other person's social media postings
Grasping any attempt to make conversation
Their voice cracking or rising in pitch when speaking to the person they like
Increased perspiration

INTERNAL SENSATIONS

A fluttering in the belly
Knees that wobble, tremble, or feel weak
The mouth flooding with moisture
An overall tingling
Aching in the chest
Feeling energized
Breath stopping or catching in the throat
An almost electrical feeling upon meeting the other person's eyes
Feeling an emotional or spiritual connection with the other person
The body feeling warm

MENTAL RESPONSES

Having their curiosity awakened, displacing other concerns or thoughts
A willingness to leave their comfort zone to be with the other person
Boldness or forwardness
Wanting to get closer to the other person
Viewing everything this special person does as highly interesting
Only seeing the positive in them
Desperately wanting to be witty or charming
Applying internal pressure to do or say the right things
Daydreaming or fantasizing about the other person
Planning out opportunities to be with the other person
Difficulty forming thoughts into speech
Feeling insecure; wondering if they have a shot with this person
Becoming competitive; sizing up potential rivals
Being jealous of the other person's friends or romantic partner
Mentally replaying recent interactions with the source of attraction
Sexual thoughts
Feeling guilt if the character is in a committed relationship with someone else

EFFORTS TO HIDE THE ATTRACTION

Pretending indifference when the other person returns their attention
Finding ways to be near the person while not directly engaging with them
Befriending the other person or getting involved in their interests
Denying having feelings for the other person (if asked)
Downplaying their personal knowledge of the other person when they come up in conversation with friends
Ramping up an existing relationship to suggest the character isn't interested in building something with the new person
Always having a reason or excuse to approach the other person
Avoiding the person the character is attracted to
Dismissive gestures and comments
Avoiding eye contact with the person
Befriending the person of interest's friends to obtain access to them

Subtly watching the person they're attracted to from a distance
Fiddling with things when the other person is around

ASSOCIATED POWER VERBS: Call, smile, approach, bait, watch, gaze, yearn, draw, shift, charm, stare, hold, enchant, tempt, relish, arrest, sway, entrance, fascinate, influence, melt, captivate, tease, joke

EMOTIONS GENERATED BY THIS AMPLIFIER: Adoration, Conflicted, Desire, Despair, Determination, Disappointment, Eagerness, Elation, Excitement, Giddiness, Guilt, Happiness, Inadequacy, Insecurity, Jealousy, Longing, Love, Lust, Obsession, Resignation, Tormented, Unappreciated, Vulnerability

DUTIES OR DESIRES THAT MAY BE MORE DIFFICULT TO FULFILL
Staying focused on tasks and goals that have nothing to do with the person of interest
Maintaining a professional working relationship with the other person
Staying faithful to a spouse or significant other
Keeping the attraction secret (if it isn't a good idea to express it openly)
Not showing bias toward the person they find attractive
Staying focused on academic or professional goals
Showing hospitality and true friendship to the person's significant other
Remaining friends with the source when there is no hope for a deeper relationship
Creating distance in hopes of the attraction fading away

SCENARIOS FOR BUILDING CONFLICT AND TENSION
Being drawn to someone in an inappropriate setting—a spouse's retirement party, for example, or at a parent-teacher conference
Being in a committed relationship and running into an old flame on a work trip in another city
The character experiencing attraction but feeling unworthy or incapable of developing the relationship
Being attracted to someone who is taboo for the character (a brother's ex, for example)
The person the character is attracted to starting a romantic relationship with someone else
A sibling or close friend expressing interest in the same person
Discovering something undesirable about the person (certain political views, a personal bias, an annoying habit, etc.) but still being attracted to them
Being in a position where a romantic relationship isn't a good idea (because of long work hours, not being allowed by parents to date, etc.)

> **WRITER'S TIP:** *With a strong reactive state like attraction, be aware that the character's expressions will vary according to sex, age, culture, and experience. Their response will also depend on whether they can be open about their feelings or if they need to hide them.*

BEING STUCK

DESCRIPTION: A character in this state is caught in a situation or bound by circumstances that feel impossible to resolve or escape from. For information on the specific scenario of being physically stuck in a certain location, see the CONFINEMENT entry.

PHYSICAL SIGNALS AND BEHAVIORS

Pacing
Scrubbing their hands through their hair
Shaking their head
Having pent up energy (tapping knuckles on a surface, bouncing a foot, etc.)
Re-asking questions (when the character knows the answers)
Spending a lot of time online or on the phone to find a way out of the situation
Talking about the situation with anyone who will listen
Soliciting advice
Asking people to act on their behalf or be their advocate
Begging others for help
Trying to bargain their way out of the situation
Talking through possible (and increasingly desperate) options
Making rash decisions with their financial assets
Muttering or mumbling
Unfocused eyes
Lines gathering on the forehead or between the eyes
Fixating on the unfairness of the situation and how others are able to move forward
Pulling at their clothing
Throwing or breaking objects
Clenching their fists and jaw
Dragging their hands down their face
Sagging posture
Arms hanging at the sides, pulling down the shoulders
Biting or picking at their nails
Failing to respond to questions
Moving from task to task without finishing anything
Losing interest in other things (hobbies, activities, socializing, etc.)
Tuning out (unless news comes in about their circumstances)
Having insomnia
Inappropriate responses (uncontrollable laughter, aggression, bursting into tears, etc.)
Snapping at those who give platitudes or say they understand
Twisting their hair
Glancing around listlessly
Looping their arms around themselves to self-comfort
Rocking back and forth to soothe themselves

INTERNAL SENSATIONS

Blurred vision
Muscle tension

Headaches
Chest pains
A rapid pulse
Nausea
Neck, back, and jaw pain from tension
Feeling jittery or restless
Shortness of breath
Dizziness
Loss of appetite
Fatigue

MENTAL RESPONSES
Feeling powerless
Wanting the uncertainty to end
Desiring closure
Regretting decisions that led to the current circumstances
Losing hope for finding a way out
Having the urge to flee
Taking unnecessary risks
Resenting others who have more freedom
Pretending things are fine to keep others calm (children, for example)
Indecisiveness; worrying an action might make things worse
Impatience
Losing track of time
Feeling isolated
Compromising their morals to get out of the situation
Wanting to hurt people standing in the way of escape
Feeling sorry for themselves
Trying to convince themselves that things are better than they seem
Blaming people they believe contributed to their circumstances
Self-blame that becomes increasingly irrational as time goes on
Feeling like no one understands how they feel
Bargaining with God
An increasing sense of dread
Considering suicide as a way out

EFFORTS TO MINIMIZE OR HIDE THE IMPACT OF BEING STUCK
Repeating phrases to try to calm themselves
Downplaying the situation to others
Being in constant motion to burn off energy
Throwing themselves into unrelated projects as a way to stay busy or ignore the problem
Using stimulants (drugs, coffee, or energy drinks) to stay awake and work on a solution
Abusing substances (alcohol, pain medication, drugs, etc.) to numb their reality
Pulling back from their daily life (work, home, school, etc.) to avoid scrutiny
Taking controlled breaths
Forcing themselves to try to sleep

Struggling to retain their visual and mental focus
Rolling their shoulders back to release tension
Engaging in reckless behavior to distract themselves
Withdrawing from others to hide the situation
False optimism with others

ASSOCIATED POWER VERBS: Bargain, beg, lie, agonize, plead, hunch, fixate, demand, snap, resent, blame, regret, blackmail, extort, dismiss, isolate, expend, numb, distract, struggle, reflect, wish, ache, retreat, ruminate, obsess, lash out

EMOTIONS GENERATED BY THIS AMPLIFIER: Acceptance, Anger, Anxiety, Concern, Defiance, Desperation, Determination, Discouragement, Envy, Fear, Frustration, Impatience, Indignation, Longing, Misery, Obsession, Powerlessness, Regret, Resignation, Self-Pity

DUTIES OR DESIRES THAT MAY BE MORE DIFFICULT TO FULFILL
Giving their all to work or school projects
Leaving the house to run errands
Returning messages
Making decisions about the situation
Taking care of personal hygiene tasks
Being happy for other people when something good happens for them
Remaining dedicated to the goal of getting out (of the marriage, the dangerous neighborhood filled with negative influences, etc.)
Moving on without answers (say, as they wait for police to solve their daughter's murder)
Actively working to improve the situation
Being honest with friends and loved ones when they ask about the problem
Protecting someone in their charge who is stuck in the situation with them
Maintaining a positive attitude about the future

SCENARIOS FOR BUILDING CONFLICT AND TENSION
Being blackmailed or extorted to keep the situation private
Experiencing a health-related event due to stress, such as a panic attack or a stroke
Having a lawsuit filed against them related to the situation
Not having the financial means to address the problem
Another character disagreeing with the course of action the character wants to take
The situation going public and affecting the character's reputation
Being abandoned by friends and family who discover the problem
Trusting the wrong confidant
Being unable to bring the truth to light because it's being covered up

WRITER'S TIP: *Characters are not always a victim of circumstance; sometimes they're part of the problem, and resisting change is causing them to be stuck. This fight against taking necessary steps to take responsibility and be accountable can oftentimes produce the most story tension.*

BEREAVEMENT

DESCRIPTION: Bereavement occurs when the character has lost something or someone of vital importance. While it often follows a physical death, this sense of loss can also be the product of a divorce, being fired, having to give up on a dream, and other painful events that create a significant void in their life.

PHYSICAL SIGNALS AND BEHAVIORS
Slackness in the face
Having red or swollen eyes
Difficulty sleeping
Neglecting personal hygiene
Wearing or holding the clothing of the one who was lost
Wandering aimlessly, with little direction or purpose
Restlessness; needing to be busy (manically cleaning, tackling a neglected project, etc.)
Avoiding certain areas of the house that awaken raw memories
Refusing to go anywhere (or, alternatively, finding it hard to be alone at home)
Praying desperately
Talking aloud to the person who has passed
Attending religious services more frequently (or avoiding them)
Voicing regrets about missed opportunities or not doing more with the time they had
Rebuffing people's attempts to reach out to the character
Getting rid of (or clinging to) items that serve as reminders
Wanting to be with others who were also impacted by the loss
Avoiding (or visiting) people and places that remind the character of their loss
Drinking more than usual
Engaging in unusual or reckless behavior
Putting off managing the affairs of the deceased (if the bereavement has to do with someone's death)
Losing interest in activities that used to bring joy
Becoming obsessed with safety or health
Seeking mental health support
Reaching out to estranged contacts (because the character recognizes how short life is)

INTERNAL SENSATIONS
An overall feeling of heaviness
Changes in appetite; seeking out certain foods or not being hungry
Difficulty breathing
Exhaustion; just wanting to sleep
Chest pains
Dry mouth
A tight throat
Frequent headaches
Sensitivity to light and sound
Insomnia

Stomach discomfort
A sense of emptiness or numbness; feeling cried out

MENTAL RESPONSES
Escaping into happy memories (especially at night)
Struggling with their own mortality
Doubting their faith
Struggling with uncertainty when making decisions
Experiencing confusion
Trying to rationalize or make sense of the loss
Rewriting or reframing the past in ways to try to minimize the loss: *He was only holding me back,* or *It was always a fight to get funding so I'm better off not working there anyway.*
Mentally replaying events leading up to the moment of loss
Looking for someone to blame
Self-blame; unfairly dredging up every fault and mistake
Guilt at not being more accessible to those also dealing with the loss
Feeling alone in their grief
Apathy; viewing life differently now
Regretting past choices
Feeling pressure to move on
Questioning their ability to go on
Experiencing disbelief
Feeling overwhelmed by ordinary responsibilities
Resenting others who move on quickly or are not experiencing the same pain
Resisting change and letting go

EFFORTS TO HIDE THE EFFECTS OF BEREAVEMENT
Toxic positivity (always being 'up,' forced happiness, etc.)
Throwing themselves into work or other responsibilities
The character assuring others that they're okay
Avoiding places or people linked to their loss
Making drastic changes, such as moving or taking an unplanned trip
Verbally rationalizing the loss
Becoming upset or irritated when people want to talk about the loss
Jumping into a new relationship, job, etc. quickly
Making changes to their physical appearance
Explaining away concerning changes (weight loss is due to a new diet, an unkempt appearance is caused by a cold, etc.)
Making *I'm so busy* excuses to avoid events that will bring grief closer
Professing that everything is fine while pulling away from others
Avoiding friends and family to escape scrutiny, pity, and unsolicited advice

ASSOCIATED POWER VERBS: Weep, mourn, moan, collapse, isolate, obsess, lash out, yell, blame, question, panic, avoid, retreat, doubt, disengage, regret, regress, weaken, yearn, ruminate, recall, wish, ache

EMOTIONS GENERATED BY THIS AMPLIFIER: Acceptance, Anger, Anguish, Anxiety, Apprehension, Bitterness, Confusion, Connectedness, Denial, Depressed, Despair, Devastation, Empathy, Fear, Guilt, Hurt, Jealousy, Loneliness, Longing, Nostalgia, Overwhelmed, Panic, Powerlessness, Regret, Resignation, Sadness, Vulnerability, Worry

DUTIES OR DESIRES THAT MAY BE MORE DIFFICULT TO FULFILL

Caring for children or pets (walking the dog regularly, being positive for the kids, etc.)

Performing academically at the level required to pass a class or keep a scholarship

Enjoying activities, such as hobbies or outings

Participating in faith-based activities, such as prayer or attending church

Dating and engaging in sexual activity (if the loss was a partner or spouse)

Planning a bereavement service

Executing the will of the deceased

Going through the deceased person's belongings and financial affairs

Preparing food for themselves or others

Dealing with affected loved ones who want to talk about the loss when the character doesn't want to think about it

Having to explain what happened to others

Dealing with a new problem regarding a child, employee, or someone else in the character's charge (especially if the person who was lost always handled such things)

Making important decisions, such as accepting a new job or moving across the country

Trying to match the same performance levels at work as they had before the loss

Turning to a new goal or dream

Trusting people (if something underhanded went on to cause the loss)

SCENARIOS FOR BUILDING CONFLICT AND TENSION

Discovering a secret about the person who has passed that casts them in a negative light

Learning that foul play was involved in the event

The loss generating a financial burden for the character

Seeing drastic or dangerous behavior from another bereaved character and not knowing how to help them

Being blamed for the loss

Slipping into a deep depression

Developing a fear or phobia related to how the loss occurred

The loss removing a buffer between the character and someone toxic—e.g., being fired and having to move in with an abusive parent

Fighting over the deceased person's will

Being surrounded by people who are opportunistic, not supportive

WRITER'S TIP: People will grieve differently based on their core beliefs, character traits, and their relationship with what or who was lost. Explore your character's personality, support system, past traumas, and any other factors that could influence their response to a deep loss so you can write their next steps with care.

BOREDOM

DESCRIPTION: This state of weariness, brought about by dullness or a lack of stimulation, causes mental and physical restlessness.

PHYSICAL SIGNALS AND BEHAVIORS

Resting the chin in the hand
Slouching over a desk or table
Staring off into space
Half-closed eyes
Sleeping or dozing
The chin resting on the chest
Limp posture
Listless movements
Slouching in a chair with their arms dangling
Restless movements (rolling the neck, tapping a foot, etc.)
Dramatic sighing or groaning
Engaging in small talk with people nearby
Watching people go about their day
Eating or drinking out of boredom rather than from hunger or thirst
Watching videos, checking social accounts, or surfing online
Taking frequent trips outside or to the bathroom
Flipping through TV channels
Aimlessly wandering or pacing
Texting or scrolling through old pictures on their phone
Picking up random and unnecessary things (rocks on a beach, for example)
Counting items (cigarette butts on the ground, people leaving a store, etc.)
Being easily amused or entertained
Complaining or whining
Yawning
Difficulty focusing on any one thing
Participating in mundane activities out of a desire to do something
Jumping at any opportunity that arises
Making lists
Indulging in habits, such as picking at fingernails or twirling the hair
Passive destructiveness (shredding paper, bending paperclips, etc.)
Mumbling under the breath
Purposely irritating others for entertainment
Pulling pranks
Getting into trouble
Talkativeness; incessantly calling others just to chat
Seeking out others, even those the character normally wouldn't interact with
The character throwing themselves into a new hobby or project
Doing more of the same things they've always done (exercising, reading, sleeping, etc.)
Cycling through new activities in an effort to find something that satisfies

Sitting or staying in one place for long periods of time
Being viewed by others as immature or silly

INTERNAL SENSATIONS
Lethargy
Heaviness in the muscles
A slow, thudding heartbeat
An awareness of things they normally wouldn't notice—a sour aftertaste of coffee, an itchy scalp, a jittery feeling in the extremities, etc.
Hyperactivity; needing to move
A sensation of emptiness inside
Feeling dizzy or spaced out
A sensation of pressure that's building to a breaking point

MENTAL RESPONSES
The mind cycling through options of what to do
Daydreaming
Random thoughts about how things work, what would happen if X happened, etc.
A tendency to notice little things
Being unable to focus on things tied to the source of boredom (work, research, etc.)
Cycling through negative thoughts
Obsessing on the boredom
The sensation of time slowing down or crawling by
Feeling frustrated
Growing impatient
Thinking about something that will happen later
Boredom giving way to apathy
The character feeling sorry for themselves
Longing for purpose

EFFORTS TO HIDE THE BOREDOM
Responding to invitations from others nonchalantly, as if the character isn't excited to have something to do
Overcommitting; agreeing to almost anything to keep from appearing bored
Staying in constant motion
Being determined to have a good time
Offering to help with tasks without being prompted to do so
Writing things down to look busy
Pretending to read a book, takeout menu, cereal box, or whatever is handy
Keeping headphones on so it looks like they're listening to something
Adhering to a strict routine so they'll look busy

ASSOCIATED POWER VERBS: Gape, yawn, stretch, flop, slouch, drag, sigh, tire, wander, doze, drift, droop, blur, smother, rest, sleep, stare, daydream, complain, whine, mumble, mutter, doodle, bother, irritate, annoy

EMOTIONS GENERATED BY THIS AMPLIFIER: Annoyance, Curiosity, Desperation, Determination, Dissatisfaction, Dread, Eagerness, Embarrassment, Frustration, Impatience, Indifference, Irritation, Loneliness, Resentment, Resignation, Sadness, Wistfulness

DUTIES OR DESIRES THAT MAY BE MORE DIFFICULT TO FULFILL

The character applying their full effort to a school or work project
Paying attention to important instructions
Taking careful notes in a vital meeting
Engaging in activities that impart purpose
Feeling fulfilled
Staying alert and awake
Getting along with others
Showing patience and understanding when someone is late
Being perceived as mature and responsible
Finding something they have a passion for
Observing something important in the environment that's easy to miss
Being social at family events
Listening to long stories and remembering the details
Driving long distances
Running a product demonstration for potential customers

SCENARIOS FOR BUILDING CONFLICT AND TENSION

Attending an important but intensely boring career-building event
Having to endure a family vacation in a place the character doesn't enjoy
Being the only bored person in the group
The character doing something while bored that has catastrophic results
A date misinterpreting the character's boredom as a lack of interest in them
Refusing to participate in a boring activity, and causing friction in a relationship
Annoying people to the point of aggravation and strife
Fighting boredom in a situation where attention is paramount (fixing airplane engines, working with chemicals, operating on a patient, etc.)
Lowering their guard due to boredom and being taken advantage of
Missing a critical threat or danger because they were inattentive or fell asleep
Being scrutinized and having to hide their boredom

WRITER'S TIP: Be careful with this amplifier, as bored characters can lead to bored readers. Use this state with purpose and brevity to work toward a specific end goal—to generate conflict, challenge the character, or cause unintended fallout they'll have to navigate. And remember that boredom can also have positive results, becoming a catalyst that pushes your character into uncovering the truth, discovering a new passion, or mending an existing fault in society or their life.

BRAINWASHING

DESCRIPTION: This is the process of a character being pressured, indoctrinated, or subtly forced to change their ideas and beliefs. It can be inflicted by an individual (an abuser, for instance) or a group (in the case of a cult), and the victim is often unaware that their adapted outlook, attitudes, and behaviors are the product of manipulation.

PHYSICAL SIGNALS AND BEHAVIORS
Adopting new habits or rituals related to their dress, diet, religious practices, etc.
Following a routine that is different (and more restricted) than it used to be
Attending regular meetings, gatherings, or retreats
Complying with rules and demands
Using new words or terms that are cryptic or not widely known
Giving up hobbies and favorite pastimes
Spending less time with loved ones
Pulling away from old friends
Missing days at work or school
Abruptly breaking off contact with people
Moving out of a home shared with family members
Keeping to themselves in the workplace
Talking incessantly about the person or group doing the brainwashing
Proselytizing; trying to get friends to join the group or embrace their way of thinking
Questioning or criticizing ideas and beliefs the character used to embrace
Getting frequent texts or phone calls the character is compelled to respond to right away
Blindly agreeing with and following the tenets of a group or group leader
Exhibiting co-dependent behaviors
Giving money, possessions, and anything else requested to the group or individual
Using drugs supplied by the brainwasher
Signs of exhaustion (dark circles under the eyes, staring blankly, nodding off during the day, etc.)
Expressing new opinions that contradict previously stated beliefs
Avoiding, ignoring, or dismissing ideas that oppose theirs (or people who do)
Not standing up for themselves
Speaking less (and fearing to speak about certain things)
The shoulders curving inward
Adopting a downward gaze
Making themselves smaller
Chewing on their lip
Fiddling with jewelry or nearby objects
A gaze that darts around (looking for monitors)
Monitoring others for disobedience
Excessive swallowing
Startling easily; being jumpy

INTERNAL SENSATIONS
Breathlessness in the presence of an influential leader or person

An expanding sensation in the chest (during good times)
Adrenaline rushes
Feeling energized
Fluttering in the stomach
A speeding heartbeat when the character is confronted by loved ones
Muscle tension (when someone the character seeks to please is upset)
A pain in the chest when the overseer's mood darkens
A tingling internal discomfort (when something is "off")

MENTAL RESPONSES
Questioning the loyalty, intentions, and unconditional love of their family
Feeling vulnerable when they're away from the person or group
Anxiety at facing situations without guidance on what to do
Feeling superior to people who believe differently than them
Carefully considering their words—what to say and not to say around certain people
Distrusting outside sources of information (the media, the internet, etc.)
Living in denial
Being easily confused by opposing ideas and arguments
Shutting down "dangerous" thoughts that question new beliefs
Difficulty thinking for themselves and making independent decisions
Self-blame for punishments they have suffered
Being confused about their identity and who they are
Forgetting memories, or remembering them wrong
Losing time
Feeling attacked when someone questions their beliefs or "protectors"
Feeling watched

EFFORTS TO AVOID OUTSIDE INTERFERENCE
Responding to questions about their new beliefs with vague answers
Hiding personal objects associated with the group
Practicing rituals in private
Telling people what they want to hear
Sneaking out to meetings and gatherings
Misrepresenting what the group or person is about
Praising the overseer to others for helping them correct "mistakes"
Hiding signs of punishment that people wouldn't understand (bruises, cuts, brandings, etc.)
Talking only about someone's positive aspects, like their work ethic or skills

ASSOCIATED POWER VERBS: Believe, censor, guard, deceive, dissemble, hide, lie, pretend, conceal, disregard, embrace, rattle, subvert, doubt, question, rearrange, reorder, avoid, cut off, sequester, isolate, promise, recommit

EMOTIONS GENERATED BY THIS AMPLIFIER: Adoration, Awe, Betrayed, Conflicted, Confusion, Connectedness, Defensiveness, Determination, Flustered, Frustration, Gratitude, Insecurity, Intimidation, Nervousness, Obsession, Paranoia, Reluctance, Remorse, Resignation

DUTIES OR DESIRES THAT MAY BE MORE DIFFICULT TO FULFILL
Feeling comfortable with people outside of the group
Interacting authentically with others
Staying connected with loved ones and friends
Persuading others to join the group or the character's new way of thinking
Pursuing a dream that involves a lot of public scrutiny, such as running for office
The character staying true to their roots, culture, or heritage
Making their own decisions
Pursuing a career or keeping a job the brainwasher doesn't agree with
Knowing what's true
Trusting people
Accessing information that isn't sanctioned or allowed
Seeking help (if the character is a prisoner or fears for their life)
Wanting to leave an organization but believing the people in charge are too powerful to cross
Protecting children from abuse
Leaving the abuser or group

SCENARIOS FOR BUILDING CONFLICT AND TENSION
Being arrested for engaging in criminal activity
Being confronted by concerned friends or family
The character's attempts to find answers outside of the group being discovered
An attempt to leave the group being thwarted
Loved ones being threatened in an effort to bring the character into submission
Their marriage falling apart
Being coerced into behaviors the character doesn't want to engage in
Encountering an argument the character struggles to refute
Being exposed to something forbidden (the internet, freedoms others enjoy, etc.)
The character questioning what they have been taught
Discovering a fundamental lie within the new teachings
Being presented with an opportunity to leave the person of influence
Being forced to leave the group—e.g., when it falls apart due to criminal charges
Discovering a child is being groomed for something that doesn't feel right

> **WRITER'S TIP:** Brainwashing is an insidious practice because the character doesn't realize it's happening to them. It is a slow process of restricting information, manipulating emotions, deconstructing core beliefs, creating isolation, and applying intimidation and fear. Then, the character is rewarded for compliance, shown conditional love, and made to feel valued, protected, and understood.
>
> If you need to extricate your character from their situation, it will take more than one person or intervention to convince them of the truth. Consider where loving opposition might come from and use multiple approaches to bring the message of change.

BURNOUT

DESCRIPTION: Burnout is a state of exhaustion (mental, emotional, and physical) brought on by excessive, prolonged stress. While it's most often associated with work, a character can experience burnout in many areas of life, such as school, volunteering, hobbies, and family.

PHYSICAL SIGNALS AND BEHAVIORS
Bags forming under the eyes
Losing weight
Hair that is thinning or going gray
A slumped or rounded posture
Lifeless eyes
Putting in the minimum effort with their appearance
Wearing disheveled or inappropriate clothing
Missing or showing up late to commitments
Eating on the go or forgoing meals
Being constantly attached to the source (a computer for work, a vehicle for required travel, a person the character must care for, etc.)
Cutting corners to save time
Making careless mistakes
Failing to communicate with others
Allowing responsibilities to pile up
Being indifferent to people, tasks, and prior passions
Blowing off responsibilities
Appearing aimless or disengaged
Becoming disorganized
Having an unkempt workspace or living space
Disengaging from relationships
Lacking interest in new developments
Snapping at others and losing patience easily
Responding to simple requests with anger because the character can't deal with one more thing
Making passive-aggressive comments
Using brash or unfiltered language
Slacking off when it comes to procedures and protocols
Procrastinating
Rejecting new ideas and responsibilities without much consideration
Getting sick frequently
Becoming reclusive; seeking to be alone

INTERNAL SENSATIONS
Headaches
Fatigue
Difficulty sleeping despite being exhausted
Low energy
Stomach discomfort

Tense muscles
Tightness or heaviness in the chest
Dizziness and body tingling (from high blood pressure, anxiety, and exhaustion)
Feeling as if a weight is pressing down on them
Panic attack symptoms (racing heartbeat, trembling, shortness of breath, etc.)

MENTAL RESPONSES
Wandering thoughts
Feeling stressed and anxious
Being irritated easily
Decreased mental focus and acuity
Feeling helpless and defeated
Viewing the world through a filter of cynicism and pessimism
Dreading daily duties and responsibilities
Feeling unappreciated and trapped
Doubting their ability to improve their situation
Talking themselves into continuing
Resenting their situation or the people who contributed to it
Regretting past choices
Not seeing the point in anything
Losing interest in activities the character used to enjoy
Longing to be doing other things
Losing their sense of joy
Low self-esteem (feeling like a disappointment for not handling things better)
Thinking about how to escape or offload burdens
Toying with the idea of self-sabotage (because poor performance and results will provide a way out, though it means disappointing others)

EFFORTS TO HIDE THE BURNOUT
Abusing substances to cope
Denying the problem
Assuring others about their own capability
Overly relying on others to complete requirements
Making excuses for failures
Blaming something (the stock market, inflation, a program, etc.) for errors or problems
Faking happiness
Keeping unusual hours (so others won't notice how little they're working)
Asking for extensions on deadlines
Stalling for additional time
Focusing on the short-term only; not participating in long-term planning
Physical cues that indicate hidden emotions (flexing the jaw, clenching fists, deep breathing, etc.)
Sacrificing personal needs to have time and energy for others
Avoiding people who might hold them accountable

ASSOCIATED POWER VERBS: Snap, withdraw, argue, criticize, complain, avoid, vent, spiral, explode, disparage, doubt, abuse, decline, disengage

EMOTIONS GENERATED BY THIS AMPLIFIER: Anxiety, Apprehension, Bitterness, Conflicted, Defeat, Depressed, Despair, Discouragement, Disillusionment, Dread, Inadequacy, Indifference, Insecurity, Powerlessness, Reluctance, Resentment, Resignation, Sadness, Skepticism, Unappreciated

DUTIES OR DESIRES THAT MAY BE MORE DIFFICULT TO FULFILL
Leading or coaching others on a team
Working on group projects with people who are excited and motivated
Maintaining enthusiasm about the source of stress
Completing a project that requires complex problem-solving
Helping ease a coworker's workload
Accepting and incorporating feedback; actively working to improve
Working full days in the work environment
Relaxing without feeling guilty for doing so
Stepping up in another area as needed
Being there for a friend in need
Taking a vacation
Participating in a meeting where new goals are set or an overall vision is cast
Finishing a project and feeling proud in knowing they did their best work
Saying *yes* to a new opportunity that is good for the character

SCENARIOS FOR BUILDING CONFLICT AND TENSION
Being assigned a mentor who will work with the character on personal growth
A coworker going on maternity leave, resulting in more work for the character
A major life event happening, such as a loved one dying or the character having a baby
Deciding to exit the situation, then being offered an attractive incentive to stay
The character's rent increasing, adding an additional financial burden
Being caught slacking off
Venting to the wrong person or in an online forum about the situation
Being placed on probation for cutting corners or other mistakes
Substance use becoming abuse, impacting the character's performance
Receiving a poor review on a project and having to redo it
A child experiencing a crisis that requires more of the character's time and energy
Being presented with a way out that is morally gray at best (temptation)

> **WRITER'S TIP:** *While stress will make a character feel "more" (overwhelmed, overworked, pressured, etc.), burnout is associated with feelings of emptiness: a lack of motivation, having no purpose, feeling apathetic or numb about the situation, negative thought patterns, and seeing no way out. The line between stress and burnout is fine, so explore both options carefully to know which side your character is on.*

CHRONIC PAIN

DESCRIPTION: This kind of pain is persistent and carries on for many months or years despite treatment. It's often seen in conjunction with a chronic health condition. For information on the generalized, temporary form of PAIN, see that entry.

PHYSICAL SIGNALS AND BEHAVIORS

Closing the eyes and letting out a breath
A pinched mouth
Wincing
A furrow forming between the eyes
Moving wrong, then hissing through clenched teeth at the pain
Stiff or jerky movements
A wavering voice
Being fidgety
Moving as little as possible
Having a slumped posture
A sheen of sweat appearing on the cheeks, chin, or forehead
Rubbing any painful areas
Taking medications regularly (possibly several types)
Having to sit, lie, or move in a certain way
Difficulty sleeping
Sleeping to escape the pain
Frequently canceling plans
Utilizing assistive devices, such as a cane, walker, or wheelchair
Making clothing choices based on comfort rather than style
Taking frequent sick days from work
Taking seats near the door at social events
Avoiding bright lights
Walking with a shuffling or shambling gait
Viewing physical activities with doubt or trepidation
Drawing their limbs in close to their body
Becoming defensive or aggressive when pushed past their comfort zone
Vocalizing blame for a condition stemming from an accident
Having a short fuse
Not engaging in sexual activity
Neglecting their children's basic needs (bathing, feeding, etc.)
Grunting and groaning when they move
Complaining about their circumstances (or suffering in silence)
Easily becoming winded
Flinching when touched

INTERNAL SENSATIONS

Ringing ears
Throbbing headaches or migraines

A sensation of pins and needles in the limbs
Experiencing weakness in the muscles
Persistent aches in the joints
A shooting pain in their back
Feeling overheated
Tingling skin
A burning sensation in the muscles
Shallow breaths
Persistent fatigue
Aching that never subsides
Ulcers
A sense of overall pain or discomfort

MENTAL RESPONSES
Having anxiety over their pain level on any given day
Being frustrated when people doubt their pain or condition
Feeling guilty for being a burden to others
Moodiness
Feeling guilty when an engagement has to be canceled
Feeling isolated from others
Worrying they're going to lose their job
Feeling misunderstood
Envying people who aren't living with chronic pain
Praying for relief
Doubting their ability to continue
Harboring anger against the person who caused the pain
Worrying about dependency on (or running out of) medications
Mounting frustration at limited medical options
Growing weary of seeing doctors and explaining their pain or condition
Giving up hope of ever feeling better
Being shocked at rare, pain-free moments
Feeling helpless
Struggling with suicidal thoughts

EFFORTS TO HIDE THE CHRONIC PAIN
Trying to work and play at other people's levels
Staying busy
Telling everyone they're fine
Making sure everything is close at hand to avoid moving too much
Refusing help
Overmedicating
Avoiding medical attention
Physical cues of inward pain (clenched teeth, wincing, sweating, trembling, etc.)
Drinking heavily
Using self-deprecating humor to deflect attention from the problem

Pulling away from others
Withdrawing from activities that used to bring joy

ASSOCIATED POWER VERBS: Agonize, clench, tense, moan, groan, complain, hyperventilate, mutter, pace, rock, shiver, strain, suffer, tremble, wail, despair, give up, avoid, seize, sweat, shake, slip, ache, cry, rub, massage, adjust, lean, wobble

EMOTIONS GENERATED BY THIS AMPLIFIER: Agitation, Amazement, Anger, Anguish, Anxiety, Apprehension, Bitterness, Defeat, Defensiveness, Despair, Determination, Discouragement, Dread, Fear, Frustration, Jealousy, Loneliness, Moodiness, Overwhelmed

DUTIES OR DESIRES THAT MAY BE MORE DIFFICULT TO FULFILL
Activities that require a lot of walking (taking a tour, navigating an airport, etc.)
Carrying or lifting items (luggage, a pet, etc.)
Sleeping through the night
Remaining in a seated position for work, travel, or leisure time
Engaging in outdoor activities
Attending concerts or theatrical shows
Running necessary errands
Bathing themselves
Attending parties and social engagements
Being an active parent or grandparent
Staying optimistic about treatment and cures
Connecting deeply with others (and having to be honest about their condition)

SCENARIOS FOR BUILDING CONFLICT AND TENSION
Someone questioning the true level of their pain
The character being forced to accept that they must depend on others
The emergence of a secondary health issue
Developing an addiction to drugs or alcohol
Being unable to adequately care for a child or pet
Being abandoned by a spouse
Medical treatments or needs no longer being covered by insurance
A procedure or treatment that makes the pain worse
The character's needs not being accommodated at work
Having to relocate to live near a caregiver or in an assisted living facility
Learning about a new treatment option but not wanting to be disappointed again
The character lashing out at loved ones and creating relationship friction

> **WRITER'S TIP:** *Go beyond the physical limitations of chronic pain and consider how it could impact important relationships. Some loved ones may enable the character while others will challenge the legitimacy of their condition. Other people's responses, as well as the character's reactions to them, can cause relational strain even within the character's support system.*

COGNITIVE BIAS

DESCRIPTION: Cognitive biases occur when a character processes new information based on their personal ideas, perceptions, and experiences rather than viewing it through an objective lens. While biases are natural inclinations (the brain's way of simplifying and sorting through an overload of data) they often result in inaccurate interpretations, skewed conclusions, and illogical decision-making.

It's important to note that bias typically occurs at the subconscious level, with the character being unaware of its existence or its influences on their thoughts and actions.

PHYSICAL SIGNALS AND BEHAVIORS
Eyebrows furrowing
Tilting or cocking the head
A flat stare
Pursing the lips or frowning
Shaking the head
Pulling at an ear lobe
Displaying restlessness (fidgeting, shifting position, pacing, etc.)
Slanting the body to the side
Putting their hands on their hips
Crossing their arms
Making assumptions
Making stereotypical statements
Waving a hand dismissively
Putting a hand up, palm out, in a *stop* gesture
Interrupting: *No, that's wrong, Let me stop you there,* etc.
Becoming confrontational
Squaring their shoulders or planting their feet
Talking over someone with a contrary view
Unconsciously taking a step back (or moving forward, if agitated)
Speaking with conviction (a sharp tone, directness, being emphatic, etc.)
Demanding proof or evidence when an alternative viewpoint is shared
Seeking information only from sources that agree with the character (confirmation bias)
Attributing bias to gut instinct: *I tossed his resume because I had a bad feeling about him.*
Glossing over information that contradicts their opinion
Applying tendencies to people based on specific criteria such as gender, race, or age
Jumping to conclusions: *They raised their prices? Talk about greedy!*
Seeing a rare news event and believing it's more common than it is
Failing to see faults in certain people (favorable bias)
Giving someone (or a group) preferential treatment
Forgiving easily (being unable to stay angry)
Dismissing mistakes and missteps of those the character respects

INTERNAL SENSATIONS

Favorable Bias:

A feeling of expansion and warmth in the chest

Relaxed muscles, being at ease

A steady heart rate

Negative Bias:

The chest growing tighter

Body temperature rising

The stomach hardening

Breathlessness due to frequently interjecting or talking over people

Tension in the muscles

A pounding heart

MENTAL RESPONSES

Sorting rapidly through existing knowledge to see how the new information fits in

Being conflicted; not knowing what to make of the information being presented

Giving greater weight to information that supports what the character wants

Thinking prejudicial thoughts about some people

Tending to believe or trust people who share the same views

Tending to disbelieve or distrust people who disagree with their views

Seeking to disprove those who disagree (instead of examining their own opinion for validity)

Having an us-versus-them mindset

Expecting an individual to behave a specific way because of a stereotype

Being closed to new information that challenges the character's beliefs

Being overly inclined to see the good (or bad) in a situation

Blaming external forces (instead of internal reasons) for personal failures

Viewing certain people as inferior

Applying deeper meaning to coincidental events

Forming opinions based on gut feeling rather than facts

Making connections between unrelated events

Believing that because something has never happened, it never will

Underestimating risks (because the character doesn't think they're a big deal)

Favoring certain ideas and decisions, even if they're not the best or "right" choices

Mentally justifying their thoughts so they can dismiss any suspicions of bias

Feeling self-righteous when someone responds as expected (because their bias is "confirmed")

Being annoyed when people disagree with them

Experiencing mental discomfort and wondering if they're being biased

Feeling like a bias might be in play but being unwilling to examine it too closely

Becoming defensive if someone suggests that the character is being biased

Waffling and second-guessing themselves

EFFORTS TO HIDE SUSPECTED OR KNOWN BIAS

Going on the offensive; accusing a challenger of being biased

Searching for data to support their ideas (so they can feel right, rather than biased)

Surrounding themselves with people who agree with them

Avoiding environments where their beliefs will be challenged

Delaying a decision so the character has time to privately examine potential biases
Using noncommittal language: *Well, I'll need to think about that.*
Disengaging from the conversation
Changing the subject

ASSOCIATED POWER VERBS: Believe, assume, argue, demand, scoff, debate, claim, cling to, state, embrace, lean, view, filter, blame, expect, doubt, question, denounce, disprove, ignore, deny, suppress

EMOTIONS GENERATED BY THIS AMPLIFIER: Agitation, Anger, Certainty, Confidence, Conflicted, Confusion, Contempt, Defensiveness, Defiance, Denial, Doubt, Flustered, Frustration, Irritation, Nervousness, Relief, Reluctance, Satisfaction, Schadenfreude, Smugness

DUTIES OR DESIRES THAT MAY BE MORE DIFFICULT TO FULFILL
Staying open-minded
Forming an objective opinion
Making the most sensible and logical decision
Viewing all people equally in terms of value and deserved respect
Doing what's right when it goes against a personal bias
Remaining impartial
Fostering a welcoming and inclusive environment
Making accurate predictions about future events
Experiencing personal growth and becoming more self-aware
Accurately interpreting data
Respecting someone's choices when they don't align with the character's views
Solving problems creatively, which requires seeing situations from different perspectives
Supporting someone's decision when the character has personal doubts

SCENARIOS FOR BUILDING CONFLICT AND TENSION
A situation with high stakes that requires an impartial decision
Someone accusing the character of bias (whether it's true or not)
Working or living with people the character is biased against
Someone else being put in charge because the character isn't trusted to think objectively
An experience that causes the character to recognize their own bias—especially if it's something they've been incentivized to embrace (as a political lobbyist, for instance)
The character voicing an opinion and being ridiculed for it
Acting on a bias and it ending badly for the character
Being called out for favoritism
Shedding a bias and having to confront those who instilled in

> **WRITER'S TIP:** *Bias runs on a spectrum, and while we often focus on its negative effects, it can also skew to the positive, such as a grandparent viewing everything their beloved grandchild does in the best light. If, however, a bias activates and amplifies a character's darker emotions, their response could cause harm for themselves or others.*

COGNITIVE DECLINE

DESCRIPTION: This condition results in decreased mental functions in the areas of memory, awareness, and acuity. It can be severe—significantly interfering with daily activities—or mild. While it's most often associated with aging and mental conditions like Parkinson's, dementia, and Alzheimer's, other factors can contribute to it, such as depression, illness, sleep deprivation, medication side effects, nutrition deficiencies, a traumatic brain injury, and diet and health choices.

PHYSICAL SIGNALS AND BEHAVIORS
The eyebrows pulling together
Biting the inside of the cheek
Fidgety movements
Glancing around in confusion
Struggling to find the right words
Easily becoming flustered
Using the wrong words when speaking
Difficulty following the conversation when several people are involved
Showing frustration when communication is difficult
Short- or long-term memory loss
Making errors during familiar tasks, such as managing household finances
Losing keys, a wallet, phone, and other items
Putting familiar items in unusual places
Forgetting about appointments
Difficulty with complex tasks that used to be relatively easy
Getting lost in a familiar place
Being unable to get to a place they've been to dozens of times
Snapping at people
Being irritated by small inconveniences
Telling the same stories and asking the same questions
Needing clarification more often than is normal
Not recognizing friends or family members
Forgetting to take medications
Leaving projects unfinished
Struggling to plan a vacation or family get-together
Driving erratically—being overly cautious or not cautious enough
Remembering events incorrectly
Showing up late to events
Struggling with everyday tasks, such as grocery shopping or cleaning the fridge
Not recognizing familiar mementos
Difficulty learning new information or skills
Declining personal care—forgetting to bathe, wearing clothes that aren't clean, etc.
Personality and behavior changes
Clumsiness; decreased muscle control

Forgetting to eat

Impulsivity

Having no sense of how much time has passed

Not wanting to go out of the home

Turning down social invitations

Difficulty keeping up with a favorite pastime, such as a baseball team's record or the plotline of a TV show

Sleeping more than is healthy

INTERNAL SENSATIONS

Feeling exhausted

An overall sense of slowing down

Dizziness

A lack of energy

Racing heartbeat due to not knowing where they are, frustration surges, etc.

MENTAL RESPONSES

Muddled thoughts

The mind wandering

Slower processing of stimuli and information

Struggling with decision-making

Difficulty solving problems

Feeling mentally fatigued as the day or a task goes on

Decreased interest in previous passions or hobbies

Being easily distracted or confused

Poor judgment—e.g., making an expensive purchase without considering the cost

Being overwhelmed by increased sensory stimuli

Becoming suspicious of loved ones

Feeling disconnected from others

Sensing that something is very wrong but not knowing what it is

Being overly fearful

Feeling agitated and uneasy outside of their comfort zone

Anxiety

Depression

EFFORTS TO HIDE THE COGNITIVE DECLINE

Brushing off a relative's concern

Relying heavily on memory aids (lists, a journal, etc.) to remember things

Setting calendar reminders for upcoming events and important tasks

Double- and triple-checking details to be sure they've been recorded correctly

Speaking less (to avoid repeating themselves)

Smiling and nodding in conversations

Blaming confusion or forgetfulness on something else, such as hearing loss

Refusing to see a doctor or have tests run

No longer participating in activities that will highlight a decline (playing chess, reciting a favorite poem, etc.)
Spending more time alone
Staying at home
Walking instead of driving

ASSOCIATED POWER VERBS: Forget, struggle, strain, grasp, fumble, stumble, flounder, grapple, grope, neglect, wander, withdraw, isolate, hide, deflect, camouflage

EMOTIONS GENERATED BY THIS AMPLIFIER: Agitation, Anger, Anxiety, Bitterness, Confusion, Connectedness, Defiance, Denial, Depressed, Discouragement, Embarrassment, Fear, Flustered, Frustration, Impatience, Inadequacy, Longing, Moodiness, Overwhelmed, Powerlessness, Resentment, Resignation, Sadness, Self-Pity

DUTIES OR DESIRES THAT MAY BE MORE DIFFICULT TO FULFILL
Engaging in activities that provide meaning and purpose
Recalling important memories
Feeling valued
Being viewed as competent and capable
Participating in activities that bring the character joy (that they no longer can do)
Keeping a job
Driving and traveling independently
Maintaining control over their life
Being involved in the decision-making process for the family
Interacting socially with others

SCENARIOS FOR BUILDING CONFLICT AND TENSION
Getting lost and not remembering who to call or how to get help
Causing a car accident
Having to move out of their familiar home
A spouse or caregiver dying
Loss of insurance benefits
Developing an allergy to an effective medication
A disaster that disrupts the character's support system, threatening their safety
A predatory family member or neighbor looking to take advantage
Being scammed and facing a financial crisis

> **WRITER'S TIP:** *Cognitive decline is a natural process, but it's by no means a welcome development. Because of denial or a desire to maintain control, your character will likely try to hide what's happening to them. In this case you'll need to carefully show the contrast between what's really happening to them and the image they're portraying to others. The former can be shown through their thoughts and emotions, while their deflection and deception can be revealed through their actions and dialogue.*

COLD

DESCRIPTION: This state is brought on by a sudden or ongoing exposure to uncomfortably low temperatures. There are a number of environmental factors that could cause a character to suffer in this way, such as being caught in a weather event, stranded in frigid waters, or locked in a freezer by someone wishing them harm.

PHYSICAL SIGNALS AND BEHAVIORS
Shivering
Lips that are tinged blue
Dry, cracked lips
Lips that tremble
Enlarged pupils
Chattering teeth
Stuttering speech
Slurred, unclear speech
Their voice dropping in volume
Skin that is noticeably cold to the touch
Clumsiness
Slow, shallow breaths
Quivering breaths
Decreased dexterity
Wrapping their arms around the torso to stay warm
Jumping, shuffling, or dancing to get the blood flowing
The character clapping their hands or stamping their feet
Shoving their hands deep into their pockets
Red and swollen patches on their skin (chilblains)
Pulling their limbs tightly against the body's core
Rubbing their hands together
Tucking their hands into their armpits
Pulling a collar or scarf up over their face
Huddling deeper into a jacket
Rounded shoulders, the chin dropped down to the chest
Cringing and squeezing the eyes shut
Repositioning themselves so their back is to the source of cold
Pulling down their sleeves to cover their hands
Curling and uncurling their toes
Rubbing the legs or arms; using friction to create warmth
Slapping themselves on the cheeks to warm them up
Shaking out their arms and legs to get blood flowing
Flexing their fingers
Stiff steps; walking slowly
Curling into a ball; making themselves small to conserve heat
Sharing body heat with others

Blowing into their cupped palms to warm them
Yawning
Eyes tearing up
Taking deep breaths in an effort to stay awake
Body motions slowing over time
Decreased activity as the character seeks to use as little energy as possible
Stumbling or falling
Checking for frostbite
Frost forming on their hair, eyelashes, eyebrows, etc. (extreme cold)
Slipping into unconsciousness

INTERNAL SENSATIONS
Fatigue or drowsiness
Feeling cold even on the inside
Numbness in the extremities
Tingling extremities
A burning sensation on their skin
Muscle tension and aches from holding themselves tightly for so long
A stiff jaw that makes speech difficult
Uncontrolled shivering
A heaviness in their limbs that makes movements difficult
A weakened or thready pulse
Loss of appetite
A burning sensation in the lungs when inhaling
An eventual cessation of pain or cold
Abnormal heart rhythms

MENTAL RESPONSES
Fantasizing about fires, sunshine, and other sources of heat
Remembering times when they were warm (at the beach, cooking over a stove, etc.)
Feeling envious of people with warmer clothing (if the character is with others)
Worrying about what will happen if they can't get warm
Muddled thinking and confusion
Impaired decision-making
Wanting to sleep
Not wanting to move
Apathy

EFFORTS TO HIDE THE EFFECTS OF BEING COLD
Wearing multiple layers of clothing
Making excuses for their unusual clothing choices
Suggesting activities that require movement so the character can subtly stay in motion
Hiding their hands so no one sees them shake
Biting down on the lips so they don't tremble
Only speaking when it's absolutely necessary

Avoiding contact with others so they won't notice the character's cold skin or shivers
Holding themselves together tightly to hide the trembling
Feigning sleep

ASSOCIATED POWER VERBS: Shake, tremble, shiver, chatter, rub, flex, numb, damp, frost, sniff, sneeze, quake, hug, nip, thaw, whiten, pierce, cough, cringe, freeze, huddle, ice, brush, vibrate, jerk, falter, stiffen, totter, stutter

EMOTIONS GENERATED BY THIS AMPLIFIER: Agitation, Anguish, Anxiety, Apprehension, Frustration, Inadequacy, Loneliness, Longing, Misery, Overwhelmed, Panic, Powerlessness, Regret, Resignation, Unease, Vulnerability, Worry

DUTIES OR DESIRES THAT MAY BE MORE DIFFICULT TO FULFILL
Tasks requiring dexterity, such as stitching up a wound or untying shoelaces
Hunting or gathering food
Chopping or hauling wood to build a fire
Maintaining a positive attitude
Keeping up the spirits of others who are stuck with the character
Getting medical care for an injured party member
Making important decisions
Coming up with an escape plan
Communicating clearly with others
Caring for loved ones who share the character's situation
Staying awake
Writing a note or message
Staying active
Driving a car

SCENARIOS FOR BUILDING CONFLICT AND TENSION
Running low on food
Falling and suffering an injury
Someone in the character's party succumbing to the cold
Developing frostbite
Hearing signs of humanity (footsteps, a car motor, etc.) but being unable to flag them down
Wild animals getting bolder and coming closer to the character
Getting rained on or falling into a river
The character's location becoming unstable, forcing them to relocate
Being pushed into the leadership role of getting everyone to safety

> **WRITER'S TIP:** *Attitude makes a difference when someone is dealing with the cold. A person who can maintain mental acuity and focus will withstand the elements much better than someone whose mental condition is compromised by negativity or worry.*

COMPETITION

DESCRIPTION: Rivalry—when a character is pitted against others who want the same thing—creates psychological strain because the outcome is uncertain. While competition is frequently associated with athletics, it can manifest at work and school (vying for a promotion or academic award), in relationships (competing for a love interest's attention or a parent's approval), and anywhere else a position of power or object of desire can be won. Regardless of the context, the character's response to this amplifier will vary depending on how prepared they are and whether they anticipate success or failure.

PHYSICAL SIGNALS AND BEHAVIORS
Sizing up the competition
Pursing the lips
Holding the gaze of their opponent
Giving their competition a nod
The character's brows lowering in concentration
Straightening their posture and thrusting out the chest
The character looking down, mentally preparing for the task ahead
Rolling the neck from side to side
Fidgety movements
Shaking out the arms and loosening up the shoulders
Bouncing in place or pacing
Behaving assertively and with confidence (even if the character is faking it)
Scanning their environment
Focusing on preparations, studying, self-improvement, or whatever else they need to do to come out on top
Setting steppingstone goals that will get them closer to success
Incessantly practicing skills the character will need to win
Learning from mistakes to avoid making them again
Being disciplined in preparing for the task ahead
Staying up late; sacrificing sleep
Pushing themselves to greater limits than ever before
Taking risks if doing so will give them an edge
Analyzing data to predict success, ascertain growth, and identify weaknesses
Shying away from activities or jobs that will reveal their weaknesses
Gathering a team of talented people to support the character
Expecting team members to work as hard as the character does
Being a control freak (needing to lead, manage the process, etc.)
Frequently checking in on a team member's progress
Prioritizing the goal by sacrificing other hobbies or habits
Spending a disproportionate amount of time working toward the goal
Becoming overwhelmed when new stressors or responsibilities come up
Flattering the decision-makers
Berating allies when mistakes are made

Blowing up over setbacks and errors
Relying on stimulants to stay awake and remain sharp
Neglecting the important people in their life
Talking trash to a rival to get into their head
Covertly undermining an opponent
Sabotaging a rival
Being a sore loser if things don't go their way

INTERNAL SENSATIONS
Adrenaline rushes
An accelerated heart rate (feeling it beat harder in the chest)
Quicker breaths
Butterflies in the stomach
A heavy feeling of dread in the core (if the opponent is seemingly better positioned)
Muscles feeling taut
Tension in the jaw
Feeling antsy, as if the character needs to be in motion

MENTAL RESPONSES
Being hyper-focused on the objective
Mentally talking themselves up as an important date or event approaches
Visualizing the win
Thinking incessantly about their goal
Feeling stressed
Comparing themselves to rivals
Being jealous of a competitor
Becoming obsessed with the rival; constantly checking on their progress
Intrusive thoughts about the rival (their skills, assets, abilities, etc.) that sabotage the character's confidence and make them doubt their abilities
Craving the win because the character believes it will fill an internal need (gaining someone's approval, proving their own worth, providing security, etc.)
Underestimating the competition
Overestimating their own abilities
Adopting unfair or unfounded biases against a rival
Being tempted to cut corners or sacrifice ethics to get ahead
Worrying about what others think
Being self-critical
Struggling with perfectionism
Fearing failure
Feeling nervous or anxious as the moment of truth draws near

EFFORTS TO HIDE THE EFFECTS OF THIS AMPLIFIER
False bravado
Claiming that the rival isn't competition at all
Skipping practices, meetings, and other preparatory events

Practicing skills alone, in private
Pretending that winning doesn't matter to the character
Complementing or embracing their opponent to downplay the rivalry
Avoiding the rival

ASSOCIATED POWER VERBS: Strive, persevere, push, toil, work, practice, hone, rehearse, exercise, train, drill, sharpen, sacrifice, prioritize, focus, fixate, concentrate, obsess, undermine, sabotage, defeat, thwart, undercut, visualize, analyze, scrutinize

EMOTIONS GENERATED BY THIS AMPLIFIER: Anticipation, Anxiety, Apprehension, Confidence, Contempt, Desire, Determination, Doubt, Dread, Embarrassment, Excitement, Fear, Hopefulness, Inadequacy, Insecurity, Intimidation, Jealousy, Nervousness, Obsession, Overwhelmed, Uncertainty, Vulnerability, Worry

DUTIES OR DESIRES THAT MAY BE MORE DIFFICULT TO FULFILL
Not becoming obsessed with the need to win (to the detriment of everything else)
Knowing and abiding by healthy limits
Having a realistic view of their own capabilities
Making time for important relationships
Succeeding independently, without anyone's help
Maintaining the proper perspective regarding mistakes and failures
Being able to live with a loss
Treating people with respect when emotions are high (the rival, team members, loved ones, an employer, etc.)

SCENARIOS FOR BUILDING CONFLICT AND TENSION
The character sustaining an injury or contracting a sickness that impedes their progress
The rival gaining a significant advantage
Losing the support of loved ones or family members
Losing a benefactor or source of income
An underdog rival appearing out of nowhere to challenge the character's success
Public opinion turning against the character
A failure that shakes the character's confidence
The benchmark for success changing in a way that makes winning more difficult
Struggling to acquire a necessary skill
The character suspecting they're being sabotaged but not being able to prove it
Being betrayed by an ally

> **WRITER'S TIP:** *For competition to be a stressor, there must be something significant at stake should the character lose. The stakes for failure need to be high and personal, so explore the possibilities and be sure you know what this looks like for the person involved. Then convey the stakes adequately so readers will know why competition has brought out the best or worst in your character.*

COMPULSION

DESCRIPTION: A compulsion is an irresistible urge to take a certain action, especially one that is irrational or even unwanted. We tend to think of compulsions in terms of a serious condition, such as obsessive-compulsive disorder or substance abuse, but the truth is that we're assailed by strong urges every day. Your character will face them, too, such as the urge to cover up a mistake, cheat on their diet, reward themselves with a coveted item, or rescue a loved one from the consequences of their actions. This entry addresses a range of possibilities for characters wrestling with urges and compulsions.

PHYSICAL SIGNALS AND BEHAVIORS

Shaking the head (as if to an internal *no* or *don't do it*)
The face reddening
Rubbing the back of the neck
Rolling the shoulders or neck to release tension
A gaze that bounces from place to place
Restless limbs
Pacing
Dilated pupils
Avoiding eye contact with others
Rapid blinking
Adjusting their clothing
Dragging the hands through the hair
Intense breathing
Filling the cheeks with air, holding it in, and then finally releasing a breath
Verbalizing or reasoning it through under the breath: *Should I?* or *I have to*
Laughter with an edge
Swallowing often
Hands that tremble or shake
Flapping the hands
Abruptly turning on their heels
Repeatedly shaking their feet
Sweat appearing on the chin, cheeks, and forehead
Making odd noises in the throat
Scratching or rubbing the skin until it is red or raw
Making fists while fighting the compulsion
Repeatedly checking switches, locks, etc.
Routinely setting several wake-up alarms rather than only one
Ordering and arranging things in the workplace or home
Trash and debris piling up in their living space (or the opposite—everything being in its place)
Not showing up to appointments and social engagements
Emotions fluctuating wildly in a short span of time
Constantly chewing on something (gum, fingernails, etc.)
Needing to perform a ritual at certain times (before bed, before leaving the house, etc.)

Over-collecting (there's too much to display, the character is going into debt, etc.)
Hoarding (forming attachments to things and being unable to let them go)
Excessive hand washing
Counting, praying, or reciting a phrase under the breath
Engaging in repetitive body behaviors, such as pulling hair or picking at the skin
Overreacting when their schedule changes or things aren't as they want them
Avoiding triggers that intensify the urge to act
Explaining why they're acting on a compulsion: *It's silly, but it just makes me feel better.*

INTERNAL SENSATIONS
A quickening pulse
Eyes that have a hard time focusing
Loss of appetite
Grinding the teeth
Sounds seeming louder than they are
Tightness in the chest
Feeling highly energized
An internal jumpiness
Sensitivity to the way clothes feel on the skin
Difficulty sleeping or relaxing
Feeling overheated
A tingling or itching sensation that won't go away
Tense muscles

MENTAL RESPONSES
Being singularly focused on the compulsion
Emotional reasoning over what to do; weighing and measuring
Justifying giving in to an urge: *Everyone lies about money. No big deal.*
Losing perspective on the consequences of their actions
Unwanted thoughts that are hard to dismiss
A phrase repeating in their mind
An inability to articulate thoughts
Trying to distract themselves
Telling themselves not to act on the compulsion
Desperately wanting relief from it
Wanting to resist but feeling unable to do so
Losing track of time
Thoughts becoming less rational as the compulsion builds
Convincing themselves they have no other option but to act
Negative self-talk: *You're crazy, You should be able to stop this*, etc.
Struggling with self-loathing and shame
Anxiety that develops into panic

EFFORTS TO HIDE THE COMPULSION

Reassuring others that things are under control
Lying about what they've been doing
Giving excuses for why they won't go to certain places or see particular people
Seeking reassurance from others
Using a controlled tone of voice
Hiding body parts that display signs of their compulsion (self-harm marks, bitten-down nails, etc.)
Cutting people out of their lives
Embracing the behavior as part of an accepted spectrum, like drinking, gambling, etc.
Reframing the behavior: *I just like everything organized, that's all.*

ASSOCIATED POWER VERBS: Bounce, consume, control, deliberate, demand, fixate, justify, rationalize, preoccupy, refuse, repeat, stalk, watch, wrestle, fight, resist, avoid, distract, follow, act, pick, straighten, move, organize, pause, delay, rush

EMOTIONS GENERATED BY THIS AMPLIFIER: Agitation, Anticipation, Anxiety, Apprehension, Conflicted, Determination, Doubt, Excitement, Guilt, Insecurity, Longing, Obsession, Remorse, Self-Loathing, Shame, Tormented

DUTIES OR DESIRES THAT MAY BE MORE DIFFICULT TO FULFILL

Resisting the urge to meddle, fix, lie, hide, interfere, or whatever form the compulsion takes
Making healthy choices
Focusing on other things when a compulsion comes on
Feeling confident, strong, and free
Being transparent and open with family members or close friends
Helping someone else deal with temptation
Admitting there's a problem and seeking help

SCENARIOS FOR BUILDING CONFLICT AND TENSION

Giving in to a compulsion, then having to explain it or apologize to someone else
Acting on an urge that leads to unintended consequences
Hiring an inept or ineffective therapist who isn't able to help
Subconsciously sabotaging a relationship to avoid having to address the compulsion
Being so focused on their own struggle they miss something happening in a child's life
Someone threatening to reveal the character's secret
Being recorded engaging in the compulsion
Having an adverse reaction to medication that is helping with the compulsions

WRITER'S TIP: *For this amplifier to work, you need to know your character's temptations and weak spots. What are their urges and compulsions and what causes them? Are they triggered by something specific—a situation, person, or emotion? How irresistible are the urges? If your character has a serious condition that causes their compulsions, do your research to write it accurately and avoid stereotypes.*

CONFINEMENT

DESCRIPTION: A character is confined when they're physically restrained, restricted to a defined area, or held against their will. The type of confinement, length of time, and isolation level will all factor into the character's physical, mental, and psychological well-being in this situation.

PHYSICAL SIGNALS AND BEHAVIORS

Pale skin
Dark hollows under the eyes
Unkempt (and possibly overgrown) hair
Losing body weight and muscle mass
Rumpled clothing
Skin at the wrists or ankles being torn, chafed, or reddened by restraints
Bruises, cuts, and other signs of being beaten
Flinching at noises and other sensory stimuli
Straining to reach a window (if there is one)
Exploring the space for openings or vulnerabilities that might offer escape
Lying in the fetal position
Sleeping frequently
Backing away or making themselves small when a captor appears
Bursting into tears
Stalking back and forth across the space
Crouching in a corner
Talking to themselves
Talking to inanimate objects
Refusing to eat
Giving short answers to questions
Bargaining with the captor
Pounding their fists against the wall
Asking for information
Marking time by scratching marks into a bedframe, writing on the wall, etc.
Shouting for help
Pulling at restraints
Hurling or banging items
Passing the time in odd ways, such as counting the bricks in the wall or plaiting twigs together
Rolling the shoulders and trying to work out aches associated with confinement
Looking for weapons, tools, or other items that could be of use
Stretching or exercising as much as their space allows
Taking stock of possible resources
Scrutinizing their space for vulnerabilities
Rebelling in small ways to maintain control over some part of their life
Engaging in self-harm as a final resort

INTERNAL SENSATIONS

Loss of appetite
Hunger (if meals are inadequate or unreliable)
Dehydration
The mouth going dry
Exhaustion
Tension headaches
Stomach pain
Aches and pain from being confined to a certain position
Heightened senses and light sensitivity
Weakness in the limbs
A head that feels too heavy to hold up
Hot eyes from crying
The throat being sore from yelling or screaming
Pain from injuries incurred during the kidnapping or confinement
Itchiness (from sweat, dirty clothes, chafing, etc.)
Being cold or hot, depending on the environment
Restlessness; wanting to move more than they can
Hypervigilance
Feeling on edge

MENTAL RESPONSES

Having no sense of the passage of time
Feeling watched
Pretending they're somewhere else
Rehearsing plans for escape
Vitriol toward their captor
Homesickness; longing to be with familiar people and in safe surroundings
Growing claustrophobia
Chafing at the worry and fear the character's loved ones must be going through
Racing thoughts that are difficult to corral
Fluctuating between hope and despair
Having to ingratiate themselves with their captor and hating themselves for it
Recalling happy memories to keep up their spirits
Praying for deliverance
Meditating as a means of relaxing
Seeking positivity and envisioning a future where the character is free
Exercising the brain to stay adroit (reciting song lyrics, doing mental math, etc.)
Negative thoughts repeating on a loop
Self-blame for the decisions that led to this predicament (even if its illogical to feel at fault)
Over time, becoming more willing to comply with their captor
Questioning their sanity

ASSOCIATED POWER VERBS: Assault, assess, comply, surrender, despair, feign, humiliate, insult, manipulate, panic, resist, restrain, scrutinize, analyze, survive, chafe, distract, prepare, flinch, pace, obey, rebel, regret, wish, plead

EMOTIONS GENERATED BY THIS AMPLIFIER: Acceptance, Agitation, Anger, Anxiety, Hopefulness, Humiliation, Impatience, Intimidation, Longing, Neglected, Powerlessness, Rage, Resignation, Self-Pity, Shame, Terror, Tormented, Vengefulness, Vulnerability

DUTIES OR DESIRES THAT MAY BE MORE DIFFICULT TO FULFILL
Getting medical attention
Getting adequate nutrition
Staying fit
Communicating with others
Finding joy or a reason to go on
Having privacy for showering, using the bathroom, or changing clothes
Having a schedule or routine
Being in control
Being constructive or productive
Setting goals
Being comfortable (not having warm clothing, difficulty staying dry, etc.)
Staying mentally sharp
Keeping a positive outlook
Protecting others (if the character is responsible for someone's welfare)

SCENARIOS FOR BUILDING CONFLICT AND TENSION
Scrapping with someone the character is confined with
Being moved to a new location
A promising negotiation falling apart
Revealing too much to the captor
A lie being uncovered, leading to punishment
The character's loved ones being threatened
The character's living space being reduced
Being betrayed by another captive
Discovering an escape opportunity but being too scared to take it
Being caught during an escape attempt
A captor discovering a hidden object (a weapon, diary, religious item, etc.)
A danger or threat closing in on the character
A medical condition taking a turn for the worse
Running out of food or water
Bad weather moving in
Sustaining an injury
Developing empathy for and a sense of connection with the captor (Stockholm syndrome)

> **WRITER'S TIP:** *It's important for every protagonist to maintain agency, but that can be challenging for a character who has lost their freedom. Consider other people and aspects within the environment that can provide opportunities for the character to exert control and direct their own path.*

DANGER

DESCRIPTION: This state develops when a character is threatened with harm, vulnerability, risk, or loss. For information on danger that risks their life or the lives of others, see MORTAL PERIL.

PHYSICAL SIGNALS AND BEHAVIORS
Pupils dilating and eyes going wide
The character's gaze fixing on the threat
Eyebrows pulling together
The head and upper body pulling back
Flushed skin
Flaring nostrils
Going still and silent
Tilting the head to listen (or watch for movement)
Scouring the environment to assess the situation
The character placing their hand over their throat
Crouching or getting low to the ground
Hiding
Glancing around for help or an escape route
Taking careful steps back; retreating slowly to not draw attention
Collapsing
Trembling or shivering
Decreased fine motor skills (from shaking)
The hands clenching into fists
Flinching if touched
Stammering or stuttering
The voice cracking and going high
Clumsy, fumbling movements
Fidgeting as time stretches out
Praying
Shouting out or sending messages to loved ones
Stating phrases of denial: *No, this isn't happening*, etc.
Murmuring phrases of encouragement: *It's okay, Everything's fine, You can do this*, etc.
Stalling for time
Gripping the wall, a counter, or furniture
Crying
Hyperventilating
Screaming for help
Maneuvering to put something between themselves and the threat
Reaching for a weapon
Going on the offensive; attacking the threat
Negotiating with the offender
Running away

INTERNAL SENSATIONS
A rush of adrenaline
The stomach "dropping"
Profuse sweating
The legs feeling wobbly
Sensitivity to stimuli
Chills
A fight, flight, or freeze response kicking in
Warmth radiating throughout the body
A tingling in the chest
The mouth going dry
Acute vision
A racing heartbeat
Cold hands
Tense muscles
A dry mouth and throat
Dizziness
Exhaustion (if the danger is prolonged)

MENTAL RESPONSES
Racing thoughts
Heightened senses, especially to sound and movement
The brain trying to make sense of the situation
The character wondering if they're overreacting
Being unable to think clearly
Questioning the credibility of the threat
Mentally weighing courses of action and risk
The character wondering if they can handle the situation
The mind leaping to worst-case scenarios
Thinking about loved ones
Regretting choices or actions that led to this situation
A rush of intense emotions (rage, terror, hatred, panic, etc.)
Being overwhelmed by panic
A willingness to violate morals to neutralize the threat

EFFORTS TO DOWNPLAY THE DANGER
Posturing (chest out, hands on hips, false nonchalance, etc.)
Holding their ground
Scoffing or rolling their eyes
Sighing dramatically
Waving a hand in dismissal
Adopting a smirk or sneer
A shaky laugh
A challenging tone
Speaking louder

Disparaging the one who is suggesting the character is in danger
Talking tough while backing up or acting in a defensive manner
Aggressiveness

ASSOCIATED POWER VERBS: Bargain, bribe, beg, negotiate, run, flee, escape, sprint, gasp, stammer, stutter, mutter, moan, scream, shout, collapse, shiver, tremble, quiver, shake, plead, squirm, struggle, avoid, evade, stare, panic, pray, protect, shield

EMOTIONS GENERATED BY THIS AMPLIFIER: Anger, Anguish, Anxiety, Confusion, Denial, Desperation, Determination, Devastation, Dread, Fear, Flustered, Hysteria, Overwhelmed, Panic, Paranoia, Powerlessness, Rage, Regret, Shock, Terror, Tormented

DUTIES OR DESIRES THAT MAY BE MORE DIFFICULT TO FULFILL
Neutralizing a significant threat
Sneaking past the threat or danger without being caught
Protecting loved ones
Appearing normal and relaxed
Being optimistic
Knowing who to trust
Thinking clearly
Focusing on other things
Controlling the actions of a fearful group (if the character is in charge)

SCENARIOS FOR BUILDING CONFLICT AND TENSION
Being the only person in the group who is willing to risk the danger
Suffering a flashback to another time of danger
Having a panic attack
Knowing danger is present but being unable to identify or confront it
Loved ones also being threatened
Facing the threat in a physically compromised state—being injured or ill, for instance
Not having the tools or skills to face the danger
Being given a way out, but it requires a significant sacrifice
Making a decision that makes things worse
The danger triggering the character's greatest fear or phobia
The character realizing they've underestimated the danger

WRITER'S TIP: *When a character is in danger, it isn't typically the physical threat that holds the reader's attention. Rather, it's what the character stands to lose in other ways—emotionally, spiritually, morally, etc. Consider the stakes involved beyond the risk of injury, illness, and their physical well-being. What else might be ruined or diminished if the character can't neutralize the threat? Who else might be hurt?*

DECEPTION

DESCRIPTION: Deception occurs when the character chooses to uphold a lie or hide the truth from someone. Their internal stress level and their effectiveness at deceiving others will depend on their personality, reasons, and moral flexibility. One factor that will always make deception harder is how close the character is to the person they must lie to. Having to deceive someone important can turn a great liar into a poor one.

PHYSICAL SIGNALS AND BEHAVIORS

Avoiding eye contact
Dilated pupils
Evading questions
Increased perspiration
Covering portions of the face while engaging with someone they're deceiving
Sudden changes in the volume of their voice
Engaging in habits (nail biting, hair twisting, etc.) or fidgeting to keep the hands busy
Touching or rubbing the lips before or while speaking
Pulling on an earlobe
Turning their body slightly away from the person they're lying to
Facial tics
Steepling their fingers
The character tilting their head to the side
Readjusting their physical position frequently
Being quieter than normal when the person being deceived is present
Nails that are bitten down to the quick
Smoking or drinking more than normal
Spending time with people who don't know the character as well
Working at off-peak times or avoiding those the character must lie to
Stammering while giving information
Saying as little as possible
Leaving a commitment prematurely (schooling, a job, a relationship, etc.)
Avoiding social gatherings
Oversharing (or rambling)
Defensive responses
Trying to win people over with unusually enthusiastic fervor
Planting seeds of blame or doubt during social interactions
Repeating the question they've been asked; giving themselves time to think
The voice rising at the end of a sentence as if they're asking a question
Offering vague or incomplete answers
Using phrases that emphasize truthfulness: *Honestly, Let me be honest,* etc.
Avoiding the person who wants to confront them
Appearing disheveled or tired—indications they're sleeping poorly

INTERNAL SENSATIONS
Feeling warmer than normal
A heaviness in the stomach
Twitchy muscles
Nausea
Accelerated breathing
A heightening of the senses
Dry mouth
A tightness in the chest
A racing heartbeat
Pain in the back of the throat
Adrenaline spikes

MENTAL RESPONSES
Thinking about why the lie is justified
Reminding themselves why holding back is necessary in the situation
Doubting themselves and their ability to deceive others
Wondering if the other person believes them
Being angry at themselves when they make a mistake
Feeling guilty for lying to loved ones
Feeling alone, as if no one really knows them
Feeling like the lies are corrupting who the character is
Crafting cover stories or excuses
Assuring themselves they won't get caught
Forcing themselves to act casual
Being easily agitated
Struggling to keep track of the lies they've told
Wanting, on some level, to be discovered so the deception can end
Viewing the other person as gullible or unintelligent
Feeling powerful for having information others do not

EFFORTS TO HIDE THE DECEPTION
Keeping a neutral expression
Carefully steering conversations toward safe topics
Appearing bored or nonchalant (lack of tension in the body, loose posture, etc.)
Purposefully making eye contact while delivering the lie
Shifting suspicion or blame to someone else
Joking with or complimenting the other person to disarm them
Evading questions
Acting hurt over being questioned; encouraging the other person to feel guilty and retreat
Creating drama (sharing a rumor, gossiping, etc.) to divert attention
Pulling someone else into the conversation as a buffer
Using a controlled voice level, tone, and word choices

ASSOCIATED POWER VERBS: Manipulate, concoct, hide, plant, obscure, ruminate, rehearse, rationalize, protect, lie, deceive, deflect, divert, redirect, avoid, shift, fidget, perspire, sweat, stammer, elaborate, mislead, withhold

EMOTIONS GENERATED BY THIS AMPLIFIER: Agitation, Anxiety, Apprehension, Conflicted, Confusion, Defensiveness, Desperation, Excitement, Fear, Flustered, Guilt, Insecurity, Loneliness, Nervousness, Paranoia, Self-Loathing, Shame, Unease, Vulnerability

DUTIES OR DESIRES THAT MAY BE MORE DIFFICULT TO FULFILL
Being interviewed by the authorities to collect the character's statement
Interacting with people who know the truth
Maintaining relationships with discerning friends or family members
Getting together with honorable friends, family, or colleagues
Protecting others who are involved in the deception
Testifying in a court of law
Accepting an award, public thank you, etc. for being a good person
Being intimate with a romantic partner the character is lying to
Being questioned by loved ones
Entering areas where the media is present
Repeating the lie to their children
Staying loyal to those who are putting the character at risk
Letting a friend who is ignorant of the truth make a mistake
Withholding the truth from someone who has always been open and honest
Participating in therapy or faith-based confession
Upholding their self-esteem and sense of worth

SCENARIOS FOR BUILDING CONFLICT AND TENSION
Having to lie to protect someone who is undeserving
The character's situation being exposed on social media
Someone figuring out the lie without the deceptive character knowing
An important relationship being threatened if the lie comes to light
Revealing the deception to a friend and making them complicit
Someone close to the character inching toward the truth
Being blackmailed by someone threatening to reveal the truth
The character discovering the secret they agreed to keep is pure fiction
The lie being used to turn the character into an unwitting scapegoat
A situation that offers the character a chance to come clean

> **WRITER'S TIP:** *Readers often engage on a moral level when we create characters they can empathize with. Rather than a character being deceptive for a selfish or malignant purpose, consider imbuing them with a heartfelt reason to deceive others.*

DEHYDRATION

DESCRIPTION: This physiological condition is caused by the body losing more water than it brings in. Many situations can cause dehydration, including sickness, some medications, physical activity, prolonged vomiting and diarrhea, and heat exposure.

PHYSICAL SIGNALS AND BEHAVIORS
Dry skin
Cracked or chapped lips
Sunken eyes
Pale "stringy" veins that are hard to see under the skin
Stumbling and clumsiness
Listlessness
Weaving when walking
Crying without tears
Blinking more than normal or rubbing at dry eyes
Shortness of breath
Twitchy muscles
Decreased muscle coordination
Trembling extremities
Decreased productivity
A slower work pace
Taking more rest breaks
A stooped posture
Massaging muscles that suddenly cramp
The character rubbing their forehead or temples (trying to quell a headache)
The character pushing a fist into their ribs when a side-stitch forms
Producing dark-colored urine
Walking with a shorter stride
Arms that hang loosely at the sides
Hair that is fragile and breaks easily
Asking the same questions or needing reminders (becoming forgetful)
A voice that grows whispery, lacking strength
Little or no sweat production
Skin that appears shriveled and lacks elasticity
Gulping water when it becomes available
Searching out sources of water
Acting irrationally
Passing out

INTERNAL SENSATIONS
Thirst
A dry or sticky mouth
Not having to urinate as often as normal

Feeling constipated
Fatigue
The need to sit or lie down
Nausea
Dizziness
Lightheadedness
Headaches
Blurred vision
Eye strain
Cramped muscles
A scratchy throat
Weak muscles
Feeling off-balance or unsteady
The heartbeat being amplified in the character's ears
A pounding or fluttering heartbeat
Elevated heartbeat and rapid breathing
Feeling feverish
Needing to sleep more than usual
Easily growing tired during physical activity
Waking from sleep feeling unrefreshed
A decreased desire for sex
Acute pain from kidney stones

MENTAL RESPONSES
Irritability
Being fixated on getting something to drink
Imagining sources of water and other consumable liquids
Decreased pickiness (becoming willing to drink almost anything)
Mental confusion
Difficulty focusing on a task
Reduced memory function
Reduced mental acuity
Moodiness
Delirium

EFFORTS TO HIDE THE DEHYDRATION
Frequently licking the lips
Chewing gum or sucking on something to increase saliva
Denying offers of beverages
Becoming defensive and agitated when someone suggests the character may be dehydrated
Making excuses to avoid physical activity
Popping aspirin to relieve headaches, muscle pain, and other symptoms
Making light of their poor memory or forgetfulness so people think it's just who the character is
Claiming other conditions (such as a sprained ankle in a race) to divert attention from their dehydration

Blaming fatigue and tiredness on other things
Moving carefully to avoid signs of clumsiness

ASSOCIATED POWER VERBS: Thirst, lick, moisten, crack, stagger, falter, stumble, weave, struggle, sweat, desire, need, faint, obsess, crave, slake, parch, trudge, tremble, quiver, tire, fixate

EMOTIONS GENERATED BY THIS AMPLIFIER: Agitation, Anger, Concern, Defensiveness, Desire, Determination, Flustered, Irritation, Longing, Moodiness, Nervousness, Obsession, Regret, Tormented, Unease

DUTIES OR DESIRES THAT MAY BE MORE DIFFICULT TO FULFILL

Carrying important equipment or supplies needed for survival
Appearing physically and mentally strong in the presence of a rival or enemy
Engaging in high-energy activities
Excelling in a sport
Finishing a marathon, triathlon, or extreme sporting event
Doing well on an exam
Thinking clearly enough to make an important decision
Passing a health physical
Performing well on the job
Activities that require stamina, concentration, and/or dexterity
Finding solutions for hard-to-solve problems
Recovering from an illness
Staying alert in a dangerous environment
Leading others to safety
Recovering from a mistake that further depletes the character's energy

SCENARIOS FOR BUILDING CONFLICT AND TENSION

Having to perform with focus and clarity—while participating in a debate, for instance
Trying to withstand intense questioning or torture
Not being able to find water
Feeling obliged to press on (while playing a sport, in a survival situation, etc.) instead of prioritizing hydration
Being forced to go up against someone who is well-hydrated
A mental health condition or eating disorder causing the character to resist drinking
Out of desperation, drinking water that may not be clean
Finding a water source, but there's a moral cost to obtaining it

WRITER'S TIP: *Depending on the age and size of a person, dehydration can become serious quite quickly. If it factors into your scene, make sure to research the effects of dehydration on the body to maintain authenticity.*

DISTRACTION

DESCRIPTION: This state of mental preoccupation mostly occurs in times of personal stress, but it can also be a byproduct of boredom. Whatever the reason, a distracted character will find it harder to concentrate and focus, and they'll be less present in the moment.

PHYSICAL SIGNALS AND BEHAVIORS

Gazing off at nothing
Slackness in the face and body
Sitting for long periods of time without doing anything
Subconsciously turning away from a conversation
Not answering when a response is requested
Doing jobs half-heartedly
Being late
Only giving partial attention to a person, conversation, or task
A slack expression, the mouth slightly agape
Scrambling last minute to do things that were forgotten
Being perceived as a procrastinator or slacker
Forgetting appointments and meetings
Being generally disorganized
Performing poorly at work or school
An inability to complete menial tasks (burning dinner, breaking something while cleaning, etc.)
Taking longer than is necessary to complete a chore
Showing up with an unkempt appearance
Wearing clothes that are buttoned up wrong
Wearing mismatched clothes
Wearing the same clothes for days in a row
Forgetting to follow personal hygiene routines
Arriving at a destination and realizing that something has been forgotten
Bumping into people or things
Trailing off while speaking
Adopting a look of extreme concentration in an effort to pay attention
Losing interest in hobbies or pastimes
Having to reread the same page of a book several times
Being unable to participate in activities that require a lot of time or focus
Oversleeping
Driving carelessly (running stop signs, veering into other lanes, etc.)
Avoiding social situations
Attending events but not joining in (standing to the side, hanging out by the snacks, etc.)
A perception of being snobby or standoffish generated by the inability to engage
Forgetting the basics (leaving doors unlocked, not feeding the dog, etc.)
Difficulty falling asleep
Asking people to repeat themselves or the question

The character rededicating themselves to a task only to become distracted again
Apologizing or making excuses for the inattention
Kids or employees getting away with things because of decreased monitoring
Losing items
Decreased intimacy with friends
Loved ones voicing concern about the character's distractibility
Being reprimanded at school or work for poor performance
Frequently having to redo subpar work
Suffering accidents caused by inattention (cutting a finger while cooking, colliding with someone on the street, etc.)

INTERNAL SENSATIONS
Hunger pangs from not eating
Dry throat from thirst
Cramped muscles from a lack of movement or stretching
A desire to get up and wander around rather than do focused work
A feeling of restlessness

MENTAL RESPONSES
Scattered thoughts; the mind jumping from one thing to another
Thoughts turning inward to problems or decisions to be made
A nagging feeling that something has been forgotten
A gnawing feeling; wanting the situation to be resolved
Obsessing over the cause of the distraction
Being unable to focus on the work at hand
Avoiding situations where concentration is required
Feeling guilty for forgetting important things
Losing time; not realizing how much has passed while they were thinking or daydreaming
The character berating themselves for not staying on task
Feeling incapable or irresponsible
Wondering why they can't focus and pay attention like other people

EFFORTS TO HIDE THE DISTRACTION
Focusing intensely on whatever or whoever the character needs to pay attention to
Narrowing the eyes
Pressing the lips together
The head jutting forward
Making general statements to cover up inattention: *Tell me more,* or *So good to see you.*
Cupping the hands around the eyes to block out distractions
Turning away from a source of distraction
Using a visual aid to stay focused (setting a timer, writing a note on the back of the hand, etc.)
Keeping the head still, with the eyes focused on whoever is talking
Continually dragging the gaze back to what the character is trying to focus on

ASSOCIATED POWER VERBS: Stray, muddle, forget, fluster, fumble, stumble, bother, grind, annoy, rattle, drop, misplace, disregard, confuse, fail, pause, drift, blur, skip, redo, blunder, botch, spoil, strain, stare, gaze, daydream, refocus

EMOTIONS GENERATED BY THIS AMPLIFIER: Agitation, Anxiety, Concern, Confusion, Defensiveness, Discouragement, Doubt, Embarrassment, Flustered, Frustration, Guilt, Inadequacy, Insecurity, Irritation, Overwhelmed, Remorse, Resignation, Self-Loathing

DUTIES OR DESIRES THAT MAY BE MORE DIFFICULT TO FULFILL

Being taken seriously
Doing well in school
Achieving a competitive milestone, such as being named captain of a team or chairperson of a local board
Making family members feel appreciated and valued
Driving responsibly
Making the most of an opportunity
Working a job where attention is paramount (operating heavy machinery, working as an air traffic controller, etc.)
Focusing on a goal, such as running for office or getting a promotion
Being responsible for a baby or young child
Successfully smoothing over a relationship mishap by being attentive and present
Remembering to pick up the kids from school or get to an appointment on time
Handling additional responsibilities assigned to them

SCENARIOS FOR BUILDING CONFLICT AND TENSION

Being distracted when the character needs to prep for an exam, meeting, or project
Knowing something is incomplete in their work but being unable to pinpoint it
Striving to focus when self-control alone won't do it—e.g., because the distraction is due to a condition like ADHD
Causing relationship strain due to inattentiveness
Learning that someone was offended by the character's lack of attention
The character's distraction impacting someone else, causing them to underperform
Facing a short deadline where the stakes are high
Losing something of vital importance
Being overlooked for a promotion or job opportunity because of poor performance
Causing a traffic accident due to distracted driving
The character waking up to discover they're late for an interview or work event
Having to make a public speech or presentation when they're unprepared
Being partnered with a diva or someone who needs lots of attention

> **WRITER'S TIP:** *Distraction can be caused by mental or physical fatigue, but more often it is the result of the mind being focused on an unresolved emotional situation. Make sure the reader always understands the cause of the distraction and the root emotion at play.*

EXHAUSTION

DESCRIPTION: This state is caused by a depletion of energy that impacts the character's cognitive and physical functioning. For information on a similar state that is less severe but can be longer-lasting, see LETHARGY.

PHYSICAL SIGNALS AND BEHAVIORS
A blank stare with eyelids half-closed
Bags or circles under the eyes
A slack expression
Heavy limbs, the shoulders pulled down
Eyes that appear glazed
Leaning against a wall or holding onto something for support
Swaying in place
Sagging in a chair
Speech that trails off
Hands loosely open at the sides
Yawning
Eyes tearing up
Rubbing at the face
An unkempt appearance
Poor communication (repeating things, incoherence, thoughts trailing off, etc.)
Disorganization
Easily dozing off
Sleeping a lot or not sleeping enough
Speaking in a subdued voice
Unshaven cheeks
Muttering or mumbling
Slouching or leaning with the shoulders bowing over the chest
Propping up their chin with a hand, or laying their head on their arms
Rumpled clothing
Clumsiness
Forgetfulness
Tipping the head back and briefly closing the eyes
Rubbing at the face or eyelids
Slowed reaction time
Jolting at sudden sounds (phones ringing, doors slamming, etc.)
Slumped posture
Dragging footsteps
Impatience and emotional volatility; getting upset quickly
Passivity: letting others take the lead
Reduced monitoring and attention (when parenting, overseeing employees, etc.)
Trouble working through multi-step tasks
Difficulty with problem-solving

Doing poorly at school or work
Reduced dexterity and fine motor skills
Falling asleep at inappropriate or dangerous times—e.g., while driving
Getting sick frequently

INTERNAL SENSATIONS
Scratchy eyes
Blurred vision
Heaviness in the limbs
Weighted eyelids
A ringing in the ears
Sounds coming as if from far away
Lack of appetite
Slowed breathing and heartbeat
Heavy muscles
Dulled senses
An extreme lack of energy
Being temporarily energized from drinking too much coffee, then crashing
A sour coffee taste in the mouth

MENTAL RESPONSES
Cognitive fuzziness; having a difficult time focusing
Wanting or needing to sit or lie down
Developing an *It's good enough* mindset
Not being able to pay attention to a task or conversation
Lack of interest in hobbies and activities
Emotional sensitivity
Being easily irritated or frustrated
Impaired judgment
A slowed processing speed when putting together cause and effect
Forgetfulness
Losing a sense of the time
Being sensitive to light and sounds

EFFORTS TO HIDE THE EXHAUSTION
Increased use of stimulants (coffee, energy drinks, loud music, drugs, etc.)
Staying in constant motion to avoid falling asleep in the wrong time or place
Using products to cover physical clues of fatigue (eye drops, cosmetics, etc.)
The character offering excuses for why they're tired
Talking more than normal to try to stay energized by conversation
Wearing sunglasses to hide the signs of exhaustion and help with light sensitivity
Lightly slapping their cheeks to wake themselves up
Avoiding morning appointments and social events

ASSOCIATED POWER VERBS: Drag, blink, droop, slouch, drop, blunder, fumble, lose, doze, stall, lean, slacken, drift, scatter, cave, crouch, hunker, stagger, stumble, bumble, lurch, pitch, reel, trip, yawn, fog, drain, sway, struggle, sleep

EMOTIONS GENERATED BY THIS AMPLIFIER: Agitation, Annoyance, Confusion, Despair, Desperation, Flustered, Frustration, Impatience, Longing, Overwhelmed, Resentment

DUTIES OR DESIRES THAT MAY BE MORE DIFFICULT TO FULFILL

Staying awake

Fulfilling job requirements that require careful thought, such as prescribing or administering medication

Lying convincingly, especially if being questioned by the authorities

Keeping a secret when the conversation is revolving around it

Doing well on an exam

Participating in an athletic competition

Working efficiently at speed

Being tolerant and patient with others

Having to fulfill duties while a spouse or partner gets to sleep

Having to drive a long distance

Not falling asleep when the character has a concussion

Having to stay alert when there's little stimulation (during a police stakeout, for example)

SCENARIOS FOR BUILDING CONFLICT AND TENSION

Being in danger and needing to exhibit stealth and care

Being responsible for the safety of others (in the aftermath of a plane crash, prepping for a flood, leading a retreat in battle, etc.)

Having to navigate a dangerous situation, such as crossing a broken-down suspension bridge or booby-trapped building

Having to escape a situation within a specific time limit

Having to navigate an area with balance and precision (crossing a minefield, avoiding pressure sensors in a secure facility, etc.)

Needing to remain vigilant because someone in the character's group is a killer

The character being scrutinized for their mental and physical conditioning (say, as a military recruit in boot camp)

Finally getting to sleep, then being awakened

> **WRITER'S TIP:** *Keep an eye out for situations where one amplifier can lead to others. For instance, a character who is exhausted can easily be injured, fall ill, or become distracted by their condition. Compounding amplifiers can cause compounding difficulties, so when you get the chance, pile on the complications.*

HANGOVER

DESCRIPTION: In this state, a character experiences unpleasant and lingering effects from overdrinking. How much consumption is required to produce these effects will depend on your character's genetics, constitution, and possibly a sensitivity to certain ingredients. For related information, see ADDICTION and SUBSTANCE WITHDRAWAL.

PHYSICAL SIGNALS AND BEHAVIORS

Squinting, the eyes reduced to slits
A pained or pinched expression (wincing, a furrowed brow, grimacing, etc.)
Slow, clunky movements
The character rubbing at their forehead or pressing fingertips to temples
Audible tongue clicking as they work up moisture to combat dry mouth
Visible shakiness and fumbling
Holding up a hand or arm to block a source of light
Mumbling and groaning
Poor balance (bumbling into walls or furniture, tripping, etc.)
A slack expression
A bent neck
The character's hair hanging in their face
Poor hand-eye coordination (knocking things over, fumbling, etc.)
Difficulty with fine motor skills
Curling up on a couch or floor
Wrapping arms around the body or head
The character grabbing at their head as if it can stop the room from spinning
Crawling (because standing and walking require too much balance)
Listless responses: grunts, a hand flap, shrugging, or a head shake
The character laying their head on their arms as they sit at a table
Flinching away from loud noises, bright lights, and movement
Wearing sunglasses, even inside
Fumbling through drawers or a medicine cabinet for pain relievers
A disheveled appearance (rumpled clothing with vomit or drink stains, running makeup, etc.)
Vomiting
Visible sweat
Rudeness
A slumped and sagging body posture
Lying very still, trying not to move
Facial puffiness
Bags under the eyes
Shuffling or shambling footsteps that drag
Rounded shoulders and arms that hang loosely
Swaying while standing
Bloodshot eyes
Pressing knuckles against the eyes for relief

Rubbing at the eyes or pinching the bridge of the nose
Trembling hands and fingers
Hiding (under the blankets, in their room, pulling the hood up on a hoodie, etc.)
Batting away people who try to shake the character awake
Waking up in unusual places (at a stranger's house, in a chair on the porch, etc.)
Drinking water straight from the tap or chugging it from a glass or bottle
Avoiding food for fear of throwing up (or eating certain things, hoping it will help)
Waking up with cuts, scrapes, or bruises the character doesn't remember getting
Waking up with a stranger
Shuffling home the next morning in the rumpled clothing that was worn the night before

INTERNAL SENSATIONS
Blurred vision
Headaches
Dry mouth
An unpleasant taste in the mouth
Sensitivity to light and noise
Stomach queasiness or heavy nausea
Pain in the stomach
Indigestion
Feeling like the room is spinning
Dizziness
Shakiness
A deep thirst
Fatigue and aching muscles (throbbing, stabbing, pounding, pulsing, etc.)
A racing heartbeat
Pulse thudding in the character's ears

MENTAL RESPONSES
Desperately wanting to sleep
Heightened irritability
Fractured thoughts; being unable to concentrate
A desire to not move
A willingness to try odd hangover cures (eating greasy food, raw eggs, etc.)
Fixating on symptom relief (avoiding light and noise, attending to thirst, etc.)
Anxiety or depression symptoms
Wanting to hide and avoid people
Guilt or shame
Mental flashes of what transpired while drinking (which may cause them concern)
Struggling to remember what happened
Wanting to talk to witnesses to ask if the character did anything stupid

EFFORTS TO HIDE THE HANGOVER
Using breath mints and mouthwash to hide the smell of their breath
Complaining they didn't sleep well (to excuse their appearance and irritability)

Calling in sick to work
Telling people they have food poisoning rather than admit to over-imbibing

ASSOCIATED POWER VERBS: Sleep, hunch, slouch, shake, tremble, slur, groan, moan, mutter, avoid, stagger, trip, slump, choke, vomit, churn, rumble, drag, shuffle, curl, totter, squint, rub, ache, twist, hide, gag, linger, urinate, weave, tumble, fade, heave, slough, struggle, seek, fumble, clutch, beg, plead, scrape, hold, flinch, sip

EMOTIONS GENERATED BY THIS AMPLIFIER: Annoyance, Appalled, Concern, Confusion, Denial, Embarrassment, Flustered, Guilt, Indifference, Irritation, Misery, Moodiness, Nervousness, Regret, Revulsion, Sadness, Self-Loathing, Self-Pity, Shame, Somberness, Unease, Vulnerability

DUTIES OR DESIRES THAT MAY BE MORE DIFFICULT TO FULFILL
Being patient with children, siblings, coworkers, and others
Performing well on a difficult exam or in a work meeting
Being reliable and responsible
Maintaining a reputation of sobriety and self-control
Gaining approval from people disappointed in the character's decision to drink
Making a positive first impression (with future in-laws, at an interview, with a big client, etc.)
Being on time and alert early in the morning
Fulfilling duties that require the character to be around food, such as cooking in a kitchen or attending a work lunch

SCENARIOS FOR BUILDING CONFLICT AND TENSION
Being hungover when a crisis hits (a fire, an earthquake, an active shooter, etc.)
Mandatory attendance (having to be at a custody hearing, a work event, etc.)
Needing to hide symptoms from loved ones or the boss
The character realizing they've broken a long streak of sobriety
Others counting on the character's abilities in a high-stakes situation
Being confronted or arrested for drunken activities the character doesn't remember
Having to participate in a loud and active event, such as a team-building retreat
Being discovered in a hungover state by someone who wouldn't approve, such as a parent, spouse, or pastor
Waking up in a remote location with no money or identification
Waking up with someone the character would never have hooked up with when sober
Having to deal with the hangover in the presence of a really annoying person

> **WRITER'S TIP:** *When a character is suffering from alcohol's effects, their thoughts are singularly focused on finding relief for their painful symptoms. Use their poor judgment and irritability to complicate their relationships or throw stressors their way when they're least able to deal with them appropriately. As a bonus, think about the kinds of regret they might carry from things done or said while under the influence.*

HEAT

DESCRIPTION: A character becomes overheated when they're exposed to elevated external temperatures that cause their internal temperature to rise. The length of time your character is exposed, and the intensity of the heat, will determine their physical, mental, and emotional responses and how quickly things devolve. So keep these things in mind, along with their overall health, condition, and disposition.

PHYSICAL SIGNALS AND BEHAVIORS
Flushed skin
Increased sweat
Chapped lips
Frizzy hair (if humidity is a factor)
Squinting or closing the eyes
The character fanning themselves with a hat or book
Peeling off excess clothing (or using it to protect exposed skin from the heat source)
Rolling up pants and long sleeves
Splotchy skin
Flapping the front of a shirt to cool the body
Weakened steps
Arms hanging limply at the sides
Shuffling
Blotting at the face and neck with a towel or tissue
The character shielding their head with whatever is at hand
Seeking out shelter or a way to block direct exposure to the heat source
The character swaying on their feet
Walking with an unsteady gait
Panting or wheezing
Turning toward even the faintest of breezes
Breaking out in a heat rash
Sweat-darkened hair
The skin taking on a puffy look
Large sweat patches spreading across the character's clothes
Increased body odor
Sunburn
Swollen feet and ankles
Eyes that appear sunken
Heat blisters or peeling skin
Impaired decision-making
Skin that ceases to sweat (due to dehydration)
A lack of coordination
Becoming non-responsive (not engaging, answering questions, etc.)
Falling down and being unable to get back up
Fainting

INTERNAL SENSATIONS
A dry or sticky mouth
Skin that feels hot
Eyes that burn (from sweat)
A tongue that feels swollen
Tasting salt (from licking sweat from the upper lip)
The body feeling weighed down
Excessive thirst
Blurred vision
Blood pounding in the skull
Lightheadedness and dizziness
Muscle weakness, cramps, or spasms
Headaches
Lethargy and fatigue
Rapid heartbeat
Nausea and vomiting

MENTAL RESPONSES
Confusion
An inability to think clearly
Lack of focus
Fantasizing about water, ice, snow, or air conditioning
A loss of appetite
The character losing their temper faster than normal
Single-minded focus on finding shade or a reprieve from the heat
Becoming apathetic
Irritation, hostility, or rage
Hallucinations
Seizures
Brain damage

EFFORTS TO HIDE BEING OVERHEATED
Deliberately lounging and relaxing the body
Getting into a pool or sitting in front of a fan to get relief
Wearing the least amount of clothes possible for the occasion
Subtly drinking lots of water
Pulling the hair up and off the face
Choosing shade over sun
Choosing cold food over hot (or avoiding spicy options)
Opening the fridge (as if hunting for a snack) just to feel the cool air inside

ASSOCIATED POWER VERBS: Sweat, gasp, burn, swelter, boil, roast, overheat, smother, blanket, steam, blister, sizzle, wither, sag, cover, whimper, broil, flush, redden, bake, fry, sear, engulf, scorch, thirst, peel, smoke, brand

EMOTIONS GENERATED BY THIS AMPLIFIER: Agitation, Anger, Anguish, Anxiety, Apprehension, Concern, Confusion, Desperation, Determination, Irritation, Nervousness, Obsession, Paranoia, Tormented, Uncertainty, Worry

DUTIES OR DESIRES THAT MAY BE MORE DIFFICULT TO FULFILL

Maintaining a polished and well-kept appearance (especially if wearing makeup)
Staying calm and patient
Finishing a race or other test of endurance
Being at their best when it's important to do so
Fulfilling obligations that require a lot of physical activity
Wanting to appear strong and capable
Standing up to scrutiny that is focused on the character's appearance
Having to mediate between parties who are already at odds—e.g., during a divorce proceeding
Preparing food using hot ovens
Getting restful sleep
Entertaining guests (or keeping children busy and happy)
De-escalating a violent situation, such as a mob or riot

SCENARIOS FOR BUILDING CONFLICT AND TENSION

Becoming overheated at an event where formal dress is required and expected
Sharing in the suffering with loved ones and being unable to help them
Being stuck in a hot situation with someone who has a short temper
Suffering unbearable temperatures during a once-in-a-lifetime event, such as the character's own wedding
Being trapped with prickly family during a heat wave
The character learning the heat event they are experiencing is intentional—a weapon deployed by an enemy to punish the character, prove a point, or weaken them
The temperature increasing over time, forcing the character to find a solution quickly
Developing an uncomfortable rash
Snapping at a loved one or ally and creating a rift
The character going into labor
Being in a situation that requires clear thinking and objectivity
Running out of water, so dehydration also becomes an issue

> **WRITER'S TIP:** *Heat is a natural amplifier, the perfect catalyst for pushing ordinary people to anger and violence. But characters and readers need a respite from the heat every once in a while. Give them a break periodically by providing relief—a chance to rest and recharge, so they're able to jump back into battle when they need to.*

HORMONAL IMBALANCE

DESCRIPTION: The human body works best when its hormones are at precise levels; an imbalance with these chemicals can result in a condition that has serious physical, mental, and emotional impacts for your character. This inner volatility may be triggered by a number of factors, such as diet, chronic stress, certain autoimmune conditions, medications, and menopause. For specific information on two common causes of hormonal imbalance, see the entries on PUBERTY and PREGNANCY.

PHYSICAL SIGNALS AND BEHAVIORS
Unexplained weight changes
Body fat accruing unevenly or in unusual places
Thinning hair (or hair growing in new places)
Night sweats
The face looking puffy
Irregular menstrual periods
Stiff movements
Reduced muscle mass
Changes in skin texture (becoming drier, oilier, etc.)
A jaundiced appearance
Difficulty sleeping
Eyes that appear to be swollen or bulging
Dark patches of skin
Increased acne
Swollen legs and feet
Wearing clothes for comfort instead of fashion
Crying more easily
Struggling with infertility
Appearing distracted
Reacting to environmental triggers (smells and sounds) that never used to bother them
Overreactions and outbursts
Engaging in riskier behaviors
Developing food sensitivities
Researching hormones and the body to learn more about what's happening
The character changing their diet to try to improve their situation
Trying home or natural remedies to alleviate symptoms
Exercising more
Taking medications to treat symptoms
Going to the doctor frequently

INTERNAL SENSATIONS
Increased anxiety
Libido changes
Unwelcome changes affecting the sex organs, such as erectile dysfunction or vaginal dryness

Muscle spasms and cramping
Changes in bowel movements
Feeling dehydrated
Craving certain foods
Exhaustion
Tingling in the fingers
The breasts feeling tender
Migraines
An insatiable hunger or thirst
Feeling shaky
Sharp pains in the pelvic area
Dizziness
Rapid heartrate (high blood pressure)
Sensitivity to heat or cold
Restlessness
New aches, pains, or areas of sensitivity

MENTAL RESPONSES
Difficulty concentrating
Feeling "foggy"
Telling themselves that their symptoms will pass
Feeling unattractive or undesirable
Irritation; being frustrated easily
Struggling with moodiness and emotional volatility
Feeling shame and embarrassment over the changes to their body
Living in denial about what's really happening
Knowing something is wrong but not knowing what it is
Wanting to hurry up and be finished with this change
Feeling like no one else understands
Paranoia (a sense of increased scrutiny)
Feeling vulnerable in a way they've never experienced before
The character fearing they'll be diagnosed with a serious health problem
The character believing they will die
Experiencing apathy—in general or in a specific area, such as work, school, family, or sex life
Worrying that their romantic partner will leave them
Struggling to recall memories
Becoming depressed

EFFORTS TO HIDE THE HORMONAL IMBALANCE
Working late because the character can't sleep but claiming it's because they need to catch up
Withdrawing from sexual activity
Frequently calling in sick from school or work
Frequently apologizing and making excuses for their moodiness
Blaming the symptoms on a lack of food or rest
Cycling through diets as a cure for their body changes

Avoiding friends and family who may notice and comment on the changes
Focusing on the symptoms, such as high cholesterol or low blood sugar
Exercising excessively
Hiding the changes (wearing hats to disguise thinning hair, makeup to cover acne, etc.)
Wearing lighter clothing (if hot flashes are an issue)
Engaging in new hygiene routines, such as washing the face to prevent breakouts

ASSOCIATED POWER VERBS: Crave, fluctuate, sweat, rage, snap, shout, yell, cry, sob, hide, deflect, zone out, fade, retreat, argue, change

EMOTIONS GENERATED BY THIS AMPLIFIER: Agitation, Anger, Anxiety, Apprehension, Confusion, Depressed, Despair, Dissatisfaction, Euphoria, Happiness, Insecurity, Moodiness, Nervousness, Nostalgia, Paranoia, Sadness, Shame, Uncertainty, Unease, Worry

DUTIES OR DESIRES THAT MAY BE MORE DIFFICULT TO FULFILL
Participating in sexual activity
Exercising (if it causes pain, energy levels shift, or weight changes)
Fitting into clothing or finding new outfits the character feels good in
Sticking to a diet
Maintaining a positive attitude
Getting dressed up and/or engaging in social activities
Getting along with others (especially when patience is required)
Being in the spotlight (say, as a politician or celebrity) where their appearance and performance are scrutinized
Fulfilling job responsibilities that require the character to maintain a certain appearance
Duties that require high energy, such as parenting toddlers or being a performer

SCENARIOS FOR BUILDING CONFLICT AND TENSION
Being diagnosed with a serious underlying condition for the imbalance, such as a tumor or disease
Frequent tension with loved ones because of the character's volatility
Discovering they're pregnant while needing treatment for a hormone imbalance
Passing out or needing medical attention in a public place
Other sources of conflict occurring when the character already feels overwhelmed (being called in for a school conference, work drama coming to a head, etc.)
Being unable to get pregnant
Being written up at work for excessive absences or lateness
Learning that the hormonal imbalance will be a chronic situation
A romantic partner leaving them

WRITER'S TIP: *Hormone imbalances often will impact the character's mood. Consider how their emotions might create unintentional conflict within their relationships—at home, in the workplace, and with friends.*

HUNGER

DESCRIPTION: Hunger can be defined as experiencing a vital need for food. The varying degrees of severity for this amplifier make it a versatile one. Whether you want to use a skipped meal to create an atmosphere of discomfort and irritability or explore hunger as a threat to the character's survival, this entry covers the full range. If hunger plays a significant role in your story, you might find the MALNUTRITION entry useful.

PHYSICAL SIGNALS AND BEHAVIORS
Glancing about for food sources (snacks laid out, a fast-food chain nearby, etc.)
Catching the scent of food and breathing in deeply
Making comments: *Those pastries look great,* or *Smells like fresh bread in here.*
Staring at food
Openly watching others eat
Trembling hands
Asking for food (from a host, asking a friend to share, at an establishment, etc.)
Hunting for a stray mint or piece of gum in a purse or pocket
Drinking something sugary to tide the character over
Seeking out free samples (at grocery stores, in a mall, etc.)
Moaning at the sight of food
Moving closer to the food source
Lips that are slightly parted
Licking or chewing the lips
Talking about food constantly
Swallowing often
Fingers twitching involuntarily toward food sources
Touching or rubbing the stomach or throat
Arms cradling the stomach
Overeating when food becomes available
The character cramming food in their mouth quickly
A lack of table manners when the need to eat is urgent
Balance issues (becoming lightheaded)
Begging for food

CUES OF ACUTE OR LONG-TERM HUNGER
Weight loss or emaciation
A distended midsection
Being willing to commit violence for food
Clothes hanging on the character's frame
Bony shoulders, fingers, or legs
Hollowed-out eyes
Facial bones becoming prominent, like a skull
Sallow skin
Sagging skin
Thinning hair

Crying
Teeth loosening in the gums
Health problems stemming from a lack of essential nutrients
Shiny, glittery eyes
Oversleeping
Exhaustion
Weak movements
Body tremors
An unhealthy complexion (greasy skin, discoloration, acne)
Unfocused thoughts
A whispery voice
A willingness to eat anything, even food that is rotten or unsafe
An uneven or racing heartbeat
Loss of consciousness

INTERNAL SENSATIONS
An empty, gnawing feeling in the belly
The stomach twisting in knots
Dry mouth
A gurgling in the belly
Nausea
Having an over-sensitive sense of smell
Quick salivation at the sight or scent of food
Lightheadedness
Headaches or migraines
Stomach pain
A hollow ache in the midsection

MENTAL RESPONSES
Obsessive thoughts of food
Losing focus; fractured thoughts
Becoming decreasingly picky about what they eat as time goes on
Making impulsive decisions regarding food
Being tempted to abandon their moral code if doing so will get them something to eat
Worrying over changes in their appearance
Lethargy; feeling like even little actions are too hard
Desperation (a willingness to eat almost anything)

EFFORTS TO HIDE THE HUNGER
Drinking lots of water in an attempt to fill the void
Avoiding looking at food
A gaze that drifts back to where food is kept or displayed
Chronic gum chewing, smoking, or other oral fixations
Trying to stay busy or occupied to avoid obsessing about the lack of food
The character claiming to be full or making excuses for why they're not eating

ASSOCIATED POWER VERBS: Stare, smell, salivate, growl, starve, gurgle, grumble, swallow, clench, pinch, crave, envy, need, ask, plead, beg, weaken, tremble, quiver, faint

EMOTIONS GENERATED BY THIS AMPLIFIER: Annoyance, Anticipation, Concern, Desire, Despair, Desperation, Determination, Disappointment, Eagerness, Excitement, Frustration, Giddiness, Hopefulness, Impatience, Jealousy, Moodiness, Obsession, Unease, Vulnerability, Worry

DUTIES OR DESIRES THAT MAY BE MORE DIFFICULT TO FULFILL
Refraining from eating (for religious reasons, prior to a medical procedure, etc.)
Giving someone their undivided attention
Not driving other people crazy (from short-temperedness or constantly complaining about their hunger)
Hiding their hunger from others
Doing their best on a standardized test or hours-long examination
Performing well at a sporting event, race, photo shoot, interview, or contest
Excelling at work (because the character's preoccupation with food makes it hard to focus, or their sour mood is affecting their team's output)
Gaining or maintaining weight
Caring for and protecting others
Having a healthy relationship with food

SCENARIOS FOR BUILDING CONFLICT AND TENSION
The character's stomach growling in a quiet room with many other people around
Snapping at someone and having to apologize
Being surrounded by food when the character is supposed to refrain from eating
Hunger reminding the character of a traumatic time in their childhood when they were denied or went without food
The character carrying on about how they're starving, only to learn that the person they were talking to hasn't eaten in days
The character being physically compromised by their hunger, and an employer or overseer reprimanding them for being weak
Sharing the situation with someone more vulnerable, such as a child or a grandparent
Seeing someone else who is hungry but being conflicted about sharing food
Encountering a food source, but the character can't verify whether it's safe to eat
Knowing a food source is not safe but being too desperate to care
Physical weakness causing the character to injure themselves
Hunger driving the character to cross a moral line
Getting sick

WRITER'S TIP: *As hunger intensifies, both common sense and determination erode. Characters will do things they normally wouldn't do if it means alleviating their hunger.*

HYPERACTIVITY

DESCRIPTION: Hyperactivity is the state of being excessively active. When it results from a medical condition or is part of the character's general personality, it can happen frequently. But it also could be situational, caused by medication, drug use, food additives, excess sugar, and even boredom and restlessness.

PHYSICAL SIGNALS AND BEHAVIORS

Speaking rapidly or rambling
Squirming while idle
Pacing
Difficulty sitting still; being in constant motion
Twitching and spasming muscles
Spontaneity
Engaging in physical activity to release the excess energy
Rapid blinking
Asking a lot of questions at once
The character verbalizing their thoughts, skipping from one idea to another
Interrupting others
Acting impatiently (dramatic sighs, nagging, mentioning something repeatedly, etc.)
Bouncing a leg or tapping the fingers
Wide eyes that try to look everywhere at once
Speaking with excitement
Monopolizing conversations
Breathlessness
Being careless in their actions
Pulling and plucking at clothing
Moving the feet—shifting, side-stepping, bouncing, etc.
Fidgeting and fiddling (playing with keys, spinning a watch or wedding ring, etc.)
Arms that shift—going from hugging the waist to rubbing the hands together to swinging, for example
Biting the tongue, lips, or cheeks
The character touching objects in the environment
Swaying and bobbing, as if listening to a musical beat
Scrubbing a hand through the hair or repeatedly rubbing at the back of the neck
Engaging in compulsive and restless habits, like nail biting
Acting impulsively without thinking things through
Switching between unfinished activities
Forgetting to clean up or put things away (or rushing the process and doing a poor job)
Struggling to finish sedentary responsibilities, such as writing a school assignment or reading a business report
Becoming aggressive
Mood swings
Disorganization
Tardiness

INTERNAL SENSATIONS
Feeling highly energized
The sensation of vibrating or buzzing inside
Feeling a compulsive urge to run, jump, pace, or do something active
An internal jittery sensation
Increased heart rate
Adrenaline rushes
Restless arms or legs
Sensitivity to lights, sounds, textures, and smells
Tension in the muscles
Heightened senses

MENTAL RESPONSES
Craving stimulation and seeking it out
Having a short attention span
Finding it hard to concentrate
Feeling constantly bored
Racing thoughts
An inability to relax
Difficulty sleeping
Being highly observant; noticing everything that's going on in the environment
Feeling guilt or shame for not being able to do things the way others do them
Self-critical thoughts
Feeling disconnected from others because of the character's differences
Experiencing intense emotions
Living in the moment, not thinking about the future
The character worrying over what people think of them
Trying to figure out and exhibit the expected behavior in a situation

EFFORTS TO HIDE THE HYPERACTIVITY
Forcibly holding the body in a state of stillness (knotting the fingers together, crossing the legs, etc.)
Incessantly clicking a pen, drumming fingers, or tapping a foot
Choosing not to speak in a conversation with others
Smiling and nodding too much
Swallowing rapidly
Feigning interest (but coming across as trying too hard)
Being still for a prescribed period of time (say, at school), then being overly active later
Energy being released through tics
The body seeming to be vibrating with built-up energy, even when the character is standing still
Becoming increasingly agitated or anxious

ASSOCIATED POWER VERBS: Twitch, jerk, move, surge, chatter, pump, race, charge, rev, clench, rush, jabber, catch, pace, streak, sprint, dash, burst out, interrupt, fidget, squirm, excite, push, activate, bug, touch, bump, grab

EMOTIONS GENERATED BY THIS AMPLIFIER: Agitation, Anxiety, Curiosity, Defiance, Eagerness, Elation, Embarrassment, Excitement, Guilt, Impatience, Insecurity, Moodiness, Nervousness, Relief, Resentment, Satisfaction, Self-Loathing, Uncertainty, Unease, Worry

DUTIES OR DESIRES THAT MAY BE MORE DIFFICULT TO FULFILL
Sitting through a meeting
Attending religious services
Listening to a lecture at school
Working a desk job
Sitting through a wedding, funeral, or other service
Actively listening to someone else for an extended period
Completing a "boring" task, such as reading a book
Keeping a neat and organized work or living space
Being on time to an appointment or social gathering
Managing time well on a project
Engaging in calm activities with a partner, like relaxing at the beach
Visiting relatives who prefer sitting and conversing to getting out and do things

SCENARIOS FOR BUILDING CONFLICT AND TENSION
Overhearing people talking negatively about the character (*He can't sit still, He doesn't take things seriously, He's childish,* etc.)
Sustaining an injury that limits mobility, such as breaking a leg
Missing an important meeting due to forgetfulness or lack of organization
Being reprimanded for always being late
Spontaneously going somewhere without telling anyone and encountering an emergency
Letting excitement carry the character toward a dangerous situation
Procrastinating on an assignment and running out of time
Friction with friends and family members who don't understand the character
Accidentally breaking something of value
Acting impulsively, resulting in an unfortunate consequence (for the character or others)

> **WRITER'S TIP:** *Hyperactivity can create a host of conflict for the character, bringing on unwanted emotions and consequences. But for this amplifier to work, there needs to be a reason for it to strike. For maximum authenticity, make sure the character has a history of hyperactivity or there's an underlying cause that makes it believable.*

HYPNOTIZED

DESCRIPTION: Hypnosis is an altered state of consciousness that makes the subject highly susceptible to suggestion. This entry contains ideas for what this could look in the various scenarios (hypnosis in a therapy session, onstage as part of a performance, etc.), as well as behaviors that might result. In fiction, there's leeway as to how a hypnotic state can be used, but we recommend researching what is and isn't possible so you don't wander too far afield.

PHYSICAL SIGNALS AND BEHAVIORS
Eyebrows pulling together
Slackness in the face
Becoming expressionless as the trance takes hold
Blinking less frequently
Eyes moving beneath closed eyelids
Swallowing less frequently
An overall stillness
The skin becoming paler or flushed (due to blood flow changes throughout the body)
Tension disappearing from the shoulders
The body going limp
The character slumping over while seated
The arms hanging at the character's sides
The head rolling to the side or nodding forward
Being unresponsive to loud noises
A cessation of common tics and twitches that usually assail the character
When the eyes are open, having a vacant or inward look (waiting for instruction)
Reddened eyes
The character responding to the hypnotist's prompt after a slight lag
Responding to questions automatically
Changing behavior based on a pre-determined cue (a sound, word, sentence, or action)
Reacting to hallucinatory sensory stimulation (behavior matching the emotional trigger)
Writing answers to questions without conscious engagement
A lack of emotion in the voice
Being compliant; agreeing with what the hypnotist says
The character describing what they're seeing when they're asked to do so
Facial expressions changing to match the emotion being suggested
Trembling when strong negative emotions surge
Calming down immediately when instructed or reassured by the hypnotist

INTERNAL SENSATIONS
Feeling deeply relaxed
The heart rate slowing
Relaxed muscles
Tingling in certain parts of the body
Increased salivation

A reduction in pain
Seeing the shape, size, and color of things differently
Slight spasms in the muscles
Slowed breathing
Feeling warmer due to an increased body temperature
Heavy limbs
Foggy or tunnel vision
An overall sense of being weighed down
Visceral sensations that match emotions tied to the experience (the character's breath quickening when they're scared, an expansive feeling in the chest during exhilaration, etc.)

MENTAL RESPONSES
Struggling to turn off thoughts and focus on the hypnotist's words and methods
Resisting the hypnosis (if the character is fearful)
Trying to set aside anxiety or fear about the hypnosis
Feeling skeptical about it working
A sense of drifting off
Reduced anxiety and stress
Being in a dream-like state
Being open to suggestion (while retaining a level of awareness and control)
Having intense focus
Recounting memories the character thought were lost
Feeling in the moment, like the suggested experience is really happening
Being unaware of the passage of time
Feeling emotions associated with what the hypnotist suggests
Being able to turn off or change emotions as instructed—e.g., the character going from fearful to calm when the hypnotist reiterates they are safe
Re-experiencing past moments with emotional distance
Enhanced creativity and imagination
Reliving pain
Waking up to a sense of well-being (if instructed to by the hypnotherapist)
Visualizing or imagining a better future (if instructed to by the hypnotherapist)
Remembering the experience, free of negative emotions (as instructed by an ethical hypnotist), or being instructed to forget (an unethical one)

EFFORTS TO RESIST THE HYPNOSIS
Not following instructions (to relax, listen to the speaker's voice, etc.)
Focusing on things that will distract them from being pulled under
The character moving or fidgeting rather than being still
Opening the eyes when they've been instructed not to
Forcing the body to remain tense
Shifting in the seat
Using pain to stay alert (pinching themselves, biting the inside of their cheek, etc.)
Talking and being disruptive
Claiming that hypnosis doesn't work on them

ASSOCIATED POWER VERBS: Calm, soften, ease, loosen, blink, relax, calm, visualize, focus, drift, sink, drop, breathe, inhale, exhale, comply, obey, agree, submit, sag, settle, slump, slouch, loll, feel, speak, recount, answer

EMOTIONS GENERATED BY THIS AMPLIFIER: Agitation, Annoyance, Anticipation, Apprehension, Determination, Doubt, Dread, Eagerness, Fear, Frustration, Guilt, Hurt, Nervousness, Powerlessness, Reluctance, Sadness, Skepticism

DUTIES OR DESIRES THAT MAY BE MORE DIFFICULT TO FULFILL
Suppressing painful memories
Resisting the hypnotist's suggestions
Maintaining control
Guarding secrets
The character being able to tell their own thoughts and emotional reactions from those planted by the hypnotist
Complying with loved ones when what they want goes against what the character has been told to do under hypnosis
Being open to the hypnotism (if the character is a skeptic)

SCENARIOS FOR BUILDING CONFLICT AND TENSION
Being directed to forget something important
Not being able to achieve a hypnotic state
Having to relive a memory the character doesn't want to remember
Being unable to physically move
Seeing something untrustworthy in the hypnotherapist
Having a negative idea planted in their mind
Revealing sensitive information during a hypnotic state
Developing a confusing post-hypnotic reaction to something
Being directed to harm themselves or others
Undergoing a medical procedure where hypnosis is being used in place of anesthesia, and coming out of the hypnotic state early
Realizing during the session that they're under hypnosis
The hypnosis not doing what it was supposed to do (get rid of a memory, help with a compulsion or addiction, etc.)
Signing a legally binding document while under hypnosis
Not being brought out of the state successfully
A sensitive recording of the session being made public

WRITER'S TIP: *If something unknown needs to emerge during a character's hypnosis, be sure to set it up with clues beforehand so the reader is prepared and can participate in the unveiling process.*

ILLNESS

DESCRIPTION: This amplifier is defined as an unhealthy condition that weakens the body. Though illnesses can focus on either the body or the mind, this entry has been limited to sicknesses that are physical in nature.

PHYSICAL SIGNALS AND BEHAVIORS
Feverish, glassy eyes
Dark smudges under the eyes (making them appear sunken and small)
A pained expression (eyebrows drawn in, creating a furrow)
Complaining about feeling poorly
A pale or sallow complexion
Dragging steps
Listless movements
Sitting with a hand supporting the head or slumped with the head on the table
Drooping shoulders
Sweat dotting the forehead and upper lip or making the skin appear greasy overall
Sneezing
Coughing up phlegm
A runny nose
Chattering teeth
Shivering and muscle tremors
Sweat stains on the character's clothing (at the neckline and beneath the arms)
Labored breathing
A loss of stamina
Needing to lie down
Skin that is dry and papery, hot and flushed, or cold and clammy
A raspy or nasal voice
Speaking in short sentences or one-word answers
Sleeping for long periods of time
Sleeping restlessly, tossing and turning
Seeking a doctor's advice
Taking medications
An overall demeanor of frailness
Weight loss
Picking at food
Smelling of sickness
Decreased attention to personal hygiene
Not eating
Vomiting and/or diarrhea
Fainting
Trying risky or unproven remedies for relief

INTERNAL SENSATIONS
Sensitive skin
Feeling feverish
Aches in localized places (head, stomach, ear, throat, etc.)
An all-over achy feeling
Nausea
Dizziness when standing up too quickly
Muscle weakness
Feeling cold or hot
The sense of taste being "off"
A loss of appetite
Dry mouth
Congested sinuses
Fatigue and lethargy
Thirst
A pins-and-needles sensation in parts of the body
Rapid or sluggish blood pressure and pulse
Feeling generally weak

MENTAL RESPONSES
Not being able to concentrate
Mental fog; forgetting things
Impatience
Wanting to rest but feeling pressured to go to work, attend school, etc.
Losing track of the passage of time
Fearing that a simple cold will turn into something worse
Attempting to distract themselves from the discomfort
Trying not to think of all the things that aren't getting done
Worrying over others getting sick
Wanting the discomfort to end
Increased irritability as the sickness lingers
Difficulty carrying on a conversation with others
Being determined to overcome
Praying for relief and healing

EFFORTS TO HIDE THE ILLNESS
Denying that anything is wrong
Continuing to work despite symptoms
Using medications and sleep aids to mask symptoms and feel better
Manufacturing excuses: *Oh, I've been lugging around boxes, that's why I'm sweating.*
Avoiding people
Canceling social engagements
Conserving energy while fulfilling responsibilities—e.g., working while lying down
Working from home
Taking a vacation day instead of calling in sick

Lying around most of the day to save energy for when the character has to go out
Wearing comfortable clothing that requires a minimum of effort

ASSOCIATED POWER VERBS: Shake, vomit, retch, cough, tremble, spew, sweat, weaken, sag, collapse, rasp, shudder, twitch, spasm, tremor, quaver, whisper, groan, sleep, limp, stagger, rest, wheeze, sneeze, blow

EMOTIONS GENERATED BY THIS AMPLIFIER: Agitation, Anguish, Annoyance, Concern, Determination, Frustration, Guilt, Impatience, Indifference, Loneliness, Misery, Moodiness, Powerlessness, Relief, Resentment, Self-Pity, Wistfulness, Worry

DUTIES OR DESIRES THAT MAY BE MORE DIFFICULT TO FULFILL
Going to work or school
Maintaining a healthy and fit physique
Looking their best
Fulfilling duties at home—cleaning, cooking, doing the laundry, etc.
Caring for an elderly relative with a compromised immune system
Caring for or playing with children and pets
Exercising
Meeting a deadline
Training for a physically demanding goal, such as a state championship game or triathlon

SCENARIOS FOR BUILDING CONFLICT AND TENSION:
An important event approaching (a son's graduation, a golden anniversary party, etc.) that the character can only attend if they're well
Being far from help—getting sick during a mountain climb or hike, for example
Falling ill somewhere outside the character's comfort zone, such as on an airplane or bus trip
Being unable to call in sick—e.g., during a scheduled evaluation
Getting worse and having no one to care for them
Dependents falling ill
Missing an anticipated trip or event because of the illness
The sickness turning into a chronic condition
Suffering a relapse
Overmedicating, or mixing medications and experiencing a horrible side effect
Being in a superstitious environment where ill people are cast out
Showing symptoms that match a known hereditary condition
Doctors being unable to diagnose the illness (or suggesting it's psychosomatic)
Treatments making the character worse, not better

WRITER'S TIP: *When rounding out a character, don't forget about their overall health and physical limitations. Are they strong or prone to illness? What kind of illness, and what brings it on? Knowing these answers will enable you to lay a foundation for things to go from bad to worse at critical times.*

INDECISION

DESCRIPTION: A character can enter an uncomfortable state of indecision when they must decide on a course of action, but they struggle to know which way to go.

PHYSICAL SIGNALS AND BEHAVIORS

A focused inward stare
Blinking more often than usual
The brow furrowing
Chewing their lips
Frowning or grimacing
Stroking their chin
Glancing around uneasily
Rolling their shoulders or cracking the neck from side to side
Pulling at their ears
Tapping a finger against the lips
Shaking their head and muttering
Nail biting or other "bad" habits
Drumming their fingers or tapping a foot
Stammering and stuttering
Squeezing the eyes shut and pinching the bridge of the nose
Avoiding people who are waiting for the character's decision
Being distracted during conversations
Showing hesitancy
Checking their watch frequently
Fact-checking or researching options
Writing down the pros and cons
Procrastinating by engaging in other tasks, such as cleaning, exercising, or organizing
Stalling for time (turning away from the person seeking an answer, asking clarification questions, promising to make a decision soon, etc.)
Making an excuse to exit when pressed for an answer
Using vague language to avoid communicating a clear choice
Closed body language (hands clenched, limbs drawn inward, etc.)
Spending more time alone, in quiet places
Talking things through with a mentor
The character's eating habits changing
Lying awake at night
Declined productivity at work or school
Taking a sabbatical to focus on the problem and decide what to do
Requesting extra time to make a decision
Ignoring phone calls and emails
Offering noncommittal answers to questions

INTERNAL SENSATIONS

Tension in the neck, shoulders, and back
A tight sensation in the chest
Tightness in the throat
Not feeling hungry
Stomach discomfort or nausea
Being filled with nervous energy
A racing heartbeat
Frequent headaches
Signs of high blood pressure (flushed skin, chest pains, shortness of breath, etc.)
Having a panic attack (if the stakes are high and a choice seems impossible)

MENTAL RESPONSES

Confusion over what to do
Mentally calculating the outcomes of specific choices
Being tempted to do other things to avoid making a decision
Experiencing a flight response when the situation is broached
Being very aware that time is limited and is slipping away
Struggling to find options beyond the obvious ones
Feeling threatened or pressured
Wanting to be alone
Feeling blocked, as if they'll never have clarity
Resenting the person requiring the character to make the choice
Being terrified of making the wrong decision
Feeling flustered and overwhelmed
Racing thoughts that are hard to control
Feeling an overall lack of motivation
Overthinking the situation
Engaging in negative self-talk (*You're no good at this*, or *There is no good decision here*)
Being plagued with self-doubt, insecurity, and plummeting self-esteem
Making the decision, then second-guessing the choice
Increased anxiety
Feeling overwhelmed when minor difficulties or problems arise

EFFORTS TO HIDE THE INDECISION

Deflecting or changing the subject when it comes up
Garnering sympathy in other areas—e.g., mentioning how stressful things are at home—so others will back off and give the character some breathing room
Making light of the decision
Buying time (claiming a decision has been made but they need to iron out the details, they need to speak to one more person, etc.)
Claiming there is no urgency, and the character will decide when they have time
Appearing apathetic, as if the decision is no big deal
Querying others for advice
Working hard to appear confident and self-assured so people won't lose faith

ASSOCIATED POWER VERBS: Avert, procrastinate, circumvent, deny, doubt, dread, elude, evade, stall, waffle, waver, fixate, hesitate, obsess, overthink, ruminate, put off, think, second-guess, wrestle, avoid, promise, regret

EMOTIONS GENERATED BY THIS AMPLIFIER: Anger, Anguish, Annoyance, Anxiety, Apprehension, Conflicted, Confusion, Discouragement, Dread, Embarrassment, Flustered, Frustration, Impatience, Inadequacy, Indifference, Insecurity, Nervousness, Overwhelmed, Powerlessness, Reluctance, Self-Loathing, Unease, Worry

DUTIES OR DESIRES THAT MAY BE MORE DIFFICULT TO FULFILL
Relaxing activities, such as reading, watching TV, or meditating
Working with the person who is awaiting the decision
Confiding in others about the inability to make a choice
Putting family first (if the right decision goes against a family edict)
Being honest and transparent (if the decision is about a secret)
Trusting their gut in other situations
Investing in relationships that could change as a result of the decision
Making other decisions
Taking a leadership role that requires decisive thinking
Being loyal (if the decision will have consequences for someone the character is close to)

SCENARIOS FOR BUILDING CONFLICT AND TENSION
A hard deadline being set for the decision
Leaning toward a choice that a loved one or respected mentor disagrees with
Friends or family being harmed by the choice
Suffering from a degenerative cognitive condition that grows worse as time goes by
Soliciting advice from an unreliable or untrustworthy person
The decision being one the character has faced before (and it didn't end well)
A relationship being strained because the character is avoiding making a decision
The indecision causing the character's capability to be questioned
Someone else stepping in with the solution the character couldn't come up with
The situation worsening as the character waffles
The character's responsibilities increasing, making it harder for them to devote time to fully understanding the problem and its possible solutions
Knowing the right choice but facing temptation to do something else
The character not having the information they need to make a sound decision

> **WRITER'S TIP:** *Decisions become more difficult when all the choices come at a cost, especially when those costs impact people close to the character. Tensions will also rise if the available options are equally good or bad or the character is at a disadvantage, lacking what they need to make a clear choice. Keep these situations in mind when your character is at a crossroads in the story.*

INJURY

DESCRIPTION: This painful state develops when a character sustains physical damage or bodily harm, either serious or minor.

PHYSICAL SIGNALS AND BEHAVIORS

A cut, scrape, burn, or other penetrative injury
Bruised or discolored skin
Swelling
Strains, sprains, broken bones, or muscle tears
An open wound where blood, tissue, and possibly bone may be visible
Sucking in air, gasping as it happens
Wincing or crying out in pain
Dilated pupils
Bending forward instinctively (to protect vital organs)
Flinching or backing away from the person or thing that caused the injury
Drawing the injured limb closer—curling a broken wrist against the chest, for example
The character forcibly slowing their breathing or taking gulps of air to manage the pain
Tears trickling from the corners of their eyes
Refraining from speaking (or speaking through clenched teeth)
Limiting movement
The character's skin going pale or becoming clammy to the touch
Trembling or shivering
Probing or examining the injury site to get a sense of how bad it is
Using a shirt or whatever is handy to wrap the injury until help arrives
Grunting and groaning
Flinching away from physical contact
Using furniture or walls to stabilize movements
Taking pain medications
Waking up frequently during the night
Developing a fever or infection
Frequently checking the area, changing bandages, or applying heat or ice
Walking with a limp
Showing signs of sleeplessness
Becoming more sedentary and less active
Snapping and snarling at people
Regularly attending medical appointments
Needing help with routine tasks
Wearing a brace or bandage
Using medical aids to stay mobile, such as a wheelchair, crutches, or cane
Giving up on activities and passions the character can no longer participate in
Visible scars or a loss of muscle tone (over time)

INTERNAL SENSATIONS

Pain in the affected area

Warmth suffusing the wound
A feeling of stiffness in that spot
Tension in the muscles
A rolling stomach (at the site of blood and tissue damage, from the pain, etc.)
Lightheadedness
Tension in the jaw from clamping the teeth together
Muscle pain due to overuse in other areas (compensating for the injury)
Reduced stamina
Discomfort that makes sleeping difficult
The character's extremities going cold
Blurred vision
Internal pain that can't be pinpointed
Temperature shifts due to fever or infection

MENTAL RESPONSES
Mental confusion due to shock or pain
Difficulty holding a conversation
Being unable to focus on anything except the pain
Worrying about how bad the injury is and its possible long-term effects
Becoming touchy and irritable
Regretting the impact the injury has on their daily life
Feeling impatient; wishing the healing process would speed up
Being angry with the person responsible for the injury
Regretting any actions that may have led to the injury
Resenting being dependent on others
Needing pain medication but worrying about becoming dependent on it
Hating the unwanted attention the injury brings (people staring, trying to help, etc.)
Reluctance to keep explaining how the injury occurred

EFFORTS TO HIDE THE INJURY
Taking carefully controlled breaths
Forcing a smile
Bracing themselves when they sneeze or cough
Learning to use the non-dominant hand or foot
Wearing clothing to accommodate for or cover an affected area
Secretly taking pain medication
Dismissing suggestions to seek medical care
Making medical appointments to appease others, then canceling them
Having an apathetic attitude
Lying about the nature of the injury
The character refusing help and emphasizing to others that they're fine
Jumping back into physical activities before they're ready
Refusing to change their daily routine
Lying about the severity of the injury
Medicating with alcohol or illegal drugs

ASSOCIATED POWER VERBS: Brace, steel, tense, stiffen, clench, cry, sob, wail, favor, flinch, gasp, grimace, grip, groan, limp, mask, protect, reel, seize, wince, burn, probe

EMOTIONS GENERATED BY THIS AMPLIFIER: Anger, Anguish, Anxiety, Appalled, Bitterness, Determination, Devastation, Disappointment, Embarrassment, Frustration, Humbled, Impatience, Irritation, Moodiness, Powerlessness, Regret, Uncertainty, Unease, Vulnerability

DUTIES OR DESIRES THAT MAY BE MORE DIFFICULT TO FULFILL

Lifting heavy objects
Walking the dog, doing yard work, or keeping up with other day-to-day responsibilities
Sitting at a desk at work or school
Getting a full and restful night's sleep
Driving a car (to the kids' school, to the grocery store, to work, etc.)
Attending an event that requires a lot of walking or standing, such as going to a concert or visiting an amusement park
Accessing services that require the character to climb a lot of stairs
Caring for or playing with children
Remaining sober
Maintaining a certain weight or level of fitness
Achieving a goal that requires physical activity and a full range of motion, such as running a marathon or climbing a mountain
Being on time for work, school, or morning appointments due to inadequate sleep or routine tasks (like getting dressed) taking more time

SCENARIOS FOR BUILDING CONFLICT AND TENSION

An injury complication that causes a secondary medical issue
Being injured during a group emergency and creating liability for others
Experiencing side effects from medication
The character being at fault for the accident and getting sued
Being unable to afford medical care
Having to move in with a toxic or difficult relative during the recovery period
The character worrying about being able to participate in an upcoming physically demanding event
The injury damaging an area of giftedness or skill of the character's
An injury not healing (or healing in a less-than-ideal fashion)
The character losing their job during their recovery
Being the primary caregiver in a household and struggling to handle those responsibilities

> **WRITER'S TIP:** *An injury—especially one requiring a long recovery—will often impact more than one of the character's basic human needs. Explore how voids in multiple areas can create conflicting needs that the character will be forced to choose between.*

INSTABILITY

DESCRIPTION: Instability develops when the character's circumstances are volatile and have a high likelihood of changing for the worse. This amplifier could become a factor in many situations, such as a change in leadership at work that will result in layoffs, a spouse slipping further into addiction, or a living environment that is unsafe or is making the character sick.

PHYSICAL SIGNALS AND BEHAVIORS
Seeming preoccupied and distracted (being unable to settle into a task for long, etc.)
Being easily startled
Rapid blinking or, alternatively, having a far-off stare
Tightness around the mouth
A stiff posture
Self-soothing gestures, such as hugging themselves or rubbing hands up and down their arms
Massaging the back of their neck
Cracking their knuckles
Blowing out a heavy breath
Pulling all the limbs inward; making themselves small
Rocking in place, displaying repetitive mannerisms, or overall jitteriness
Sleeping fitfully
Taking less care than usual with their appearance
Checking and rechecking information sources (a news outlet, text messages, etc.) for updates
Clinging to the people and situations in life that are stable and dependable
Experiencing wild mood swings
Crying with little provocation
Snapping at people
Avoiding making future commitments
Backing out of social plans
Inventorying resources (food, water, money, etc.) and planning for scarcity
Consolidating their belongings
Spending a lot of time researching possible solutions
Not investing in new friendships
Engaging in compulsive behaviors (as a form of control)
Micromanaging others
The home environment becoming cluttered and messy
Not returning calls or emails
Not completing assignments at work
Reaching out to others for help
Losing weight
Getting sick often
Seeking ways to disengage, even when doing so makes things worse (hanging out with the wrong people, abusing drugs or alcohol, spending money they don't have, etc.)

INTERNAL SENSATIONS
A lack of appetite
Headaches
Aches and pains in the muscles
Shortness of breath
Heaviness (or tightness) in the chest
Feeling cold
An inability to relax
Chest pressure
Dry mouth
Heavy shoulders

MENTAL RESPONSES
Fearing the future
Chafing at the loss of control
Feeling like they're on high alert
Becoming risk-averse
Wishing they knew how to fix the problem
Trying to make plans but being unable to do so
Being angry at the people or circumstances that created the instability
Having pessimistic thoughts
Overthinking; endlessly hunting for options to stabilize the situation
Feeling rushed and pressured
Mentally preparing for the worst
Praying for relief
Struggling with impatience and irritability
Every little thing feeling like the last straw
Being triggered by those who may make the situation worse (a landlord, the police, etc.)
Feeling alone, like no one else is struggling the same way or would understand
Wondering if they're overreacting (if others would handle the situation better)
Being drawn to stress-relieving distractions

EFFORTS TO HIDE THE INSTABILITY
Offering half-smiles
Binge eating in private
Downplaying the severity of the situation to others
Telling themselves that everything's fine
Redirecting conversations away from the situation
Speaking in an overly perky and upbeat tone
Making jokes about the situation
Increased interest in self-help books, faith, and relaxation techniques
Spending a lot of time alone
Staying busy
Engaging in activities that take the character away from the situation
Increased drug or alcohol use

ASSOCIATED POWER VERBS: Distract, divert, stress, flinch, disconnect, doubt, drum, fidget, ignore, mask, downplay, neglect, plead, ruminate, worry, fret, weigh, retreat, withdraw, fear, fuss, watch, pace, lie, soothe, promise, pray

EMOTIONS GENERATED BY THIS AMPLIFIER: Agitation, Anxiety, Apprehension, Betrayed, Bitterness, Desperation, Determination, Doubt, Dread, Fear, Guilt, Hatred, Humbled, Humiliation, Impatience, Inadequacy, Jealousy, Moodiness, Overwhelmed, Powerlessness, Skepticism, Tormented, Vulnerability, Worry

DUTIES OR DESIRES THAT MAY BE MORE DIFFICULT TO FULFILL
Keeping people calm (if the character is leading others)
Planning for the future
Pursuing a dream or passion
Investing in personal relationships
Maintaining a sense of hope and optimism
Making decisions that carry risk
Continuing with an academic program
Spending money on non-essentials
Being an attentive host
Practicing self-care and relaxing
Focusing on anything except the unstable situation

SCENARIOS FOR BUILDING CONFLICT AND TENSION
Being confronted about their poor performance at school or work
The situation coming to light when the character sought to hide it
Becoming overly dependent on alcohol
Having a panic attack in a public place
Having to make a drastic change to relieve the problem (downsizing their living quarters, changing jobs, etc.)
Instability becoming a catalyst for other negative events (like losing custody of a child)
Finding a possible solution that has drawbacks or strings attached
Having to do a hard reset (start over financially, walk away from a marriage, etc.)
Making a choice that worsens the situation
The character having to sacrifice their morals to make the situation better

WRITER'S TIP: *Instability can creep into all areas of a character's life, causing additional strain. This amplifier is also great for removing an advantage—say, disrupting their access to something they need or destroying a resource they depend on—which will force them to think creatively to get things back on track.*

INTOXICATION

DESCRIPTION: Intoxication is the state of being mentally and physically impaired due to drug or alcohol use. If this amplifier plays a part in your story, you may also find useful information in the HANGOVER entry.

PHYSICAL SIGNALS AND BEHAVIORS

The character slurring their words or struggling to pronounce certain words
Eyes that are red or watery
Pupils that are too big or too small
Rapid eye movements
Blinking rapidly to focus on something
A too-long stare
Slowed reflexes and movements
Bad breath
Smiling at nothing
Weaving slightly in place
Unsteady or shuffling steps
Giggling and excessive laughter
Speaking unfiltered thoughts and truths
The character making a concentrated effort to find their balance
Poor hand-eye coordination
Poor depth perception (stumbling over obstacles, missing a chair when sitting, etc.)
Leaning in to talk to people
Invading people's personal space
Becoming physically touchy with others
A relaxed posture (slouching, slumping, rounded shoulders, arms that hang loose, etc.)
Overreacting to stimuli (or, alternatively, not reacting to stimuli)
Falling into people and crashing into objects
Hooting, yelling, shouting, and swearing
Holding onto the wall when walking
Trembling hands
Sloppy eating
The eyes drifting closed
Shifting the body back and forth to find balance
Leaning, standing, or sitting at an angle
Excessive sweating
Talking too loudly, never shutting up, or frequently interrupting others as they speak
Asking random questions or making odd observations
Answering questions in a way that makes no sense
Easy camaraderie, even with strangers
Pulling pranks or committing petty crimes for fun
Falling down
Personality changes (becoming very talkative, gregarious, surly, weepy, etc.)

Falling asleep or passing out
Vomiting
Loss of bladder control

INTERNAL SENSATIONS

Colors, sounds, and other stimuli seeming to be brighter, louder, etc.
Feeling very relaxed or very amped-up
Heightened or depressed senses
Dry mouth
Tunnel vision
A tingling or fuzzy feeling in the body
A feeling of pleasant warmth and heaviness
Increased or decreased hunger
Nausea
Feeling like the room is spinning
Blacking out

MENTAL RESPONSES

Enhanced (or decreased, depending on the substance) mental clarity
Euphoria
A surge of creativity
Wanting to socialize, talk with, and interact with others
Taking risks
Exhibiting poor judgment
Feeling brave
Experiencing time distortions
Increased aggression
Difficulty following a conversation
Thinking deeply about everyday things
Missing or misinterpreting body language cues
A loss of inhibitions
Experiencing an increased sense of kinship and affection: *I love you, man!*
Being immune to embarrassment
The character believing they're more suave, charming, or intelligent than they are
Assuming that everyone else is just as intoxicated as they are
Struggling with paranoia
Hallucinating

EFFORTS TO HIDE THE INTOXICATION

The character insisting they're sober
Attempting to prove soberness (walking a line, touching the nose, etc.)
Forcing the eyes as wide as they'll go
Deflecting: *He's way more drunk than me*
Becoming defensive when they're accused of intoxication
Laughing off the accusation

Avoiding eye contact
Using eyes drops, breath mints, or cigarettes to mask telltale signs of intoxication
Pretending to be asleep

ASSOCIATED POWER VERBS: Weave, slip, lurch, jerk, smirk, smile, flirt, swill, gulp, slug, toss, slurp, sip, smoke, puff, pop, stumble, point, gesture, slur, mumble, ramble, wave, hug, touch, laugh, joke, shout, grin, snort, lean, pass out

EMOTIONS GENERATED BY THIS AMPLIFIER: Adoration, Amazement, Amusement, Anger, Appalled, Confidence, Confusion, Connectedness, Curiosity, Euphoria, Excitement, Giddiness, Guilt, Humiliation, Indifference, Indignation, Irritation, Moodiness, Paranoia, Sadness, Self-Loathing, Shame, Smugness

DUTIES OR DESIRES THAT MAY BE MORE DIFFICULT TO FULFILL
Proving their responsibility or maturity to someone (a parent, a mentor, etc.)
Living according to a long-held moral code
Traveling from one place to another
Committing to sobriety (if the character has an addiction)
Being a good role model for a child or younger relative
Thinking clearly enough to make an important decision
Performing at their best (to win a scholarship, be a credible witness in court, etc.)
Navigating an emergency that requires a clear head, dexterity, or quick reflexes

SCENARIOS FOR BUILDING CONFLICT AND TENSION
Revealing someone else's secret while intoxicated
Flirting with strangers or coworkers
Oversharing intimate details about their own life
Offering honest, unfiltered thoughts in a way that strains relationships
Being seen by someone who can make the character's life difficult (a parent, teacher, coach, talent scout, the paparazzi, etc.)
Being recorded in a compromising or embarrassing position
Being pulled over for driving while intoxicated
Getting into a fight or hurting someone while intoxicated
The character being separated from their designated driver
Encountering a dangerous scenario while being physically or mentally compromised
Having to fend off an attack while impaired

WRITER'S TIP: *Many factors determine how a character will respond to drugs or alcohol. Weight, body chemistry, and genetics will play a role, along with their personality. Before writing your character into this situation, know if they'll become more introverted or extroverted, whether they'll be emotionally reactive or muted, and how much product it will take to intoxicate them.*

ISOLATION

DESCRIPTION: Isolation occurs when the character is involuntarily cut off from others. It could be location-specific (e.g., happening only at work), occur within a group (say, a rift in the family), or arise from sickness, a mental health condition, or oppression. The resulting absence of emotional, mental, and physical support can result in loneliness, low self-esteem, and unmet needs.

PHYSICAL SIGNALS AND BEHAVIORS

A downward gaze, avoiding eye contact
A lowered chin
A lax facial expression (or slight frown)
Bags or dark smudges under the eyes
Arms hanging at the sides
Hands hidden in pockets
A walk that lacks energy
Bowed shoulders and a caved-in chest
Crossing the arms and cupping the elbows (to feel held)
Absently rubbing a hand over an arm in a self-soothing gesture
Swallowing frequently
Spending a lot of time online
Limiting public outings
Avoiding people who caused the character's isolation (staying out of an abusive spouse's way, for example)
Giving short answers to questions
Speaking in a voice that lacks energy and emotion
Awkward interactions from being out of practice socially
Shopping online or in person during off-peak hours
Inappropriate social responses, such as laughing or crying at unusual times
Clearing the throat before speaking
Wearing dark or muted colors
Not putting much effort into their appearance
Drawing their curtains or blinds
Hesitating before approaching someone or answering a question
Talking to themselves
Poor posture
Eating unhealthy food (fast food, processed food, etc.)
Developing an obsession or bad habit
Nervous head, hand, or feet movements
Using head motions, shrugs, and hand gestures to communicate
Watching excessive amounts of TV
A smile that doesn't reach their eyes
Reading or gaming as an escape
Adhering to a mental health routine (getting daily exercise, volunteering, etc.)

Paying attention to things others miss
Building "relationships" from afar—e.g., watching people go about their day
Random interactions sparking joy (a dog approaching for a head pat, a child waving from a stroller, etc.)
Being overly sensitive or unresponsive to sensory stimuli
Noticeable weight loss or gain
Withdrawing from activities they formerly enjoyed
Becoming agoraphobic or developing other fears and anxieties around people, public places, and interactions

INTERNAL SENSATIONS
Tension in the throat and neck
Not feeling hungry
Lethargy
Sweating when interacting with others
Not being able to cry
Blurry vision from frequent crying
A sensation of emptiness in the chest
Body aches

MENTAL RESPONSES
Obsessing over the cause of the isolation
Having internal conversations
Becoming lost to memories (prior to the isolation)
Fantasizing; mentally constructing a reality where things are different
Struggling to stay motivated and on task
Wondering what loved ones or old friends are up to
Becoming obsessed with things that represent what they don't have
Wondering what other people are thinking and feeling
Worrying about being judged or pitied
Loneliness or hopelessness
Embracing conspiracy theories
Developing a fear of driving
Critical self-thoughts (and possibly an impulse to self-harm)
Questioning their own sanity
Losing their sense of self
Depression

EFFORTS TO HIDE THE ISOLATION
Making excuses for not returning a call or attending an event
Claiming busyness as a reason for avoiding social events
Fabricating tales of a social life so loved ones won't worry
Lying about having plans for the weekend or a holiday
Taking on more work so they'll have a built-in excuse for a lack of relationships

Pretending to be an introvert to deny those causing the isolation any satisfaction
Hiding signs of neglect, abuse, or self-harm

ASSOCIATED POWER VERBS: Watch, wish, yearn, detach, disconnect, avoid, dodge, excuse, flee, hide, insulate, neglect, probe, retreat, regress, withdraw, struggle

EMOTIONS GENERATED BY THIS AMPLIFIER: Agitation, Anxiety, Apprehension, Betrayed, Depressed, Despair, Discouragement, Dread, Homesickness, Jealousy, Loneliness, Longing, Neglected, Nostalgia, Overwhelmed, Powerlessness, Regret, Sadness, Unappreciated

DUTIES OR DESIRES THAT MAY BE MORE DIFFICULT TO FULFILL
Socializing with people and building in-person friendships
Sharing common interests in the real world (not just online)
Dating and developing intimacy
Fully enjoying holidays that embody family and fellowship
Getting professional help from a doctor, police officer, a therapist (because these people aren't available or the character is being kept from accessing them)
Staying in touch with friends or family
Attending sporting events, concerts, museums, or other congested places
Taking a pet out of the house
Volunteering in public settings
Practicing their religion
Using someone as a sounding board for ideas
Providing adequate socialization opportunities for their children

SCENARIOS FOR BUILDING CONFLICT AND TENSION
A medical emergency that requires intervention
Witnessing something concerning that must be reported to the authorities
Losing their source of personal transportation
Losing their job and needing to find a new one
A crisis that challenges an estrangement—e.g., a parent being close to death
Having to tackle a difficult or dangerous situation without support
Recognizing they're in a toxic relationship and need to escape it
Authorities showing up for a welfare check
Developing dependency upon a substance
Being summoned for jury duty

> **WRITER'S TIP:** *While forced isolation is different from chosen solitude, this entry may also apply if a character is self-isolating out of fear. Over time, this behavior should cost them, so they'll see how a lack of connection with others is keeping them from their goal. This will force a choice: keep to the status quo and give up on their objective or face the fear that is stopping them from reaching out for help.*

LETHARGY

DESCRIPTION: A character suffering from lethargy can be described as drowsy, listless, and/or apathetic. This state has a variety of causes (both physical and mental) including illness and disease, specific mental health conditions, ongoing stress, insomnia, poor diet, and side effects from medication. For a related amplifier, see EXHAUSTION.

PHYSICAL SIGNALS AND BEHAVIORS
Slow, deep breaths
Half-closed eyes
An unfocused or lifeless gaze
Staring at nothing
Poor body posture (slouching, slumping, shoulders curling forward, etc.)
Lying prone or sagging in a seat
The body conforming to whatever surface it rests on
Ponderous movements; steps that drag
Propping the head up with a hand
Limp limbs and an overall lack of body tension
Hands and feet that are still
Signs the character is letting themselves go (unwashed hair, wrinkled clothes, etc.)
Using the least amount of physical exertion possible, such as taking the elevator instead of the stairs or eating pizza from the box rather than getting a plate
Drinking caffeinated beverages or energy drinks to stay energized
Sitting or lying for long periods of time without moving
Yawning and stretching
Moving only to shift position
Going without instead of getting up to get something, such as a drink or snack
Asking others to do things that require effort
Canceling appointments
Turning down social opportunities
Withdrawing from others
Choosing activities that have little physical or mental stimulation
Not engaging in conversations
Answering questions with a mumble or shrug
Not being picky; the character accepting whatever is available
Living in a cluttered environment
Exhibiting symptoms of an underlying illness that is causing the lethargy
Sleeping much more than usual
Weight gain or loss
Atrophied muscles
Avoiding people; displaying hermit-like tendencies

INTERNAL SENSATIONS
A heaviness in the limbs
A sensation of not wanting to move

Feeling sluggish
The character feeling like they're moving in slow motion
Loss of appetite
Sleepiness or fatigue

MENTAL RESPONSES
A lack of motivation
Apathy
Difficulty focusing on a task
Having to mentally talk themselves into a better mood
Wondering why they feel this way
Worrying over a possible sickness or disease causing the lethargy
Losing interest in things that used to be fun and enjoyable
Brain fog; thoughts that feel thick and slow
A desire to do nothing, to not think
A tendency to zone out and lose track of time
Not noticing what's going on with other people
Being unable to help loved ones with their problems
Feeling like even small tasks are too much trouble
Procrastinating until something reaches a state of urgency
Difficulty making decisions
Feeling guilty for not caring enough to help out or fix noticeable problems
Irritability at being judged
Feeling like they always have to defend themselves
Becoming depressed

EFFORTS TO HIDE THE LETHARGY
Denying there's a problem
Blaming the behavior on boredom or being overworked
Claiming that all they need is a good night's sleep
Putting on a happy face around others, then crashing when they're alone
Claiming to have participated in physical activities that no one has witnessed
Waving off the concerns of others
Claiming to have an illness or disorder that would explain the lethargy, such as a hormone imbalance or anemia
Refusing to see a doctor out of fear of the results

ASSOCIATED POWER VERBS: Slouch, drag, laze, sigh, sag, lean, droop, withdraw, reel, sleep, daydream, drift, waste, slacken, fan, sway, abandon, reject, give up

EMOTIONS GENERATED BY THIS AMPLIFIER: Anxiety, Apprehension, Concern, Conflicted, Defensiveness, Desire, Determination, Discouragement, Embarrassment, Inadequacy, Indifference, Powerlessness, Regret, Self-Pity, Shame, Uncertainty

DUTIES OR DESIRES THAT MAY BE MORE DIFFICULT TO FULFILL

Caring for an energetic child or pet
Completing tasks that require a high level of observation
Being seen as capable and responsible
Preparing sufficiently for a test or certification
Being excited for and celebrating with loved ones
Going on a family vacation with lots of planned activities
Engaging with other people for significant periods of time—say, at a work conference or family reunion
Staying focused during a meeting, lecture, or parent-teacher interview
Exercising and keeping fit
Being creative
Sticking to a routine or following a to-do list
Upholding the "giving" end of a balanced give-and-receive relationship
Tasks that require mental focus, such as managing finances or planning a wedding
Meeting an important deadline
Picking up on behavioral red flags that should serve as warnings

SCENARIOS FOR BUILDING CONFLICT AND TENSION

Neglecting something important and accidentally creating a safety issue
Being passed over for a promotion or high-profile assignment
Making a big mistake because they didn't pay close enough attention
Experiencing a break-in because the character forgot to lock their door
Missing out on a much-needed opportunity to impress someone or get ahead
A big change that requires a lot of energy, such as having a baby
Forgetting a loved one's birthday
Being given an ultimatum: get help and make a change or face consequences
Being called out for turning in sloppy work by someone the character respects
Wanting to do better but not knowing how to get past the apathy
The character seeing people living their best lives and wanting more for themselves but not being able to muster the energy to make it happen
Being unable to convince a doctor their condition is tied to something more serious
Not being there for someone (a distraught friend, a suicidal sister, etc.) when help was needed most

> **WRITER'S TIP:** *Lethargy is largely a physical ailment, but it has a profound effect on a person's psyche, compounding the physical problem with self-doubt, anxiety, and even depression. When dealing with a condition like lethargy, remember to address the emotional and mental effects, too.*

MALNUTRITION

DESCRIPTION: Malnutrition results from a deficiency of essential vitamins and nutrients the body and mind need to function properly. Underlying causes could include poverty, decreased mobility that makes obtaining food difficult, mental health conditions, eating disorders and conditions, or food scarcity. The severity and signs of malnutrition, as well as the character's responses to it, will vary depending on its cause and personal factors, such as their health, genetics, and whether they're deliberately avoiding calories or not. For related (though less extreme) information, see HUNGER.

PHYSICAL SIGNALS AND BEHAVIORS
Having little or no muscle tone
Hollow cheeks
Sunken eyes
Thinning or brittle hair
An unfocused gaze
Pronounced bone structures
A character's skin changing in color, texture, or health
A swollen or cracked tongue
Decaying teeth
Bad breath
Wheezing or shortness of breath
A head that lolls, as if it's too heavy to hold up
Slow movements
Having to sit or lie down frequently
Tripping over their own feet; clumsiness
Visible tremors in the limbs
Stabilizing themselves against walls, countertops, or furniture
Speaking less (lacking the energy to do so)
Slurred speech
Hypersensitivity to bright lights
Clothing hanging off the character's body
No longer participating in hobbies or areas of interest
Difficulty following the thread of a conversation
Diarrhea
Vomiting
Persistent illnesses
Wounds healing slower than they should
Bruising easily
Crying frequently
A bloated abdomen
Isolating themselves
Wearing layers of clothing to stay warm
Drinking lots of water to fill the belly

Stunted growth
Absence of menses

INTERNAL SENSATIONS
Dizziness
Muscle weakness
Blurred vision
Mouth pain
Feeling emotionally "on edge"
Pain in the joints
A fluttering heartbeat
An inability to stay warm
Lethargy
Feeling tired all the time
Difficulty swallowing
Nausea
A burning sensation around the eyes
Moving between extreme hunger to not being hungry at all
Decreased sense of taste and smell
Symptoms associated with high blood pressure

MENTAL RESPONSES
Incoherent thoughts
Mental fogginess that makes it difficult to focus
Memory loss
Drifting in and out of awareness
Anxiety and worrying (about how to get food or their failing health)
Thinking frequently about food
Worrying about others who share the character's situation (children, siblings, etc.)
Ignoring the possibility that there's an underlying condition at work
Drawing strength from the feeling of control (if the character is starving themselves)
Body dysmorphia
Feeling helpless to change their situation

EFFORTS TO HIDE THE MALNUTRITION
Wearing clothes that de-emphasize their weight loss
Making excuses for their dietary choices
Avoiding going to the doctor
Downplaying the truth about their condition
Avoiding social gatherings where food might be present
Joking about their appearance to deflect attention from the severity of the situation
Making a token effort to eat (or eat healthy foods) in public
Trying to continue as if nothing is wrong
Reassuring others that things are under control

Avoiding physically challenging activities
Telling others they just ate

EMOTIONS GENERATED BY THIS AMPLIFIER: Anguish, Anxiety, Apprehension, Bitterness, Concern, Embarrassment, Defeat, Depressed, Despair, Desperation, Disillusionment, Fear, Loneliness, Longing, Misery, Neglected, Powerlessness, Resentment, Resignation, Self-Pity, Skepticism, Uncertainty, Worry

ASSOCIATED POWER VERBS: Waste away, shrink, shrivel, hide, avoid, forgo, deflect, rationalize, justify, beg, plead, ache, bruise, lay, sleep, tremble, drink, collapse

DUTIES OR DESIRES THAT MAY BE MORE DIFFICULT TO FULFILL
Completing routine home maintenance jobs, such as cleaning or landscaping
Receiving visitors and socializing
Working to their full potential on the job or at school
Thinking through problems effectively
Breastfeeding
Escaping captors or facing a test of endurance
Changing clothes when others are around
Being around loved ones who will notice the vast changes and try to intervene (if the character is actively avoiding food)
Hiding the source of the malnutrition
Gaining weight or maintaining a healthy weight
Being happy with their appearance
Providing adequate nutrition for loved ones who are caught in the same situation

SCENARIOS FOR BUILDING CONFLICT AND TENSION
Receiving a diagnosis of a serious underlying medical problem
Being ordered by a court to complete a mental health evaluation or attend therapy
Child protective services inquiring about the home environment
A partner enabling the behavior
The character seeing signs of malnutrition in their children
A food bank the character relies upon being closed
Being denied medical care that could change their situation
An accident requiring the character to go to the hospital, where their condition will be discovered
Becoming pregnant
Being diagnosed with a condition that depletes calories, such as cancer

WRITER'S TIP: *While malnutrition, at its most basic, is a lack of necessary nutrients, it is always a symptom of another, more pressing issue. Know the reasons for your character's condition and map out their journey in relation to that root problem.*

MENTAL HEALTH CONDITION

DESCRIPTION: Mental health conditions are common and cover a wide range of symptoms, behaviors, and tendencies. While many characters live full and happy lives with these conditions, certain events can be more challenging for them. For instance, a character whose condition causes difficulty with regulating emotions, making abstract connections, or deciding on a course of action may find some situations harder to navigate. In this case, their existing mental health condition may become an amplifier.

When writing about a character's mental health, research is imperative. Each condition will have physical, mental, and emotional markers that vary depending on the type and individual. This entry consists of a broad range of possible indicators and ideas to help with general brainstorming.

PHYSICAL SIGNALS AND BEHAVIORS

Showing empathy for others with mental health conditions
Engaging in artistic or creative endeavors
Advocating for underdogs and those who are marginalized
Finding success through nontraditional methods and avenues
Excelling at outside-the-box thinking
Offering fresh perspectives
Advocating for themselves (or struggling to do so)
Wearing clothing based on comfort or personal style rather than popular fashion
Attending support groups
Speaking encouraging words to others
Struggling to read other people's body language
Acting impulsively
Disorganization
Forgetfulness
Interrupting others
Not engaging in conversations
Bouncing, jittering, jumping, and other signs of hyperactivity or restlessness
Sleeping a lot (or not enough)
Taking medication for their condition
Appearing socially anxious or awkward
Responding in an odd way, such as laughing at a situation that isn't funny
Having physical tics (rapid blinking, a repetitive head shake or hand gesture, etc.)
Being overly aggressive toward others
A rapidly shifting mood
Being sensitive to textures, sounds, foods, lights, and other stimuli
Engaging in repetitive soothing behaviors (pacing in a circle, rocking, swaying, etc.)
Speaking unfiltered thoughts
Having a messy work or living space
Needing things to be just so
Crying often

Having big emotional reactions (to a loud sound, a schedule change, certain triggers, etc.)
Struggling to manage their time
Having a small circle of friends
Interacting with people online rather than in person
Withdrawing from others
Obsessive-compulsive behaviors

INTERNAL SENSATIONS
Exhaustion and fatigue
Feeling antsy and restless
Feeling jittery
Feeling lethargic
Having no energy
Stomach pain
Insomnia

MENTAL RESPONSES
Appreciating the little things
Being grateful for small wins
Feeling in control and safe when certain rituals, habits, or routines are followed
Using self-talk to calm themselves, keep a positive mindset, or reaffirm what's true
Experiencing fluctuating emotions
Being assailed frequently with certain emotions, such as sadness, anxiety, or confusion
Feeling misunderstood; not knowing how to discuss what they're experiencing
Becoming easily overwhelmed
Racing or pinballing thoughts that are hard to analyze and control
Questioning their own perceptions; doubting themselves
Feeling judged by others
Wanting to change but not knowing how
Frustration with their own patterns of thinking
Feeling shame or embarrassment from their condition
Intrusive thoughts
Questioning the motivations of others
Experiencing delusions or hallucinations
Seeking escape through various means

EFFORTS TO HIDE THE MENTAL HEALTH CONDITION
Avoiding people who express concern about the character's well-being
Keeping medications and treatments (such as therapy appointments) secret
Blaming other people or circumstances for their behavior
Pretending to go to work or school
Avoiding doctors
Not allowing people into their home
Keeping their perceptions and ideas to themselves
Increased drug or alcohol use

ASSOCIATED POWER VERBS: Fixate, obsess, panic, spiral, struggle, isolate, overreact, overwhelm, worry, self-soothe, medicate, interrupt, blurt, pace, rock

EMOTIONS GENERATED BY THIS AMPLIFIER: Agitation, Anger, Anguish, Anxiety, Apprehension, Concern, Confusion, Connectedness, Denial, Despair, Determination, Disbelief, Doubt, Dread, Fear, Frustration, Insecurity, Loneliness, Nervousness, Overwhelmed, Paranoia, Powerlessness, Rage, Self-Loathing, Sympathy

DUTIES OR DESIRES THAT MAY BE MORE DIFFICULT TO FULFILL
Sticking to a schedule
Choosing realistic goals
Being on time to work, school, or appointments
Collaborating with others
Attending social events
Staying calm in stressful situations
Having enough energy for daily activities
Completing tasks in a timely manner
Reading other people and their social cues
Talking about or analyzing their own emotions
Practicing self-care
Controlling their emotions
Letting people in

SCENARIOS FOR BUILDING CONFLICT AND TENSION
Being hospitalized or losing personal autonomy in some way
Running out of medication
The character overhearing people talking disparagingly about them
Becoming pregnant
Losing control in a public place
Developing an additional condition
Receiving the wrong diagnosis
Being taken advantage of
Being trapped in a situation that is highly triggering
Experiencing disloyalty or another form of personal betrayal
Developing a coping habit, such as gambling, hoarding, or self-harming

> **WRITER'S TIP:** *As authors, we're always looking to create fresh characters and think outside the box regarding their behaviors and reactions. But when it comes to a character's mental health journey—especially when we're writing about real-life conditions—responsibility and respectfulness come first. Read up on your character's diagnosis. Talk to people living with that condition to get first-hand information on how it manifests and what it's like living with it. Then you'll know how to portray it.*

MORTAL PERIL

DESCRIPTION: Some mortal peril scenarios—dangerous situations that put the character's life at risk—play out over time, such as being taken hostage by violent people or being injured in a way that assures death is coming. Other scenarios happen quickly: the character being robbed at gunpoint, an oncoming car veering into their lane, or the like. For clarity purposes, this entry focuses on the latter. And for related information, you may find the DANGER entry useful.

PHYSICAL SIGNALS AND BEHAVIORS
Freezing in place
Not responding to stimuli
Dilated pupils
The eyes going wide or squeezing shut
Uncontrollable trembling
Tears forming
Stammering and struggling to find words
Vocal changes: the voice cracking, rising in pitch, taking on a panicked tone, etc.
Losing the ability to speak
Releasing a moan or other sound of terror
Goosebumps rising on the skin
Remaining as still as possible; avoiding moving or making sounds
Cutting the eyes to see the source of terror without facing it head on
The character sliding or dropping to the ground
Curling into a fetal position, protecting the head and vital organs
Backing up, creating distance
Being unsteady on their feet
Moving to put objects between themselves and the threat
Taking actions that only pertain to the here and now
Acting by instinct rather than with conscious thought
Jerking away from physical touches
Verbally reassuring themselves that things will be okay
Impulsivity
Losing control of bodily functions
Showing high emotion (screaming, sobbing, collapsing, attacking, etc.)
Begging and pleading (for help, for an attacker to reconsider, for mercy, etc.)
Running away in terror
Hyperventilating
Expressing regrets (if there is time for reflection)
Scribbling a quick note of love or apology to family members

INTERNAL SENSATIONS
Tunnel vision
Adrenaline racing through the system
Muffled hearing

A rabbity heartbeat
Cold sweats
The mouth going dry
Feeling sick to the stomach
Feeling the urge to urinate
Breaths quickly sawing in and out
Muscles that feel weak
Tightness in the chest
Decreased fine motor skills
Restlessness

MENTAL RESPONSES
Being hyper-focused on the threat
Forgetting about anything that isn't vitally important
Being unable to process what's happening
Experiencing shock, confusion, or disbelief
An intense urge to flee
Replaying events leading up to the situation
The mind darting between possible escape solutions
Feeling helpless and powerless
Being overcome with rage
Being unable to accept the situation
Hoping for a miracle
Praying for deliverance
Playing out what-comes-next scenarios
Their life flashing before their eyes
Being filled with regret over past mistakes
Fearing death and the afterlife
Grieving the loss of the life they knew or will never have
Giving up control and feeling an unexpected peace about whatever happens next
Experiencing a supernatural sense of calm and clarity

EFFORTS TO DOWNPLAY THE SEVERITY OF THE SITUATION
The character carefully modulating their voice's tone and volume
Taking deliberately deep breaths to appear in control
Relaxing their posture and forcing tension from their body
Hiding body tremors (making a fist, crossing their legs to keep them still, etc.)
Forcing laughter to appear unfazed
Carefully approaching the threat
Reasoning and bargaining (the character highlighting their usefulness, suggesting a compromise, redirecting attention to another target, etc.)
Playing for time (asking questions, keeping the threat talking, etc.)
Smiling at those around them as if everything is okay
The character distracting themselves and others from imminent danger

ASSOCIATED POWER VERBS: Stammer, stutter, bargain, beg, curl up, disassociate, evade, fade, faint, collapse, fall, fight, flee, freeze, moan, mutter, panic, plead, retreat, back away, withdraw, risk, run, scream, shake, hyperventilate, sink, shrink, tremble

EMOTIONS GENERATED BY THIS AMPLIFIER: Acceptance, Anger, Anguish, Anxiety, Defeat, Defiance, Denial, Despair, Determination, Dread, Fear, Grief, Hysteria, Longing, Overwhelmed, Panic, Regret, Resignation, Sadness, Shock, Terror, Tormented

DUTIES OR DESIRES THAT MAY BE MORE DIFFICULT TO FULFILL
Maintaining personal safety
Supporting others who are facing the same mortal scenario
Protecting loved ones
Being strong for loved ones who share the dangerous situation
Thinking clearly
Controlling their fear in hopes they can escape the situation or neutralize the threat
Speaking persuasively and coherently
Surviving the situation without breaking their own moral code
Fixing the past (undoing old mistakes, apologizing for wrongs, erasing regrets, etc.)
Saying what needs to be said to loved ones when there's no time to do so
Dying with dignity

SCENARIOS FOR BUILDING CONFLICT AND TENSION
Making an unkeepable promise to stave off death
Someone else being unexpectedly killed
The character losing their leverage (an ally, weapon, a skill they rely on, etc.)
Being able to save themselves, but only if they sacrifice someone else
A ticking-clock scenario complicating the situation
Making a split-second decision that ends up being a mistake
An injury that turns the character into a liability
Being offered a chance to escape and botching it
Being forced to choose who to save
Someone else paying the price because the character was too paralyzed to act
The character discovering their own actions led to their current situation
Being the only one to survive, and being overcome with guilt

> **WRITER'S TIP:** *How your character reacts in a mortal peril situation will depend on a number of factors, including their personality, the particulars of their moral code, their fight-flight-or-freeze tendency, and whether they're alone or with others who are also at risk. Run a full inventory on your character so you'll know how they'll respond to an imminent-death scenario.*

PAIN

DESCRIPTION: While there are different kinds of discomfort a character could suffer, this entry focuses on physical pain, which is most often associated with an injury or illness. For discomfort that continues for a prolonged period, see CHRONIC PAIN.

PHYSICAL SIGNALS AND BEHAVIORS
Pale or blotchy skin
Glassy eyes with visible redness
A pained expression
Dark hollows under the eyes
Lips pressed tight, the mouth appearing smaller
An audible pained breath (at moving too fast, accidentally touching an injury, etc.)
The character grinding their teeth
Sweat beading on the character's forehead and causing their face to appear slick
A bent back and caved-in chest
Shoulders hunched, drawn in close to the body
Walking with stiff movements
A visible trembling in the limbs
A weakened grasp
Probing, rubbing, or grabbing at the affected area
Wincing
Flinching when touched
Leaning back and grimacing
Expelling a grunt or hiss upon exertion
Shaking or flapping a limb that's been injured (when the pain is minor)
Asking for aid (to move, get something, call for help, etc.)
Hobbling about; taking tentative steps
The injury site swelling up
The skin around a wound going red
Crying
Taking a pain medication
Breaths that saw in and out
Taking deliberate deep breaths
Flaring nostrils
Trying to sleep the pain away
Gripping people or nearby objects for support
Cradling the wounded body part
The character's voice sounding pinched or strained
Speaking in short, clipped phrases
Answering questions with head nods and shakes
Screaming, moaning, or groaning
Rocking back and forth
Panting

Repeating the same phrase over and over
Squeezing the eyes shut; refusing to look
Squirming in discomfort
Arching the back
Passing out

INTERNAL SENSATIONS
Various pain sensations (sharp, slicing, coming in waves, pulsing, etc.)
The affected skin or joint feeling tight as inflammation sets in
The wounded area feeling warm or hot to the touch
Nausea
Hyperventilating
The character feeling lightheaded at the sight of blood
Starbursts behind their eyelids
Tight muscles
Dizziness; feeling faint
Cramping muscles
Feeling cold or feverish (from infection)
A dry or coppery taste in their mouth
Trembling hands and feet
Uncontrolled shivering
Feeling an overwhelming need to sit or lie down
A tight chest; the character finding it hard to catch their breath
Being overly sensitive to stimuli (light, sound, pressure, etc.)

MENTAL RESPONSES
Engaging in mental self-talk (to stay calm, to remind themselves the pain will pass, etc.)
Short-temperedness
Trying not to think about the pain
Conjuring up memories and experiences that were worse than this
Looking for signs that the pain is waning
A sense of time distortion (losing track of time, feeling it's passing more slowly, etc.)
Worrying about worst-case scenarios (if the pain is new and the source is unclear)
Worrying about people in the character's charge or others who might also be hurt
The mind going over possible negative effects of the injury or illness—if it will impact an upcoming trip, for instance
A single-minded focus on relieving the pain
Masking the pain in certain situations—so children don't panic, for example, or to keep an enemy from knowing the true extent of the character's injuries
Finding it difficult to concentrate, problem solve, or remember things
Being unable to answer questions or engage with others
Panic

EFFORTS TO HIDE THE PAIN
The character clenching their jaw
Lips pressing tight and becoming bloodless
Smiling quickly and waving off the pain
The character lying down or sitting to avoid showing weakness
Remaining perfectly still
Avoiding talking to others
Cradling the injured area close to the body to protect it
Turning away from others to hide their expression or the injury
Clenched hands
Hands bunching up a blanket or clutching at clothing
Wrapping the injury to hide how bad it is
Finding a way to be alone to deal with the pain in private

ASSOCIATED POWER VERBS: Ache, throb, burn, tremor, sweat, twitch, hurt, sting, stiffen, moan, grit, bite, keen, cry, tear, groan, scream, stab, erupt, prick, writhe, wail, cramp, chafe, rub, agonize, pinch, grate, wince, weep, heave, faint, blister, redden, fester, bruise, cut, slice, support, lean, drag, crumple, hobble, shake, infect, tremble

EMOTIONS GENERATED BY THIS AMPLIFIER: Anger, Anguish, Anxiety, Appalled, Apprehension, Denial, Desperation, Determination, Devastation, Disappointment, Dread, Fear, Flustered, Frustration, Hysteria, Impatience, Irritation, Moodiness, Overwhelmed, Panic

DUTIES OR DESIRES THAT MAY BE MORE DIFFICULT TO FULFILL
Excelling in a sporting event
Being patient and understanding with loved ones
Being viewed as strong and invincible
Engaging in a physical activity that requires a lot of movement or stamina
Traveling a long distance
Serving or protecting others
Staying alert and awake

SCENARIOS FOR BUILDING CONFLICT AND TENSION
Having to rely on someone they don't like or trust
The character being responsible for someone else while they're struggling with their pain
Experiencing pain in a remote place without treatment resources
An environmental danger forcing the character to relocate despite their discomfort
Having to make an important decision while their brain is fogged by pain
Having to push through the pain (in a race or to escape danger, for example)

> **WRITER'S TIP:** *Everyone responds to pain differently; some express it freely while others will try to downplay it. When writing about your character's response, think about their pain tolerance and their personality, as well as the circumstances surrounding their discomfort.*

PANIC ATTACK

DESCRIPTION: A panic attack is a sudden onset of intense fear or dread that is accompanied by worrisome physical symptoms, impaired reasoning, and illogical thinking. It may occur as an isolated event or happen regularly as part of a panic disorder.

PHYSICAL SIGNALS AND BEHAVIORS
Flushed skin
Increased perspiration
Eyes darting around, looking for danger
The character's gaze going distant
Tremors in their extremities
Abruptly sitting down
Becoming quiet in conversation
Pulling at a collar or shirt
Removing layers of clothing
Clutching the chest
Grabbing at their throat
Squeezing the eyes shut
Gasping for air
Shivering
Jumping at loud noises
Grabbing at a surface to stabilize themselves
Taking deliberately deep, calming breaths
Inhaling through the nose and exhaling out of the mouth
Swallowing deeply
Fanning themselves with a hand
Swaying on their feet
Rolling the neck and shoulders
Holding onto a comfort item
Clutching a pet or trusted person
Insisting that windows and doors remain open
Exiting a social gathering and looking for privacy
Avoiding social get-togethers

INTERNAL SENSATIONS
Difficulty drawing a full breath
Weakness in the limbs
A sharpness in the chest
The hands going numb or tingly
The pulse or heartbeat being magnified in the character's ears
Chills
Feeling faint
Seeing spots

A dry mouth
A pounding heart
Abdominal cramping
The throat tightening, feeling like it's closing
A spike in adrenaline
Feeling overheated
Muscles tightening
The character's vision narrowing
Vertigo

MENTAL RESPONSES
The flight response kicking in
Feeling a sense of impending danger or doom
Muddled thoughts
Losing all sense of place and time
Being overwhelmed with anxiety and fear
Thoughts rushing to worst-case scenarios
The character fearing they're losing control
Embarrassment (if the character experiences an attack around others)
Worrying about what other people think of them
Trying to calm themselves down
Focusing on breathing or grounding exercises
Mentally working to relax the muscles
The character thinking they're losing their mind
Fearing they're not getting better and there is no hope for improvement
Praying for deliverance
Believing they're suffering a severe medical event, such as a heart attack
Dissociating from reality

EFFORTS TO HIDE THE PANIC ATTACK
A forced smile
The character excusing themselves for "fresh air"
Claiming that an emergency has come up so they can leave
Wrapping their arms around themselves
Turning away from others
Dismissing other people's concerns or questions
Abruptly quitting an activity (shopping, a work project, a game, etc.)
Diverting attention away from triggering conversations or subjects
Subtly trying to slow their breaths
Meditating or practicing mindfulness

ASSOCIATED POWER VERBS: Clench, breathe, inhale, exhale, ground, dread, focus, concentrate, gasp, hyperventilate, overheat, palpitate, thud, hammer, seize, shudder, tremble, withdraw, exit, flee

EMOTIONS GENERATED BY THIS AMPLIFIER: Anxiety, Apprehension, Concern, Desperation, Discouragement, Dread, Embarrassment, Fear, Frustration, Inadequacy, Panic, Powerlessness, Resentment, Self-Pity, Shame, Vulnerability, Worry

DUTIES OR DESIRES THAT MAY BE MORE DIFFICULT TO FULFILL

Independence and self-reliance; wanting to manage on their own
Staying informed about current events (which is difficult because of the anxiety that comes from watching the news)
Being perceived as strong and capable
Getting a full night's sleep
Not relying on medication to cope
Avoiding a past trauma at the root of the panic attacks
Attending social gatherings with family and friends
Traveling by plane, train, or bus
Visiting specific places that have triggered attacks in the past
Speaking to a large group
Achieving a dream that would be threatened by a mental health condition, such as fostering a child or engaging in military service
Being spontaneous and trying new things

SCENARIOS FOR BUILDING CONFLICT AND TENSION

Working with a person who stresses the character
An unforeseen financial burden, such as a car repair or medical expense
Becoming intolerant to medication that controls the attacks
A friend or family member freaking out during an attack and calling an ambulance
Sensing that a panic attack is coming on in a public place
Having to explain to people what's going on
Needing to visit a triggering location
Being in an abusive relationship with someone who enjoys triggering the character
The character's panic attack frightening someone in their care
Feeling the onset of an attack before an interview, legal proceeding, or speaking event
Being alone and needing help or support
Others dismissing the panic as something minor the character should be able to control
Needing to be alone to recover after the attack but being surrounded by people
Suffering an attack in the middle of an emergency

> **WRITER'S TIP:** *If a panic attack is impending for your character, carefully consider the location. While an attack is terrifying wherever it occurs, it can be more difficult in public or at time when they want to make a good impression. It can also be helpful to think about who is present. Will the character be surrounded by sympathetic and supportive people, or will they have to go through it with someone characterized by intolerance and ignorance?*

PHYSICAL DISORIENTATION

DESCRIPTION: Physical disorientation arises when the character doesn't know where they are, or they're confused about their current location. This can happen if they get lost, suffer a head injury, become disoriented due to being intoxicated, or pass out (or are knocked out) and wake up in a new place. It can also occur with a character experiencing cognitive decline who returns to clarity and doesn't know where they are.

PHYSICAL SIGNALS AND BEHAVIORS

Staring about blankly
Blinking quickly
Squinting the eyes to look into the distance
Turning around to look in all directions
Studying a map or compass
Looking for someone who can provide information (a police officer, taxi driver, etc.)
Approaching strangers for help
Retracing their steps
Laughing nervously
Looking for landmarks
Clearing their throat
Following other people, hoping they'll lead the character to a landmark
Checking their phone to see how many bars it has
Biting the lips or inside of the cheek
Leaning over with their hands on their knees
Mumbling under the breath
Their voice changing in pitch, tone, or volume
Taking meandering steps
Touching their fingers to their lips
Stumbling over their words
Putting their head in their hands
Dropping their bag(s) to the ground
Pacing back and forth
Loosening their clothing
Dropping their head back
Swearing
Apologizing to others in their group
Snapping at other people in the party
Blaming others for this situation
Heading toward high ground (to get better reception, see the whole area, etc.)
Scanning the horizon
Checking the sky for planes or helicopters
Shouting for help
Devolving into tears
Following worn paths, streams, or roads
Gathering materials to start a signal fire

INTERNAL SENSATIONS
Breaths coming faster
Tightness in the throat
A rush of adrenaline
A tightening abdomen
The mouth going dry
Having no appetite
Feeling waves of cold or heat
Weakness in the legs
Heart palpitations
Lightheadedness
Narrowed vision

MENTAL RESPONSES
Erratic thought processes
Shock and confusion; being unable to understand how this happened
Regretting not being better prepared
Wishing for comfort and familiarity
Becoming more observant; noticing specific details about the environment
Looking for familiar signs or anything the character might remember
Retreating inward
Feeling unsafe
Telling themselves it's going to be okay
Being so focused on the situation it's difficult to respond to other people
Trying to remember past conversations, experiences, and knowledge that may help
Mentally beating themselves up for ending up in this situation
Not trusting their senses
Second-guessing their decisions
Mentally inventorying supplies to see if they're going to run out
Thinking of people who might notice they're missing and come looking for them
Oscillating between hope and despair
Fretting over loved ones worrying about what's happened to the character
Resenting the person responsible for getting the party lost
Increased connection with the people the character is with
Fearing they'll never find their way home
Panic

EFFORTS TO HIDE THE DISORIENTATION
The character claiming they know where they are and where to go
Maintaining possession of the map or compass for easy reference
Keeping up a steady stream of lighthearted conversation
False enthusiasm and positivity
Faking a smile and cracking jokes
Avoiding eye contact with others
The character's gaze casting about furtively as they look for something familiar

Seeking privacy to consult a map
Moving with false purpose and confidence

ASSOCIATED POWER VERBS: Drift, observe, ramble, reassure, replay, retrace, roam, signal, study, wander, yell, listen, panic, worry, scramble, track, mark, scan, inventory, seek, ask, follow, retreat, search, conserve, pace

EMOTIONS GENERATED BY THIS AMPLIFIER: Agitation, Anger, Apprehension, Confusion, Defensiveness, Desperation, Determination, Dread, Fear, Flustered, Frustration, Guilt, Homesickness, Inadequacy, Insecurity, Loneliness, Longing, Nervousness, Overwhelmed, Regret, Resentment, Resignation, Stunned, Vulnerability

DUTIES OR DESIRES THAT MAY BE MORE DIFFICULT TO FULFILL
Maintaining a leadership role
Being on time for a scheduled engagement
Proving capability and responsibility
Remaining safe (since the character doesn't know what areas to avoid and may not have necessary supplies)
Reconnecting with friends or family
Staying calm and reassuring others
Being patient with the people the character is with
Retaining their independence (if loved ones or authorities believe the character is no longer safe to be on their own)

SCENARIOS FOR BUILDING CONFLICT AND TENSION
Being unable to remember how they got to where they are
Running out of money, food, or water
Having no cellular service
Weather conditions dramatically worsening
A fellow lost traveler needing medication (for asthma, a heart condition, etc.)
Group members turning against the character and choosing to follow someone untrustworthy or incapable
Accidentally moving into a dangerous area
Becoming injured
The character realizing they're not clothed appropriately
A group member wandering off without telling anyone
Approaching the wrong person for help
Seeking help and encountering a language barrier

> **WRITER'S TIP:** *Physical disorientation is often seen in storylines where being lost is part of the overall plot. But it can also be used effectively at the scene level when you want to take your character out of their comfort zone and challenge them.*

PHYSICAL HEALTH CONDITION

DESCRIPTION: Physical health conditions and disabilities are common and cover a wide range of tendencies, compensations, and in some cases, limitations. But while certain endeavors will be challenging and expectations may need to be modified, a condition only becomes an amplifier when the character feels it is an impediment, and a heightened emotional state is triggered. This may occur when they encounter ableism (for example, in the form of social prejudice, a lack of accessibility to public spaces, or being segregated) or face a hazard that is difficult or impossible for someone with their condition.

Please note that this entry is highly generalized and is meant only to kickstart the brainstorming process for characters with specific health profiles. Research your character's condition carefully and tailor your ideas to fit so you can avoid stereotypes associated with their health factors.

PHYSICAL SIGNALS AND BEHAVIORS

Using assistive mobility equipment such as a wheelchair, walker, or scooter
Taking medications that are specific to the condition
Having a service dog
Being assisted with certain activities by a family member, nurse, or caregiver
Wearing custom footwear, braces, or prosthetics for greater comfort and mobility
Walking with a distinctive gait
Moving slowly and carefully
Knowing what activities will take extra time, and scheduling accordingly
Following a set diet
Following a regimen of stretches and exercise, etc.
Wincing, moving stiffly, or displaying other signs of invisible symptoms
Avoiding foods that will make the condition worse
Seeing doctors frequently
Having to undergo surgery or treatments
Employing time- and energy-saving methods (using paper plates to avoid washing dishes, etc.)
Needing to rest frequently
Suffering from bruises or scrapes (if mobility or impaired vision is an issue)
Experiencing speech struggles
Visible tremors
Venting frustrations to those who feel safe
Having to cancel social plans because of a flare-up
Avoiding activities that would be too taxing
Avoiding scrutiny and the spotlight
Having to abandon an anticipated outing because it's impossible to access the venue
Becoming exhausted or being overwhelmed by pain and having to leave an event early
Making excuses for turning down a social invitation
Staying home because it's easier and more comfortable than going out
Pushing themselves harder than they should to avoid being pitied
Putting on a happy front for others

INTERNAL SENSATIONS
Physical exhaustion
Various degrees of localized or generalized pain
Muscle fatigue or weakness
Feeling unsteady on their feet
Dizziness and lightheadedness
Digestive issues (constipation, irritable bowel syndrome, cramping, etc.)
Muscles or extremities feeling heavy and clumsy
Ringing in the ears
Blurry vision
Sensory sensitivities
Feeling like the skin is crawling or tingling

MENTAL RESPONSES
Frequent frustration at the lack of public services or support
Feeling misunderstood, as if no one knows or appreciates their situation
Dreading a flare-up, illness, or regression of the condition
Feeling embarrassed or angry when people stare at or ignore the character
Heightened anxiety in public spaces
Tending to compare themselves to others
Feeling a profound sense of unfairness
Being envious of people who don't have health struggles
Feeling as if their differences are on display
Feeling different from everyone else
Worrying that a condition is getting worse
Feeling like a burden to others
Wishing they could do more
Struggling with low self-esteem and feelings of worthlessness
Worrying about finances and being able to afford medications, accommodations, etc.
Not talking about their experiences to avoid being viewed as a complainer
Emotional exhaustion
Developing a mental health condition, such as depression or a panic disorder
Recognizing bleak moods and trying to turn them around through enjoyable activities
Embracing hobbies
Appreciating the little things (and good health days)
Practicing mindfulness and gratitude
Celebrating personal achievements
Living life one day at a time

EFFORTS TO HIDE THIS AMPLIFIER
Bottling up emotions
Lying about how they feel
Lashing out about other things
Rejecting help
Being agreeable and compromising rather than calling out ableism
Withdrawing from others

ASSOCIATED POWER VERBS: Lash out, vent, question, argue, compromise, avoid, wish, daydream, promise, reject, forgive, resent, hobble, maneuver, navigate, test, explain, reach, call out, problem-solve, adapt

EMOTIONS GENERATED BY THIS AMPLIFIER: Anger, Annoyance, Anxiety, Apprehension, Bitterness, Contempt, Defeat, Defiance, Determination, Disappointment, Panic, Powerlessness, Resignation

DUTIES OR DESIRES THAT MAY BE MORE DIFFICULT TO FULFILL

Cleaning and other household chores
Being spontaneous
Living independently
Finding work that accommodates their condition instead of working against it
Fully helping and supporting others
Accessing higher education (due to cost and inaccessibility issues)
Traveling, especially long distances or to locations with poor infrastructure
Being free financially
Relying on public transportation to get around
Attending events where the character is on display (if they're uncomfortable with this)
Navigating independently (getting to work, handling challenging daily tasks, etc.)
Self-advocating
Dating
Communicating (if speech is an issue or the character has a hard time opening up)

SCENARIOS FOR BUILDING CONFLICT AND TENSION

Encountering an accessibility barrier that keeps the character from enjoying an activity, getting the most from their education, or being able to compete with others
Pointing out ableism and being attacked for it, increasing the character's trauma
A falling out with a friend or family member within their support system
Having to navigate the health system alone
Being bullied and harassed by others
Being taken advantage of
Being discriminated against
Feeling unsafe in a situation because of a lack of support, malfunctioning aids (such as wheelchair's battery dying), or a threat they don't think they can fight alone
Spending time with family members who are superficial, spoiled, lazy, or always negative

> **WRITER'S TIP:** *When writing a character's responses to this amplifier, consider their personality traits and how long they've had their condition or disability. A person still learning to adapt to their circumstances may be more reactive than someone who has lived with it longer. Likewise, a character who tends to embrace optimism over pessimism may have stronger emotional control in challenging moments.*

POSSESSION

DESCRIPTION: Possession occurs when the character's body and mind are invaded and controlled by a supernatural entity. While there are fictional instances of characters being overtaken by positive or neutral beings, this entry covers possessions by evil entities.

PHYSICAL SIGNALS AND BEHAVIORS
The character acting in ways that don't match their personality
The character acting too old or young for their age
The eye or skin color shifting
Engaging in risky or unacceptable behaviors
Being reckless
Becoming more promiscuous than is typical for the character
Avoiding religious items, people, and locations
Speaking blasphemously about God and religious figures
Having outbursts that are inappropriate for the situation
The voice changing in tone, pitch, volume, and timbre
Complaining of nightmares
Avoiding eye contact with others
Possessing unusual physical strength
The character sharing information they couldn't have access to
Speaking in unknown languages
The eyes moving around uncontrollably
Choking
Being reluctant to wear clothes
Not sleeping
Calling themselves by another name
Making prophecies that come true
Abandoning personal hygiene routines
Raging
Screaming
Uncontrollable shaking
Having convulsions
The body contorting
Going into a trance
Acting callously toward others
Doing and saying things for shock value
Displaying an unnerving smile or too-long stare to make others uncomfortable
Marks on the skin that indicate self-harm
Committing violent acts

INTERNAL SENSATIONS
Restlessness
Muscle tension

Headaches
Being hypersensitive to touch
Dulled senses
The throat narrowing or closing
Dizziness
Chest pain
A throbbing heartbeat
Suddenly going blind
Being unable to speak
Sensations of physical pressure, pain, burning, blistering, or tearing
Feeling too nauseous to eat
Utter exhaustion

MENTAL RESPONSES
Being confused about what's happening to them
The character feeling powerless over their thoughts
Feeling compelled to engage in unhealthy or unethical behaviors
Experiencing strong feelings of hatred toward someone
Fearing God
Hearing voices speaking in their head
Experiencing delusions
Wanting to hurt someone else
Paranoia
Experiencing night terrors
Having suicidal thoughts
"Blacking out;" being unable to account for chunks of time
Struggling to determine what's real and what's not
Being terrified of being left alone
Feeling unsafe to the point of panic

EFFORTS (ON THE ENTITY'S PART) TO HIDE THE POSSESSION
Blaming others for things that happen
Feigning innocence
Gaslighting the people around the character
Offering false apologies
Leveraging the insecurities of others
Playing people against each other
Blaming their behavior on a lack of sleep, sickness, grief, trauma, or whatever fits
Using the character's knowledge and memories to manipulate people around them

ASSOCIATED POWER VERBS: Blaspheme, criticize, insult, attack, scorn, convulse, contort, distort, gag, intrude, shudder, shake, tremble, torment, prophesy, predict, blurt, rage, choke, scream, taunt, scrape, twist, levitate, shout, lie, wither, vomit

EMOTIONS GENERATED BY THIS AMPLIFIER: Anger, Anguish, Anxiety, Appalled, Apprehension, Awe, Humiliation, Loneliness, Paranoia, Powerlessness, Self-Pity, Skepticism, Tormented, Vulnerability

DUTIES OR DESIRES THAT MAY BE MORE DIFFICULT TO FULFILL

Staying in control and keeping the entity from taking over
Attending church
Praying and keeping their faith
Concentrating on projects for school or work
Showing love to those around them
Maintaining hope and optimism
Building up their self-worth and avoiding self-blame for what's happening
Expressing themselves clearly
Staying healthy (eating enough, getting quality sleep, etc.)
Being a good role model for others

SCENARIOS FOR BUILDING CONFLICT AND TENSION

Injuring themselves or someone else
Meeting someone who is possessed by a spirit that is antagonistic toward the entity living within the character
Instilling terror in a child or young sibling and driving them away
Being recorded saying something hateful about another group of people
Not being able to remember what happened during a blackout
Having knowledge and memories and not knowing where they came from
Having marks on their body and being unable to remember when or how they happened
Being arrested for a crime they don't remember committing
Being overwhelmed with guilt and shame for their actions because the character doesn't know they've been possessed
The possession episodes becoming more severe or long-lasting over time
Being isolated or shunned by others
Seeking help to understand what's happening, and the issue being misdiagnosed
Having experienced a possession in the past and suspecting it might be happening again
Failing out of school
Telling the truth and not being believed
Acting in a way that contradicts the character's stated morals and values
Strained personal relationships because of the character's behavior during possession
The character's non-religious family denying what's happening and refusing to seek out the church for help

> **WRITER'S TIP:** *Possession as a state of being is widely contested; some people believe it happens while others don't, and there is no verified set of characteristics to define it. As authors, this gives us great leeway in how it can be portrayed. If this amplifier fits for your story, give your creativity free rein and customize it to fit your character and situation.*

PREGNANCY

DESCRIPTION: Pregnancy is the process of growing a child within the body. A character's response to it will be determined by various factors such as age, overall health, genetics, and whether the pregnancy is welcome or not. Due to the physiological nature of this condition, you may find also find the HORMONAL IMBALANCE entry helpful.

PHYSICAL SIGNALS AND BEHAVIORS
Developing an abdominal "bump"
Gaining weight
The hair becoming thicker
Ankles, face, and fingers swelling
Having to pee frequently
Patches of dark skin forming on the face
The breasts swelling
Increased acne
Eating unusual food combinations or foods the character didn't like before
Taking prenatal vitamins
Going to the doctor more frequently for regular checkups
Reading pregnancy and parenting books
Researching what to eat and not eat
Quitting nicotine or alcohol
Buying baby supplies
Nesting behaviors (setting up the baby's room, preparing the house for arrival, etc.)
Sleeping frequently
Vomiting (especially in the first trimester)
Increased nasal congestion
Spider veins appearing on the legs
Crying more often than usual
Difficulty sleeping
Wearing maternity clothes
Wearing flat-heeled shoes
Walking with a wider gait
A dark line forming from the belly button to the pubic hairline
Stretch marks appearing on the abdomen, thighs, or breasts
Gently touching or stroking the abdomen
Sinking laboriously into a chair
Needing help getting up and down
Becoming winded from physical exertion
Being less flexible

INTERNAL SENSATIONS
Craving certain foods
Being repulsed by foods the character used to like
Sensitivity toward odors
Feeling short of breath

Contractions and cramping
Headaches
Nausea
Constipation
Body aches
Itchiness and tingling in the soles of the feet, hands, and abdomen
Kidney and bladder infections
Exhaustion
Heartburn
Feeling bloated
Hemorrhoids
Breasts that are tender and sore
Restless legs
The sensation of movement as the baby turns in the uterus
The body feeling cumbersome, awkward, and clumsy

MENTAL RESPONSES
Disbelief over being in this situation (if the pregnancy is unexpected)
Anxiety regarding what to do about the pregnancy (if this is a factor)
Worrying over how others will react to the news
Wanting to be excited but being afraid (due to a past miscarriage)
Being happy about the baby while also grieving the loss of independence and certain freedoms
Growing feelings of joy, elation, or a sense of euphoria
Eagerly checking for body changes associated with the pregnancy
Daydreaming about being a parent
Being excited to tell people about the pregnancy
Feeling conflicted about the pregnancy
Worrying about how to balance work with family
Being anxious about the process of giving birth
Feeling overwhelmed by the responsibility of being a parent
Obsessing over the baby's health and development
Impatience (to see the baby, to stop having pregnancy symptoms, etc.)
Worrying about being able to care for a baby
Experiencing wild mood swings
Fearing that something might be wrong

EFFORTS TO HIDE THE PREGNANCY
Avoiding people who might notice any physical changes and become suspicious
Not seeking medical attention
Continuing to exercise heavily
Wearing loose clothing
Making excuses for weight gain
Making excuses for having less energy and needing more sleep
Hiding signs of morning sickness
Refusing to give people hugs

Refusing to prepare for the baby's arrival (not buying supplies, not creating a birth plan, etc.)
Avoiding romantic relationships
Avoiding situations that will expose the belly—not changing clothes in a locker room or going to the beach, for instance

ASSOCIATED POWER VERBS: Abstain, devour, expand, grow, gain, fluctuate, cry, worry, fear, procrastinate, prepare, nest, plan, reposition, second-guess, waddle, vomit, ache, shift, stretch, rub, sing, daydream, lounge, indulge, exercise

EMOTIONS GENERATED BY THIS AMPLIFIER: Amazement, Anticipation, Anxiety, Apprehension, Conflicted, Connectedness, Denial, Despair, Desperation, Dread, Eagerness, Elation, Excitement, Fear, Happiness, Jealousy, Love, Moodiness, Overwhelmed, Panic, Regret

DUTIES OR DESIRES THAT MAY BE MORE DIFFICULT TO FULFILL
Sharing the news (if the pregnancy is unwanted)
Getting adequate rest and replenishment
Maintaining a healthy weight
Keeping up with work demands
Choosing what to do about the baby (if the character's wishes don't align with what a partner or other family members want)
Finishing an educational program before the baby is born
Pursuing a dream that isn't family-related
Having financial freedom; not having to worry about money

SCENARIOS FOR BUILDING CONFLICT AND TENSION
Being diagnosed with a medical condition that requires a drug that could harm the baby
Seeing a sonogram that shows more than one baby
Being placed on bed rest
Putting off the decision about what to do
Having to move in with family
Being cheated on during the pregnancy
Spotting or bleeding during the pregnancy
Being pressured to make a certain decision about the pregnancy
Suspecting there's something wrong with the baby
Having a genetic condition that makes a birth defect likely
Approaching a benchmark at which the character has miscarried in the past
Not being supported by family
Receiving unwanted advice from loved ones
Drifting apart from friends because the character's life is moving in a different direction

WRITER'S TIP: *While pregnancy presents many physical and emotional challenges, it can be difficult in other areas of life, as well. Consider how this diagnosis could impact the character's career, lifestyle, religion, age, and romantic situation.*

PRESSURE

DESCRIPTION: Pressure arises when a character is pushed to act or decide on something before they're ready to do so. This situation is often accompanied by an expectation that their choice will align with what others believe should happen.

PHYSICAL SIGNALS AND BEHAVIORS

Signs of nervousness or discomfort: fidgeting, biting a fingernail, rubbing the back of the neck, etc.

Asking questions to gain more information

Glancing down and pressing the lips into a thin line

Wrapping their arms around themselves

Taking slow breaths

Increased swallowing

Adjusting their stance

Pacing

Wetting the lips and biting down on them

Becoming silent

Lines appearing on the forehead, around the mouth, and near the eyes

Increased perspiration

Focusing on a location, object, person, or symbol tied to the choice or action

Moving more slowly than usual

Repeatedly rotating a ring, button, or other object

Running a hand up and down their arm

Crossing and uncrossing the legs

Running the palms down their pantlegs to remove sweat

Adjusting clothing as if it isn't comfortable

Undoing their collar or belt

Tightly gripping a meaningful object, as if to draw strength from it

Being jittery and easily startled

Checking the time often

Repeatedly checking their phone or email for messages

Skipping meals

Flipping through TV channels or scrolling mindlessly through social media

Abandoning their daily routine

Avoiding the person who is applying the pressure

Stalling for extra time

Making excuses for delaying

Trying to bargain their way out of a decision or find a compromise

Being distracted in conversations

Staring off at nothing, lost in thought

Asking for extensions on work or school projects

Taking medication to help with sleep

Seeking advice from others

Getting defensive or aggressive with the person responsible for the pressure
Blowing up over little things

INTERNAL SENSATIONS
A heaviness in the chest and stomach
Having excess energy that makes the character feel antsy
An insatiable hunger and thirst
A loss of appetite
Rapid breathing
A roiling stomach
Stomach pain
The heart beating faster than normal
Tingling extremities
Lightheadedness
Insomnia
Feeling overheated
Heartburn
Ulcers

MENTAL RESPONSES
Procrastinating
Fixating on the possible choices
Time feeling as if it's rushing by
Dreading the deadline for the decision to be made
Feeling unprepared and incapable
Being overwhelmed by little things
Mounting frustration
Feeling panicky
Regretting choices that put the character in this situation
Feeling out of their depth or doubting their ability to do the right thing
Weighing all the pros and cons
Worrying about letting others down
Feeling frustration, resentment, or anger toward the person applying the pressure
Worrying over the worst-case scenario
Making a decision, then changing their mind
Justifying a decision or course of action that will please others

EFFORTS TO HIDE THE PRESSURE
Wearing a fake grin
Pretending to be relaxed or asleep, as if nothing is urgent
Throwing themselves into physical activities, such as exercise or household chores
Laughing the situation off; acting as if it's no big deal
Lying about having made progress on the decision
Subtly changing the subject when it comes up
Claiming they're waiting on information or for someone to get back to them
Spending more time alone

Binge eating
Drinking more alcohol than they usually would

ASSOCIATED POWER VERBS: Avoid, evade, ignore, procrastinate, put off, excuse, deflect, divert, distract, pretend, bargain, exhale, dread, hyperventilate, rock, ruminate, worry, waiver, weigh, reason, distance, wring, fidget, startle, snap, overreact, explode

EMOTIONS GENERATED BY THIS AMPLIFIER: Agitation, Anguish, Anxiety, Conflicted, Confusion, Desperation, Doubt, Dread, Fear, Flustered, Guilt, Inadequacy, Insecurity, Intimidation, Moodiness, Overwhelmed, Reluctance, Uncertainty, Worry

DUTIES OR DESIRES THAT MAY BE MORE DIFFICULT TO FULFILL
Responding well to new stressors
Relaxing and taking things easy; being able to enjoy a book, movie, or family game night
Being present and attentive in relationships
Keeping up with daily responsibilities and work duties so they don't pile up
Remembering appointments and meetings
Controlling their blood pressure
Making a decision that makes everyone happy
Supporting someone else who's going through a difficult time
Planning for the future

SCENARIOS FOR BUILDING CONFLICT AND TENSION
The deadline for the decision being moved up
Being confronted by the boss about their distractibility
Forgetting a critical obligation that causes a problem at work or at home
Blowing up over something minor
A new problem arising that the character has to deal with
A situation becoming more dire or difficult because the character didn't act right away
Emotional volatility causing friction with a spouse, sibling, or child
Having to regularly see the person exerting the pressure
Being criticized in a way that makes the character doubt their abilities
Making an impulsive decision (to get it over with) that has disastrous results

> **WRITER'S TIP:** When we think of this amplifier, peer pressure is the first thing that comes to mind. But there are many other ways it can be applied to a character: the pressure to make a big change, deny something they know to be true, alter their moral stance, betray someone, do something unethical, give up on a dream . . . the list goes on and on. And the amount of time the character has to take action will also shape their responses. Whatever the situation, consider all the possible external sources of pressure and the resulting inner conflict it may cause.

PSYCHOSIS

DESCRIPTION: This is the state of losing touch with reality, which often includes hallucinations or delusions. A character's psychosis associated with a mental health condition may crop up frequently or for long periods of time. But episodes can also be isolated when they happen because of drug use or a physical illness.

PHYSICAL SIGNALS AND BEHAVIORS

Wide, darting eyes
Flinching at noises
The character frequently turning around to look behind them
Staring at things others don't see
Heavy breathing
Shaking or trembling
Tension and stiffness throughout the body
Shifts in personality—the character acting in ways that are unexpected for them
Saying things that don't make sense
Mumbling under their breath
Using the wrong words to describe something
Speaking rapidly and incessantly
Not finishing their thoughts
Reacting to stimuli that no one else is experiencing
Inappropriate social behaviors (shouting, invading someone's personal space, etc.)
Fixating on a certain topic in conversation
An unkempt appearance (disheveled hair, wearing the same clothes for days, etc.)
Body odor and bad breath
Being active in the middle of the night
Not showing up for appointments and social engagements
Appearing unemotional
Falsely believing that something is wrong with their body
Flinching away from physical contact; protecting their personal space
Embracing conspiracy theories
Becoming defensive or agitated when their beliefs are challenged
Trying to convince others that what the character believes is real
Having wild mood swings
Struggling with structure and scrutiny at school, work, or in other environments
Blowing small things out of proportion
Spending much of their time alone
Abusing drugs or alcohol
Claiming to have special powers
Blaming unusual behavior on outside forces, such as aliens or the government
Claiming to be someone they're not, such as Jesus Christ or the president of the United States
Violent outbursts

INTERNAL SENSATIONS
Feeling, hearing, and seeing things that aren't real
An inability to fall or stay asleep
Lacking energy
Shakiness in the limbs
Spikes in adrenaline
Being uninterested in food
Tense, tight muscles
An inability to speak
A racing heartbeat
A snapping sensation in the head
Goosebumps on the skin

MENTAL RESPONSES
Confusion and/or paranoia
Being overstimulated to the point of distraction
Being overwhelmed by a compulsion
Feeling distanced from others
Misinterpreting what they're seeing, hearing, tasting, etc.
Doubting the intentions of others
Losing motivation regarding previously set goals
Not being able to trust anyone
Feeling criticized and judged by others
Believing their behaviors are justified because what they do keeps them safe or they're on a mission (to fight evil, reveal the truth to the public, save the world, etc.)
Not understanding why other people don't believe them
Agitation, anger, or rage
Believing that someone or something is after them
Believing that someone or something else is controlling them
Fear and distress at not knowing what's real and what's not
Feeling endangered all the time

EFFORTS TO HIDE THE PSYCHOSIS
Making note of ideas and actions they know are off-putting to others and keeping those to themselves
Not letting others into their personal spaces
Changing the topic in a conversation to divert attention from themselves to others
Seeking to match their behavior to everyone else's
Indulging in delusions and psychosis in private
Avoiding friends and family, then making excuses for being a no-show
Not engaging in conversation (so they won't say something others will take issue with)
Matching other people's emotions
Trying to ignore suspected hallucinations
Forcing a light tone into their voice
Dismissing suggestions from others that something is off

ASSOCIATED POWER VERBS: Control, threaten, deny, disturb, laugh, cackle, garble, hallucinate, interpret, perceive, question, suspect, doubt, fear, examine, accuse, withdraw, isolate, protect, distance, convince, persuade, beg, shout, avoid, flinch

EMOTIONS GENERATED BY THIS AMPLIFIER: Agitation, Amazement, Anger, Betrayed, Confusion, Contempt, Defensiveness, Determination, Doubt, Fear, Flustered, Frustration, Irritation, Loneliness, Obsession, Panic, Paranoia, Resentment, Skepticism

DUTIES OR DESIRES THAT MAY BE MORE DIFFICULT TO FULFILL
Maintaining discipline and self-control around others
Caring for a newborn or parenting children of any age
Maintaining privacy (which is hard when you believe you're being watched)
Taking things at face value or trusting what people say
Engaging in a conversation without it devolving into frustration and paranoia
Enjoying public spaces
Sticking to a daily routine without being sidetracked
Fulfilling a dream
Maintaining a good reputation
Developing friendships or a romantic relationship
Being taken seriously
Protecting others from the threats the character believes are there
Avoiding hospitalization
Knowing truth from delusion

SCENARIOS FOR BUILDING CONFLICT AND TENSION
Seeking help but failing to receive care (due to a lack of finances, an incompetent therapist, etc.)
Unintentionally hurting someone
Being reported to the police or a mental health institution
Being taken advantage of in a vulnerable state
A friend or family member trying to coerce the character into getting help
The character secretly ceasing to take their medication
Crossing a moral line that will be devastating to the character when they become clear-headed enough to realize it
Child protective services appearing at the character's home
A psychotic episode being shared through video on social media
Loved ones pulling away because they don't know how to help or what to do
Getting involved with a radical group
Encountering a new situation where the character doesn't know what's real

WRITER'S TIP: *Psychosis is a tricky condition to write because the character often doesn't know it's happening to them. The delusions they believe and the hallucinations they experience are as authentic to them as the real world is to others. Because of this, it will be more important than ever to make point-of-view decisions carefully and know your character inside-out so you can write their story consistently and believably.*

PUBERTY

DESCRIPTION: This is the natural maturing process whereby the character's body becomes capable of reproduction. It involves many physical and chemical changes and marks a significant rite of passage in human development.

PHYSICAL SIGNALS AND BEHAVIORS

Changes in voice tonality
Increased acne
Oily skin
Growth spurts
Body hair growing in new places
Wild mood swings
Crying more easily
Starting to shave (the face, legs, armpits, etc.)
The body producing more sweat
Body odor
Weight fluctuations
Gender-specific body changes, such as widening hips, breast development, increased muscle mass, a deepening voice, frequent erections, and changes to sexual organs
Signs of discomfort with body changes (hunching over, slouching, wearing baggy clothes, etc.)
Neglecting certain aspects of personal grooming because of a lack of experience
Sleeping for longer periods of time
Moving awkwardly or clumsily
Frequently (but privately) checking for changes in height, hair growth, etc.
Menstruation
Ejaculation during sleep
Experimenting with masturbation
Pulling away from their parents
Becoming resistant or combative toward authority figures
Decreased eye contact with others
Becoming highly dramatic or prone to emotional outbursts
Becoming more peer-oriented
The character experimenting with their appearance to express their identity
Retreating to places of solitude
Taking an interest in clothing and fashion
Passions, interests, and hobbies changing
Becoming romantically interested in other people
Flirting with peers
Pursuing independence and requiring more privacy
Experimenting with drugs, alcohol, or other "adult" interests or activities
Engaging on a deeper level with social media
Becoming more aggressive or assertive

INTERNAL SENSATIONS
Fatigue and tiredness
Nausea
Uterine cramping
Feeling bloated
Growing pains in the legs and arms
Increased muscle strength
A loss of energy
An awkwardness with their own body
Frequent hunger pangs (from an increased appetite or purposeful food limiting)
Headaches or migraines
Sexual urges

MENTAL RESPONSES
Sudden mood changes
Taking more risks
Increased social anxiety
An overwhelming sense of self-consciousness
Comparing themselves to others
Being uneasy about the changes they're undergoing
Feeling emotions intensely
Worrying about what other people think of them
Daydreaming—about crushes, being able to drive, dreams, etc.
Difficulty thinking things through
Living in the moment; not thinking about how current actions impact the future
Wondering if they're developing at the proper rate
Becoming hyperfocused on perceived flaws in their appearance and behavior
Feeling misunderstood
Having questions but not feeling comfortable discussing them with others
Thinking that everything is a big deal
Jealousy; wishing they could be more like someone else
Feeling like they have no control over their lives
Resenting authority figures
Feeling nostalgic for their childhood
Questioning their sexual and/or gender identity

EFFORTS TO HIDE PUBERTY
Living in denial of the changes they're going through
Wearing baggy clothing
Hiding behind their hair
Saying they're too sick to go to school
Hiding an erection
Ignoring the changes in their body; pretending nothing has changed
Hiding laundry with bodily fluids on it
Holding onto childhood items

Acting confident when they don't feel that way
Avoiding "the talk" with their parents

ASSOCIATED POWER VERBS: Arouse, attract, conceal, hide, examine, evade, downplay, envy, exaggerate, mimic, snap, strain, tease, touch, trip, fumble, withdraw, isolate, reject, rebel, push back, yearn, question, doubt, overreact, explode, melt down

EMOTIONS GENERATED BY THIS AMPLIFIER: Appalled, Apprehension, Confidence, Confusion, Curiosity, Denial, Discouragement, Doubt, Dread, Eagerness, Elation, Embarrassment, Excitement, Insecurity, Resignation, Shame, Unease

DUTIES OR DESIRES THAT MAY BE MORE DIFFICULT TO FULFILL
Gaining the independence they think they deserve
Focusing on schoolwork and other responsibilities
Waking up early
Understanding and/or expressing their emotions
Responding appropriately to peer pressure
Impressing friends and crushes
Maintaining a healthy self-esteem
Remaining patient when things don't go their way
Feeling comfortable in their body and being happy with how they look
Being honest with their parents
Spending time with their family
Knowing who they are

SCENARIOS FOR BUILDING CONFLICT AND TENSION
Going through puberty well before or after their friends
Being sexually harassed or preyed upon
Not having a stable home life as they're going through puberty
Developing a crush on the same person as their friend
Developing a crush on someone who is bad for them
Being expected to act older than they are (because they look older than they are)
Having to undress in front of others
Unrequited love
Being bullied or becoming a bully
Having a hormonal imbalance that makes the effects of puberty more difficult
Developing a mental health condition, such as body dysmorphia or an eating disorder
A friend tempting the character to engage in risky behavior (sex, drugs, gambling, etc.)

WRITER'S TIP: Puberty is a time of many firsts, and its effect on a character will depend on various factors, such as their age when it hits, their preparedness for it, and the level of support they have. Take these into account when planning this important event for your teen or pre-teen character.

SCRUTINY

DESCRIPTION: Scrutiny occurs when a character becomes acutely aware that they're being observed or critically examined. This state is an uncomfortable one categorized by feelings of unease, uncertainty, and annoyance.

PHYSICAL SIGNALS AND BEHAVIORS

Becoming unnaturally stiff
The character's face reddening
Rubbing the back of their neck or rolling their shoulders
Raising a shoulder up and ducking their head
The character casting side-eye glances at the observer
Visible swallowing
Sweating
Tucking their chin against their neck
Tilting their head down, cheek-to-shoulder
Pulling at clothes (suddenly feeling hot)
Nervously flashing a polite smile at the observer
Taking care with what they say
Blinking more often
Licking their lips
Touching their face or the skin at their throat
Avoiding eye contact (or maintaining it, to show compliance)
Stuttering or speaking too fast
Buying time to quell their fear—e.g., pretending not to hear a question
Avoiding suspicion by saying and doing what's expected
Double-checking their work, appearance, etc.
Looking around casually to locate an observer (or see if they've moved on)
Being friendly and polite
Overcompensating (with words, actions, effort, etc.) to appear "normal"
Making an excuse or supplying information without being prompted for it
Movements changing (a hitch in their stride, etc.) when they become aware of the scrutiny
Mumbling under their breath to avoid being overheard
Trying to blend in by doing what others are doing
Turning away from the watcher
Flinching and twitching more than normal
Rushing through tasks
Fumbling or dropping things
Taking their frustration out on others (through rudeness, being short-tempered, etc.)
An inability to relax or be still
Wiping away sweat from their brow
Giving themselves a once-over to ensure they are presentable
Fixing their hair or smoothing wrinkles from clothing
Taking a breath and standing tall when approached by the observer
Angling the body or feet (or both) toward an exit

Making an excuse to leave
Breaking down under the scrutiny (pleading, apologizing, etc.)
Raising the chin and making direct eye contact (if defiance fits their personality)
Passive-aggressiveness (using sarcasm, backhanded compliments, etc.)

INTERNAL SENSATIONS
The throat going dry
Becoming lightheaded
The body temperature rising
The skin feeling itchy (as sweat pops up)
Tightness in the chest that makes it hard to pull in a full breath
Body tension
Tightness in the throat as they swallow
The character feeling their heart rate speed up in their chest
A rushing in the ears (elevated blood pressure)
Heat in the cheeks

MENTAL RESPONSES
Difficulty concentrating
A heightened awareness of being watched
A compulsion to avoid scrutiny (by turning away, using hair to hide the face, etc.)
Being overly aware of their behaviors and observable flaws
Irrational worries and concerns
Resenting the scrutiny and wanting to be left alone
Their mind going to the worst-case scenario
Mentally telling themselves to calm down
Planning what to do or say to help them align with expectations
Planning what to do or say that will make them stand out (if this is an opportunity)
Fear of repercussions should they fail or disappoint the observer
The urge to hurry up
Focusing intensely on the task at hand to block the sensation of being watched

EFFORTS TO HIDE THE DISCOMFORT OF BEING SCRUTINIZED
Faking a stretch or yawn
The character deliberately taking their time
Unhurriedly crossing a room
Stopping to exchange pleasantries with someone as if no one is watching
Showing a lack of concern by engaging in everyday behaviors, such as bending down to tie a shoe
Deliberately not looking around
Smiling and adopting a light tone of voice
Forcing their body to appear relaxed
Keeping a neutral facial expression
Making bold, challenging eye contact
Confronting the observer: *Oh, did you need something?* or *Can I help you?*
Going on the offensive: *So glad you're here. Have I done this correctly?*

ASSOCIATED POWER VERBS: Ignore, dismiss, pretend, shrink, hide, sweat, fidget, chafe, flinch, twist, shake, veer off, worry, rush, analyze, audit, call out, check, examine, monitor, observe, pick apart, probe, question, review, scan, study, take stock, test, watch

EMOTIONS GENERATED BY THIS AMPLIFIER: Agitation, Amazement, Anger, Anxiety, Apprehension, Betrayed, Bitterness, Defiance, Determination, Dread, Fear, Insecurity, Intimidation, Paranoia, Powerlessness, Resentment, Unease

DUTIES OR DESIRES THAT MAY BE MORE DIFFICULT TO FULFILL
Having to lie convincingly
Attending a forbidden meeting (with a lover, a spy, etc.)
Pretending everything is fine when a crisis hits
Fooling family members or a spouse
Doing something that is illegal or against the rules
Escaping confinement (or helping others escape)
Carrying out plans that others will not approve of
Secretly learning a skill or completing a task
Faking emotion convincingly (affection, happiness, loyalty, etc.)
Leading a double life

SCENARIOS FOR BUILDING CONFLICT AND TENSION
Having to pickpocket someone (or plant evidence) while being watched
Trying to keep their true identity a secret
Having to pass a note, key, or instructions when everyone is watching
Having to exit an area while being observed
Conveying instructions when the character's conversation is being monitored
Needing to ditch a weapon or incriminating item
Cheating on a test
Having to perform well under scrutiny
Having to pass for someone else, fooling that person's inner circle
The character needing to talk their way past a guard or gatekeeper
Having to smuggle something past security guards or police
Needing to break someone out of a secure cell or facility
Having to fool someone who is a master of deception
Being questioned by police about a crime the character was involved in

WRITER'S TIP: *The character's ability to stay calm under pressure will depend on whether they've handled scrutiny before, what's at stake, their personality, and how skilled they are at mastering their emotions. Make sure how well (or poorly) they manage scrutiny lines up with who they are and their range of experience in this regard.*

SENSORY OVERLOAD

DESCRIPTION: Sensory overload happens when a person is exposed to more information than their brain can process. This overload can be caused by excessive visual inputs, too many sounds or loud noises, strong smells, textural triggers, and even tastes. Some characters, due to their physical and mental makeup, will be naturally sensitive in this area while others may only become overwhelmed in certain environments and situations.

PHYSICAL SIGNALS AND BEHAVIORS

The body going still and tense
Eyes going wide and darting about, trying to take everything in
Voicing discomfort about things that aren't bothering other people
Shielding the part of the body that's being affected (the eyes, ears, nose, etc.)
Shrinking away from the stimulus; making the body small and tight
Wincing and closing the eyes
Flinching or micro twitches
Taking a step back
Turning away from the source of discomfort
Sweating profusely
Breaths coming fast and short
The character's chest rising and falling rapidly
Difficulty following and contributing to conversations
Not responding to questions
The character's eyes not focusing on the person who's speaking to them
Self-soothing gestures (humming quietly, wringing the hands, cracking knuckles, etc.)
Clenching and unclenching the hands
Staggering and stumbling as they walk
Being easily startled
Agitated movements; moving clumsily
Grabbing at the sides of their head
Shutting down; being unable to participate or cooperate in the environment
Asking that a certain stimulus be modified (turning down music, changing the temperature in a room, etc.)
Moving from one place to another without purpose or before tasks are finished
Overreacting to stimuli
Leaving the area

INTERNAL SENSATIONS

Feeling hyper and high-strung
Muscle tension and shaking
The character feeling like their skin is crawling, itching, or burning
A ringing in their ears
Hearing the amplified sounds of their own heartbeat and breathing
Experiencing a sense of paralysis
Feeling like the room is spinning

Sounds being jumbled and indistinct
Headaches
The throat closing up
Breaths scraping in and out of the throat and lungs
The body overheating
Feeling like they're going to explode
A sensation of being stretched too tight
The eyes, ears, etc. feeling as if they're physically hurting
Exhaustion

MENTAL RESPONSES
Being unable to process the sights, sounds, etc. that are coming in
Difficulty stringing a coherent thought together
Feeling irritable and having less patience with people
Being mentally drained
Being preoccupied with getting away
Feeling overwhelmed and anxious
Difficulty focusing and making even the simplest decisions
Struggling to determine what to pay attention to and what to dismiss
Feeling alone; forgetting that anyone else is there
Engaging in negative self-talk that doesn't help
Disorientation
Fear or panic
Blanking out; feeling detached from the situation

EFFORTS TO HIDE THE SENSORY OVERLOAD
Restless cues: plucking at clothing, feet shifting, rolling the neck, etc.
Taking subtle deep breaths
Mashing the lips together
Clenching the jaws
Subtly avoiding triggering venues
The character disappearing frequently or for long stretches
The character always being unavailable for outings to certain places (concerts, amusement parks, crowded events, etc.)
Wearing noise-canceling earbuds but claiming they're for music
Wearing dark sunglasses so they can close their eyes as needed
Claiming to have a cold so the character can maintain a physical distance from others
Making excuses for being distracted or not being able to follow a conversation

ASSOCIATED POWER VERBS: Bombard, shock, overwhelm, overpower, blind, deafen, chafe, spin, assault, attack, glare, blare, crawl, itch, hurt, blast, explode, deluge, engulf, barrage, batter, paralyze, startle, scare, irritate, roar, clamor, panic, enrage, escape

EMOTIONS GENERATED BY THIS AMPLIFIER: Agitation, Anger, Annoyance, Anxiety, Confusion, Desperation, Dread, Embarrassment, Fear, Flustered, Hysteria, Misery, Moodiness, Overwhelmed, Panic, Powerlessness, Unease

DUTIES OR DESIRES THAT MAY BE MORE DIFFICULT TO FULFILL

Completing a task that requires focus and attention to detail

Hiding their sensitivity from others

Attending an event that's loud, bright, or crowded

Having an important conversation, such as confronting someone about an issue or reconciling with an estranged loved one

Winning a competition or contest that's held in a distracting venue

Working in a field where the character must visit locations that will trigger the sensitivity

Caring for someone who is noisy and impulsive or tends to act out (such as a toddler)

Attending a worship service

Chaperoning a child's field trip to an amusement park or carnival

Wearing a work uniform made of triggering material

Leading others (as a tour guide, on a group project, etc.)

Doing well on an important examination

Passing a test to obtain a driver's license

SCENARIOS FOR BUILDING CONFLICT AND TENSION

Being accused by a family member of being melodramatic

A noisy construction project starting at the house next door

Being hugged by someone the character has asked repeatedly not to hug them

Getting to an event and discovering they've lost their dark sunglasses, noise-canceling earbuds, or whatever they use to cope

Being stared or laughed at during an episode

Being around someone who doesn't respect the character's boundaries or personal space

Snapping at someone during a triggering event and having to apologize

Having to meet someone new at a problematic venue

Being late to work, an interview, or a client lunch because the character had to take a few minutes on the way to calm themselves

Canceling an outing with a friend (again) and making up an excuse, resulting in relationship friction

Scrolling social media at home and seeing people out and about and having a great time

> **WRITER'S TIP:** *When writing about any potential mental health condition, careful research is vital. For instance, a character experiencing a one-time sensory overload will have different mental responses and intensity of reactions than someone who deals with it frequently. Learn as much as you can about both scenarios so you'll know how it should play out for your character.*

SLEEP DEPRIVATION

DESCRIPTION: A character can be categorized as sleep deprived when they've been denied quality sleep for an extended period. This state could be due to a sensory disruption (regarding lights or sounds, for instance), prolonged pain, substance use, a mental health condition, torture, disrupted sleep rhythms, a sleep disorder, or high stress and anxiety. For related information, see EXHAUSTION.

PHYSICAL SIGNALS AND BEHAVIORS

A slack expression
Half-open eyes that are bloodshot
Dark circles beneath the eyes
Skin that has an unhealthy, waxy cast
The character looking older than they are
Frequent yawning
Rubbing at the eyes and face
Shaking themselves in an effort to wake up
Putting little to no effort into their appearance (looking rough)
The eyes tearing up constantly
Conversations that are punctuated with yawns
Slurring or stumbling over certain words
The character losing track of what they were saying
Being slow to respond to directions
Reduced strength (a weaker grip, being unable to carry as much as normal, etc.)
Slow reaction time
Limp movements that lack energy
Reduced endurance and stamina
Always having a coffee on hand
Purchasing energy drinks and supplements
A lack of tension in the body (slumping, arms that drag at the character's sides, etc.)
A bent neck, as if the head is too heavy to hold up
Taking shuffling steps (rather than lifting and placing each foot carefully)
Instability; poor balance, weaving in place, etc.
Nodding off frequently (but not achieving restful sleep)
Falling asleep on bus rides, during meetings, and after eating
Hypnic jerks that wake up the character as they're falling asleep
Trying anything to be able to sleep
Seeking out medications to help with sleep
Being too tired to exercise
Misplacing and losing things
Snapping at people over inconsequential things (irritability)
Insomnia
Begging (God, a captor, etc.) to be allowed to sleep
An inability to stop crying

Collapsing and passing out
Weight gain (from using sugar to boost energy or a hormonal dysfunction that causes an increase in appetite)
Getting sick often
Suffering from delusions and hallucinations
Developing serious health conditions

INTERNAL SENSATIONS
High blood pressure
Headaches
Dry, burning eyes
Eyes that are always wet and dripping tears
Feeling spaced out and disconnected from reality
A bone-deep level of fatigue that makes movements harder
Pain flare-ups
Heaviness or pain in the chest
Racing heartbeat
An upset stomach and heartburn (from caffeine and poor food choices)
A buzzing feeling or vibration in the head and body
Exploding head syndrome (experiencing a bursting sensation or a loud internal sound upon waking or falling asleep)

MENTAL RESPONSES
Reduced alertness
An impaired memory
Disorganized thoughts
Being constantly groggy and unable to think quickly
Struggling to concentrate; having a short attention span
Being unable to work through multi-step processes efficiently
Unpredictable emotions that swing to extremes
Increased moodiness and anxiety
Poor decision-making (which leads to taking more risks)
Resenting people who can and do sleep (even loved ones)
Stressing and worrying about not sleeping
Losing interest in sex
Forgetting to do routine things (locking the door, shutting off the oven, feeding the dog, etc.)
Missing appointments
Being unable to spot dangers or discern threats in a timely manner
Thoughts that grow more depressed and frantic
Losing motivation (to achieve meaningful goals, perform at work or school, etc.)
Developing paranoia or mental health conditions

EFFORTS TO HIDE THE IMPACT OF SLEEP DEPRIVATION
Relying on coffee or stimulants and becoming jittery
Turning to drugs and sleep aids to be able to function

Delegating responsibilities (because the character is too tired to follow through or they don't want people to see them doing a subpar job)

Calling in sick to get some extra rest

Passing up good opportunities so the impacts of their sleep deficit won't be obvious

Wearing makeup to hide the signs of fatigue

Avoiding driving or other activities that will be dangerous to perform

Avoiding activities that will highlight their fatigue-induced deficiencies, such as competitive sports or mental contests

Letting others take the lead

ASSOCIATED POWER VERBS: Daze, doze, exhaust, yawn, stumble, drag, shuffle, weave, rock, sag, sleep, stammer, stutter, repeat, forget, plead, droop, slouch, lean, beg, cry, shake, tremble, tremor, slump, limp, ache, distract, worry, nod off, mumble, lose, deteriorate, collapse

EMOTIONS GENERATED BY THIS AMPLIFIER: Agitation, Anguish, Anxiety, Bitterness, Defeat, Depressed, Despair, Desperation, Dread, Envy, Flustered, Frustration, Impatience, Longing, Moodiness, Overwhelmed, Panic, Paranoia, Powerlessness, Resentment, Self-Pity

DUTIES OR DESIRES THAT MAY BE MORE DIFFICULT TO FULFILL

Organizing events and processes

Managing people

Getting pregnant (due to sleep deprivation-induced infertility)

Learning and retaining new information

Driving safely and attentively

Being responsible for loved ones (as a caregiver or parent, for instance)

Being there for family and friends when it matters most

Relaxing and enjoying life

Being active and healthy

SCENARIOS FOR BUILDING CONFLICT AND TENSION

The character suffering a break with reality that requires hospitalization

Developing a sleep disorder from the overuse of sleep medication

Being offered a way to end the torment by passing it on to someone else

Being tortured with sleep deprivation and warned that if the character can't stay awake, a loved one will also be tortured

Getting into an accident because the character fell asleep while driving

Another person being hurt because the character forgot to secure a hazard

Breaking under the strain of sleep-deprivation torture and revealing a secret

WRITER'S TIP: *Everyone loses sleep at one time or another, but eventually, they will get enough sleep and their energy will be restored. This ability to reset lulls people into believing that sleep is something they can count on, so use deprivation to show them the terrifying opposite: that sleep isn't the guarantee they think it is.*

STRESS

DESCRIPTION: This state of tension or strain can impact a character in multiple ways. Prolonged stress can be especially detrimental, leading to serious complications both cognitively and physically.

PHYSICAL SIGNALS AND BEHAVIORS
Rigid muscles
A clenched jaw
Tendons standing out
A gaze that doesn't settle, darting from place to place
A grim turn of the mouth
The character appearing older or more haggard than normal
Shrugging and rolling the shoulders as if to shake off the weight of stress
Rubbing the neck or cracking it from side to side
Running the hands through the hair
Shaking out the hands and arms to release energy
Leaning forward with a stiff neck
Pacing back and forth
Rushing from place to place with a hurried stride
Using shorter sentences and speaking more quickly
Barking orders at people
Speaking loudly or with force
Making demands instead of requests
Not being as organized and prepared as others
Being in constant motion
Approaching mundane tasks mechanically and efficiently
Complaining constantly about little things that go wrong
Relieving stress through aggressive gum chewing, popping the knuckles, etc.
Skipping meals
Being quick to criticize other people or their work
Cutting out nonessential activities (going to the gym, volunteering, etc.)
Driving offensively or recklessly
Yelling at people
Becoming short-tempered
Listening to loud, angry music
Becoming more aggressive
Losing or gaining weight
Picking at their food but not eating it
Procrastination; putting off nonessential or stressful duties
Avoiding responsibilities
Bursting into tears with little provocation
Grinding the teeth while sleeping
Sleeping fitfully (and waking up sore)

Frequently getting sick
Relying on alcohol or medication to sleep

INTERNAL SENSATIONS
Being jittery; feeling restless
Neck and back pain
Muscle strain or spasms
Jaw pain from clenching the jaw or grinding the teeth
Frequent headaches
Loss of appetite
Knots and cramping in the stomach
Digestive issues
A rapid heartbeat (high blood pressure)
Heartburn
Awaking from sleep feeling unrested
Decreased energy and libido
Exhaustion
Ulcers
Chest pains

MENTAL RESPONSES
Impatience
An inability to turn the mind off (especially at night, causing sleep issues)
Difficulty concentrating
Defensiveness
Becoming argumentative
Having no creative juice in the tank
Seeing every little thing as a huge problem
Experiencing irritability that rarely wanes
Developing an increasingly negative attitude
An inability to see value or experience joy in the little things
Feeling overwhelmed and anxious
Believing they are constantly dropping the ball and not handling things well
Not wanting to have to make any decisions
Feeling guilt for having no energy for loved ones
Feeling ashamed for being stressed out by circumstances that don't bother other people
Worry that borders on paranoia

EFFORTS TO HIDE THE STRESS
Telling people *Oh, I'm fine, really.*
Saying yes to things (when no is the better answer)
Closing the eyes and taking deep breaths to relax
Practicing relaxation techniques when others are not around
Seeking release by taking up yoga or intensifying an exercise routine
Giving up free time, hobbies, and activities to reallocate money and energy

Acting capable in public but breaking down in private
Going back to work when the family is asleep
Making excuses for being exhausted, yelling, or other stress-caused behavior
Continuing with the overwhelming workload without making changes
The character apologizing for their tone or actions

ASSOCIATED POWER VERBS: Strain, pressure, drive, pinch, push, wear, drain, harass, distort, worry, demand, force, strive, sacrifice, frustrate, balance, juggle, stretch, filter, churn, dump, burst, wring, heave, sort, choose, avoid, disassociate, fret

EMOTIONS GENERATED BY THIS AMPLIFIER: Agitation, Anger, Anxiety, Defeat, Defensiveness, Depressed, Discouragement, Doubt, Dread, Flustered, Frustration, Impatience, Inadequacy, Moodiness, Overwhelmed, Rage, Resentment, Unappreciated, Worry

DUTIES OR DESIRES THAT MAY BE MORE DIFFICULT TO FULFILL
Staying calm and cool
Focusing on necessary responsibilities
Sleeping well and restfully
Doing a job thoroughly without making mistakes
Communicating clearly, with respect
Making well-thought-out decisions
Unwinding and being able to relax (self-care)
Fixing marriage or family problems

SCENARIOS FOR BUILDING CONFLICT AND TENSION
Taking out frustrations on a loved one who doesn't deserve it
The character canceling an anticipated family outing because they're exhausted
A new issue cropping up, such as the dog going missing or a car breaking down
Having to apologize for being impatient, critical, or short-tempered
Making a crucial error
A ticking-clock scenario that worsens an already stressful situation
Loved ones making demands when the character is already stretched to their limit
The character being pulled over for a traffic violation and losing their temper
Overreacting and being rude to a volatile or unstable person
Losing an advantage that makes things more difficult
Getting sick and being sidelined when time is of the essence
Breaking an important promise

WRITER'S TIP: *If your character is experiencing body tension (a common result of stress) make sure to show the root cause and how the character's emotions and judgment have also been altered. This will provide readers with a more complete picture of what the character is going through and how their physical cues relate to the amplifier being applied.*

SUBSTANCE WITHDRAWAL

DESCRIPTION: Withdrawal includes the physical, mental, and emotional symptoms that arise when an addict stops taking drugs or alcohol. It can be voluntary (if the character is willingly trying to become sober) or forced (because they're being pressured to go without or they've lost access to the substance). For related information, see ADDICTION.

PHYSICAL SIGNALS AND BEHAVIORS
The character sleeping too much or not enough
Erratic moods
Trembling in the extremities
Dilated pupils and quick eye movements
Restlessness
Being overly reactive to stimuli
The character appearing disoriented
Struggling with fine motor skills
Excessive sweating
Yawning and other signs of sleepiness
Spending a lot of time in bed
Experiencing body twitches
Crying frequently
Retreating to a quiet, dimly lit place
Not returning phone calls and texts; going radio silent
Needing frequent breaks from activities
Vomiting
Becoming combative and confrontational
Avoiding places where the substance is present (if the character is trying to quit)
Removing all alcohol or drugs from their home
Changing social patterns
Attending therapy or counseling
Scheduling an unexplained break from work (to get through the withdrawal)
Attending support meetings and frequently calling their sponsor
Showing an increased interest in faith and religion
Clinging to people who offer support

INTERNAL SENSATIONS
Fever and chills
Exhaustion
Changes in appetite
Widespread aches and pain
The pulse quickening or decreasing as the drug leaves the system
Nausea and stomach cramping
Headaches
Excessive thirst

Feeling shaky and weak
Craving the substance
Feeling claustrophobic
Hot and cold flashes
Muscle cramps
The heart pounding erratically
Having vivid dreams and nightmares

MENTAL RESPONSES
Being afraid (of dying, of not being able to quit, etc.)
Reassuring themselves that they are stronger than the substance
Taking responsibility for the part they've played in their current situation
Believing they can quit on their own (cold turkey)
An inability to concentrate
Being unable to think clearly or coherently
Increased emotional volatility
Experiencing high levels of agitation, anxiety, and panic as withdrawal progresses
Believing they're dying
Hallucinating
Paranoia
Trying to focus on their reasons for quitting
Questioning their sanity
Resenting people who are pushing them to give up the substance
Believing they can't function without the substance
Rationalizing occasional use, such as after work, on special occasions, etc.
Feeling lost without the substance
Slipping into depression
Experiencing a spiritual awakening

EFFORTS TO HIDE THE EFFECTS OF WITHDRAWAL
Pulling away from people so no one will witness the withdrawal
Going away to a treatment facility and lying about the reason for their absence
Downplaying the severity of their symptoms
Leaving suddenly (to obtain the substance) and then lying about where they were
Visiting a methadone clinic in a different neighborhood to avoid being recognized
Lashing out due to withdrawal, then apologizing and citing stress as the cause
Avoiding the people and places associated with their substance of choice
Only going on social outings that are close to home or ones that won't last long
Developing a dependence on a new substance to replace the old one
Wearing sunglasses or earbuds to cope with sensory sensitivities
Claiming to be sick with a cold or the flu

ASSOCIATED POWER VERBS: Abuse, avoid, withdraw, pull away, cry, deflect, deny, hallucinate, isolate, quiver, writhe, convulse, regret, retreat, shake, struggle, suffer, sweat, tremble, twitch, use, hide, vomit, ache, crave, need, yearn, fight, obsess, panic, plead

EMOTIONS GENERATED BY THIS AMPLIFIER: Anguish, Anxiety, Apprehension, Depressed, Desire, Despair, Determination, Discouragement, Fear, Frustration, Guilt, Hopefulness, Inadequacy, Longing, Misery, Moodiness, Overwhelmed, Regret, Relief, Remorse, Resentment, Resignation, Sadness, Self-Loathing, Self-Pity, Shame

DUTIES OR DESIRES THAT MAY BE MORE DIFFICULT TO FULFILL
Staying away from people who will supply the substance the character craves
Staying sober
Engaging in physically demanding activities
Going out with friends to restaurants, bars, wineries, or breweries
Engaging in calming practices, such as meditation
Functioning at a productive level at work, school, or home
Being present in the moment with loved ones
Solving problems and thinking critically
Activities that require patience and focus
Attending gatherings where addictive substances will be present (weddings, birthday parties, networking events, bachelor parties, etc.)
Being at their best—mentally, physically, or emotionally
Fulfilling family responsibilities, such as feeding a baby at night or driving kids to school

SCENARIOS FOR BUILDING CONFLICT AND TENSION
Failing to remain sober
The character discovering revelatory truths about a past wounding event or suppressed memory that must be dealt with
Causing harm to someone while going through withdrawal
Naysayers doubting the character's ability to get clean
Remembering past unsuccessful attempts at getting sober
The character's custodial rights being threatened
Having an underlying medical problem that conflicts with withdrawal treatment
A loved one reaching their breaking point and leaving the relationship
Being offered the substance in a weak moment
Their private treatment being made public
The withdrawal becoming life-threatening
Deciding to use and crossing a moral line to obtain the substance (theft, cheating on a partner, leaving too-young children at home to get what they need, etc.)

WRITER'S TIP: If a character is intentionally going through withdrawal, their motivation will impact their ability to stay sober. If an external factor spawns the process (a legal requirement, limited finances, etc.), their success may play out differently than if something deeply personal is at stake. However, even having powerful reasons doesn't make sobriety a certainty, especially if unresolved trauma is a factor. To write your character's journey authentically, understand their past hurts and possible barriers that might make it difficult to remain sober.

TORTURE

DESCRIPTION: Torture is the act of someone being purposely subjected to intense physical pain and psychological suffering. The intensity, length, and severity will vary depending on the torturer's methods and what they're hoping to achieve.

PHYSICAL SIGNALS AND BEHAVIORS

The character's head hanging down, their face bruised and bleeding
A split lip and blood-stained teeth
Skin lacerations, bruises, burns, and scars
Blackened and swollen eyes
Hair that appears stringy, matted, and dark
Their skin chafing and bruising where restraints have been applied
The character holding up their hands defensively
Covering their head or neck with their hands
Bleeding from multiple wounds
Dislocated joints
Bruises and cuts on the torso
Broken bones
Profuse sweating
Shaking the head from side to side
Cutting the eyes toward the source of the torment
Rubbing at the forehead or temples
Swearing in defiance
A quivering lip
Fast, shallow breathing
Backing away from the torturer (if the character is able to move)
Bracing themselves against another attack
Answering questions with vague or noncommittal answers
A strained or tense voice that lacks strength
Speaking in slow, broken sentences
Curling their body up (if they can)
Tensing up before blows
Struggling (or sagging) against restraints
Telling the abuser whatever they want to hear
Physically shaking
Crying
Bargaining
Flinching away from physical touches
Starting at sudden movements and sounds
Groaning, moaning, and whimpering
The character's breathing beginning to rattle or gurgle
Begging for mercy or relief
Screaming
Looking for exits or weapons (when left alone)

Sleeping fitfully when rest is permitted
Suffering from nightmares
Passing out from the pain

INTERNAL SENSATIONS
The heart thundering in the chest
Heightened temperature and adrenaline surges
Vision or hearing problems
Localized, persistent pain
Muscle tension
Salivating heavily, tasting blood
Coughing that causes sharp pain
Feeling a rattling in the lungs when breathing
Burning or stinging skin
Exhaustion and muscle fatigue
Throat pain (from screaming, heavy breathing, and dehydration)
Eventually hurting everywhere, being unable to tell where the pain starts or ends
Illness symptoms (fever, inflammation, skin that's hot to the touch, chills, etc.)

MENTAL RESPONSES
Extreme fear and terror
Having heightened senses, especially regarding noise and movement
Racing thoughts as the character chooses what to say and what not to
Focusing on rage to get through the pain
Focusing on what's at stake
Trying to find vulnerabilities in the torturer
Feeling hatred toward the person inflicting the pain
Planning retribution
Feeling forsaken and utterly alone
Drifting in and out of consciousness
Mentally going someplace else; dissociating
Questioning their ability to stay strong
Being confused about what's true or right
Questioning things they were told by people they trusted
Feeling their resolve slipping
Losing track of time
Being tempted to surrender and give the torturer what they want
Being confused about their own identity
Being willing to do anything to end the torment
Reflecting on death (giving up)

EFFORTS TO HIDE THE EFFECTS OF THE TORTURE
Asking questions to get into the torturer's head and find common ground
Keeping up a steady stream of small talk or chit chat
Downplaying the pain

Telling a joke
Laughing instead of screaming
Lobbing insults or deploying sarcasm

ASSOCIATED POWER VERBS: Agonize, argue, endure, excuse, moan, groan, whimper, beg, plead, bargain, persuade, protect, shield, surrender, suffer, hurt, tremble, ache, scrape, cut, flinch, withstand, yell, scream, shout, bleed, collapse, sag

EMOTIONS GENERATED BY THIS AMPLIFIER: Anguish, Anxiety, Confusion, Defeat, Depressed, Determination, Discouragement, Dread, Emasculated, Fear, Hatred, Horror, Humiliation, Hysteria, Intimidation, Loneliness, Panic, Paranoia, Powerlessness

DUTIES OR DESIRES THAT MAY BE MORE DIFFICULT TO FULFILL

Fighting off the effects of an administered drug
Not succumbing and giving in to the torturer
Getting enough rest to heal
Being emotionally available to others (if the torture is periodic and the character has family they are responsible for)
Correctly recalling details of events the torturer wants to know about
Keeping track of time
Staying physically strong and mentally hopeful
Escaping imprisonment
Retaining their faith
Determining reality from fantasy
Staying loyal to a person or cause (if the character has been abandoned to their fate)
Maintaining the will to live

SCENARIOS FOR BUILDING CONFLICT AND TENSION

A loved one being brought into the situation to encourage compliance
Fighting back and failing
Being pregnant
Possessing highly sensitive information that can't be shared
Developing attachment or empathy for the person administering the torture
Suffering a permanent injury
Falling ill and needing medical attention
Trying to escape but not being mentally, physically, or emotionally strong enough
Being forced to partake in an activity that the character finds reprehensible
Escaping, but struggling with survivor's guilt

> **WRITER'S TIP:** *When a character is being tortured, it's important to consider your point of view and how close you want to bring readers in. A too-close viewpoint can put readers off, especially if it goes on for a long time, so a more distant perspective in these scenes may serve your story better.*

TRAUMA

DESCRIPTION: Trauma is a severe event that causes lasting physical and psychological damage. Whether the character is experiencing trauma during the story or they've been triggered into reliving a past event, the physical and mental responses will be similar.

PHYSICAL SIGNALS AND BEHAVIORS

Freezing in place; becoming paralyzed
Uncontrollable shivering or trembling
The character's eyes going wide, showing the whites all the way around
Veins standing out in the arms, hands, or neck
Making odd noises in the throat
Whimpering
Gibbering nonsensically
Being unable to look away from the source
Arms going stiff at the character's sides
Hands clenching and unclenching
Not responding to stimuli or questions
Recoiling, backing up, or turning away from the source
Shaking the head slowly, as if to deny what's happening
The character's skin flushing or blanching
A quaver entering the voice
The character's voice rising in pitch, becoming shrill
The character's knees giving out
Being too scared to move as a threat closes in
Focusing on a fixed point and not looking away from it
The jaw clenching tightly
The character's chest heaving as breaths saw in and out
Tears welling up and spilling over the character's eyelids
Sweating profusely
Becoming unsteady; weaving in place
Flinching if touched
Clutching someone else for comfort or protection
Hands reaching for a source of comfort (a passed-down locket, a friendship bracelet, a folded knife in the character's front pocket, etc.)
The body curling in on itself
Fleeing
Crying uncontrollably
Screaming for help
Begging for mercy
Adopting a posture that will enable the character to jump into action
Becoming combative; fighting back
Yelling at the perpetrator
Becoming hysterical

Losing bladder control
Hyperventilating
Passing out

INTERNAL SENSATIONS

The sensation of hair raising on the back of the neck and arms
Chills and goosebumps
Tingling skin
Tension in the muscles
A racing heart
Adrenaline surges; feeling wired inside
Lightheadedness
Eyes burning and blurring with tears
Tunnel vision
Excess saliva
Not registering pain or injuries the same way they usually do (shock)
The legs feeling weak, as if they're about to give out
Bladder pressure; a sudden need to urinate
Nausea

MENTAL RESPONSES

Becoming hyperaware and alert
Disbelief that this is happening to them
Thoughts becoming muddy and slow
Not knowing what to do
Feeling extreme anxiety, fear, and powerlessness
Ordering themselves to stay calm
Wanting to scream but being unable to make a sound
The character's life flashing before their eyes
Focusing on survival (looking for a way out, people, a weapon—whatever might apply)
Running through fight-or-flight options
Wondering if they're going to survive
Being terrified to move or act but knowing that they must
Deliberately trying to think of other things
Disassociating; going numb
Thinking about regrets and things they wish they could do differently
Thinking about *what ifs* that would have kept the trauma from happening

EFFORTS TO MASK HOW VULNERABLE THEY FEEL

Complying with directions
Not speaking
Avoiding eye contact
Taking deliberate breaths
Clearing the throat so their voice doesn't crack or waver
Unshed tears standing in the eyes

Using protective body language (arms crossing the torso, shoulders hunched, etc.)
Clenching or sitting on their hands to hide their trembling
Focusing on helping others who are also experiencing the event
Watching for an opportunity to escape, stop what's happening, get help, etc.
Going on the offensive (if the trauma is being caused by someone)
Seeking privacy or a place of safety (if past trauma memories are being triggered)
Not telling anyone what they're struggling with (if the character is reliving trauma)

ASSOCIATED POWER VERBS: Freeze, stare, gape, flinch, break, run, back up, stumble, deny, turn, startle, tremble, panic, avoid, retreat, escape, gasp, hyperventilate, tense, clutch, reach, moan, whimper, yell, scream, cry, beg, shake, cope, defend, disconnect, isolate, numb, protect, regulate, calm, attack, fight, help, rescue

EMOTIONS GENERATED BY THIS AMPLIFIER: Anger, Anguish, Anxiety, Defeat, Defiance, Denial, Determination, Doubt, Dread, Fear, Grief, Guilt, Shame, Terror, Tormented, Vengefulness, Vulnerability, Worry

DUTIES OR DESIRES THAT MAY BE MORE DIFFICULT TO FULFILL
Being there for or protecting others caught in this situation
Staying calm
Thinking clearly and carefully
Being still so a physical wound won't be aggravated
Controlling their emotions
Thinking about the future (or anything beyond the current situation)
Not acting rashly or impulsively
Acting unaffected (if others are around when trauma memories hit)
Controlling their own life and destiny

SCENARIOS FOR BUILDING CONFLICT AND TENSION
A ticking-clock scenario that forces the character to do something quickly
An escape opportunity becoming available that comes with great risk
The character having to rely on skills they haven't used in a long time or have purposely rejected
Having to sacrifice their own moral code to survive
Having to sacrifice someone else to survive
Being gaslit by the perpetrator into thinking the trauma is the character's fault
Developing an injury that makes fleeing impossible and fighting the only option
Being triggered during an interview, performance, or other important event

WRITER'S TIP: *Trauma is such a dramatic amplifier that it can't be employed too often. Sometimes it's enough to simply remind your character of a past traumatic event. Triggers can result in flashbacks, flight responses, and avoidance behaviors that can push them off-balance and create volatility.*

APPENDIX A: HOW EMOTION AMPLIFIERS DE-STABILIZE A CHARACTER

When internal strain becomes too much, rational thought and behavioral control can go out the window. And while giving in to big feelings may provide someone with momentary relief, it usually carries a price tag. If you need ideas on how emotional volatility can alter your character's responses and put them on a crash course with regret, browse this list.

IMPAIRED DECISION-MAKING

- Common sense blindness
- Irrational thinking and bias
- Jumping to conclusions
- All-or-nothing thinking
- Being unable to compromise

COMPROMISED VALUES

- Crossing moral lines
- Breaking laws
- Being controlled by bias
- Giving in to violence
- Doing what's easy, not what's right

MAKING THINGS WORSE

- Taking risks
- Rashness
- Acting on emotion, not logic
- Failing to spot a threat, mistake, or danger.
- Endangering others

QUESTIONING THEMSELVES

- A loss of self-esteem
- Feeling vulnerable
- Inadequacy
- Regret and self-blame
- Becoming self-destructive

DAMAGED RELATIONSHIPS

- Impatience
- Lashing out
- Questioning motives or loyalty
- Misunderstandings
- Shutting people out

REPUTATIONAL DAMAGE

- Displaying flawed logic
- Making mistakes
- Losing their temper
- Forgetting their filter
- Breaking under pressure

APPENDIX B: QUESTIONS FOR YOUR CHARACTER'S WEIGH-AND-MEASURE PROCESS

A character experiences dissonance when two or more of their beliefs are at odds in their current situation. To resolve this, they'll need to do some soul searching, asking themselves questions to get to the heart of what matters most. This weighing and measuring of different factors will be unique to them and their situation, but you can use the questions below to start thinking about their possible concerns. Consider, too, if fears about potential consequences of a choice or action might cause self-limiting thoughts to arise.

Why am I upset right now?

Which of my emotions are heightened, and are any too painful to bear?

Am I overreacting or overthinking?

Would other people in this situation be upset or would they let it go?

What am I most afraid of?

Is this any of my business—should I get involved?

What's better, safer, and easier: the staus quo or change?

Will someone I care about be hurt by this situation?

What will the consequences be if I keep things the same or don't become involved?

What will the consequences be if I make a change, get involved, or speak out?

Which of my beliefs are too important for me to sacrifice?

Where do my loyalties lie?

What would _____ (the person I respect the most) do in this case?

If I do what's easy instead of what's right, will I regret it?

Can I live with the end result?

SELF-LIMITING THOUGHTS THAT COULD GET IN THE WAY

✘ I can't make a difference.

✘ If I get involved, I'll only make it worse.

✘ Making a change is risky. I should stick to what I know.

✘ It's better to go along with others than be judged or alienated for my beliefs.

✘ I don't know what to do, so it's probably better to do nothing.

✘ Whenever I try to make a change, I fail.

APPENDIX C:
DECISION-MAKING CROSSROADS TOOL

When your character learns, experiences, or realizes something that challenges what they believe, it causes cognitive dissonance. To resolve this inner discomfort, they must rationalize what to do about their conflicting thoughts, beliefs, or inconsistent behavior. Draw readers in by writing these four elements into the character's decision-making process.

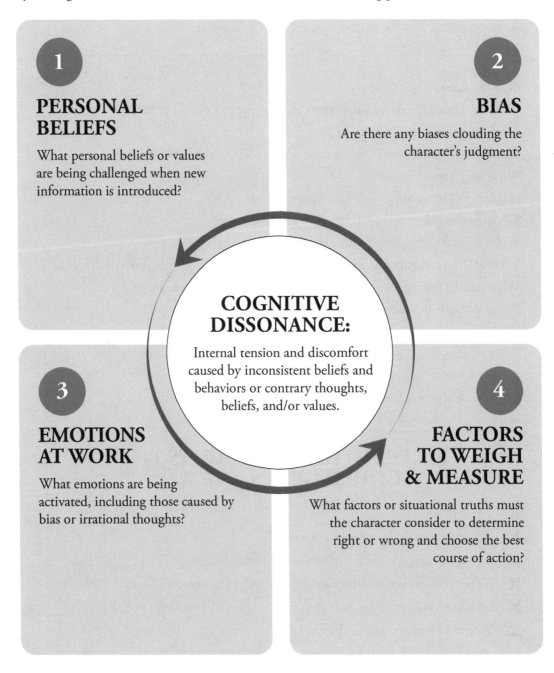

1

PERSONAL BELIEFS

What personal beliefs or values are being challenged when new information is introduced?

2

BIAS

Are there any biases clouding the character's judgment?

COGNITIVE DISSONANCE:

Internal tension and discomfort caused by inconsistent beliefs and behaviors or contrary thoughts, beliefs, and/or values.

3

EMOTIONS AT WORK

What emotions are being activated, including those caused by bias or irrational thoughts?

4

FACTORS TO WEIGH & MEASURE

What factors or situational truths must the character consider to determine right or wrong and choose the best course of action?

Use this worksheet to brainstorm the elements tied to your character's inner discomfort (cognitive dissonance) so you can show how they arrive at an important decision.

1

PERSONAL BELIEFS

_____

_____

_____

_____

_____

2

BIAS

_____

_____

_____

_____

_____

COGNITIVE DISSONANCE:

Internal tension and discomfort caused by inconsistent beliefs and behaviors or contrary thoughts, beliefs, and/or values.

3

EMOTIONS AT WORK

_____

_____

_____

_____

_____

4

FACTORS TO WEIGH & MEASURE

_____

_____

_____

_____

_____

Download additional copies of this template at https://writershelpingwriters.net/writing-tools.

LEARN TO SHOW (NOT TELL) CHARACTER EMOTION WITH THE 2ND EDITION OF *THE EMOTION THESAURUS*

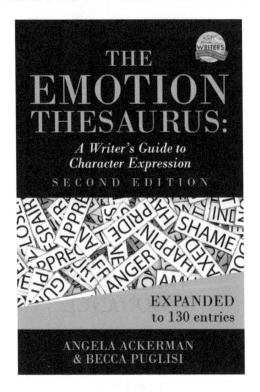

If you've found *The Emotion Amplifier Thesaurus* helpful, you should know that it's best used in tandem with *The Emotion Thesaurus: A Writer's Guide to Character Expression*. This guide spotlights 130 emotions and the body language, thoughts, visceral responses, and vocal cues for each. It also contains a masterclass of information on writing believable emotion, how to convey hidden feelings and subtext, solutions for common emotion-related writing problems, and more.

The Emotion Thesaurus encourages writers to show (not tell) their characters' feelings and is a brainstorming resource to help you as you write and refine your story. For more information on all our publications, please visit the Writers Helping Writers' bookstore page (https://writershelpingwriters.net/bookstore/).

Emotions Covered in *The Emotion Thesaurus*:

Acceptance
Admiration
Adoration
Agitation
Amazement
Amusement
Anger
Anguish
Annoyance
Anticipation
Anxiety
Appalled
Apprehension
Awe
Betrayed
Bitterness
Certainty
Concern
Confidence
Conflicted
Confusion
Connectedness
Contempt
Curiosity
Defeat
Defensiveness
Defiance
Denial
Depressed
Desire
Despair
Desperation
Determination
Devastation
Disappointment
Disbelief
Discouragement
Disgust
Disillusionment
Dissatisfaction
Doubt
Dread
Eagerness
Elation

Emasculation
Embarrassment
Empathy
Envy
Euphoria
Excitement
Fear
Fearlessness
Flustered
Frustration
Gratitude
Grief
Guilt
Happiness
Hatred
Homesickness
Hopefulness
Horror
Humbled
Humiliation
Hurt
Hysteria
Impatience
Inadequacy
Indifference
Insecurity
Inspired
Intimidation
Irritation
Jealousy
Loneliness
Longing
Love
Lust
Moodiness
Moved
Neglected
Nervousness
Nostalgia
Obsession
Overwhelmed
Panic
Paranoia
Peacefulness

Pity
Pleased
Powerlessness
Pride
Rage
Regret
Relief
Reluctance
Remorse
Resentment
Resignation
Sadness
Sappiness
Satisfaction
Schadenfreude
Scorn
Self-Loathing
Self-Pity
Shame
Shock
Skepticism
Smugness
Somberness
Stunned
Surprise
Suspicion
Sympathy
Terror
Tormented
Unappreciated
Uncertainty
Unease
Validation
Valued
Vengefulness
Vindication
Vulnerability
Wanderlust
Wariness
Wistfulness
Worry
Worthlessness

SAMPLE ENTRY: FEAR

PHYSICAL SIGNALS AND BEHAVIORS:
The face turning ashen, white, or pallid
Body odor and cold sweats
Wiping clammy hands on one's clothing to rid them of sweat
Trembling lips and chin
Tendons standing out in the neck
Veins beating a visible pulse beneath the skin
Elbows pressing into the sides, making one's body as small as possible
Freezing, feeling rooted to the spot
An inability to speak
Rapid blinking
Tight shoulders
Staring but not seeing
Eyes that are shut or crying
Hands jammed into armpits or self-hugging
One's breaths bursting in and out
Leg muscles tightening as the body gets ready to run
Looking all around, especially behind oneself
A shrill voice that one cannot control
Lowering the voice to a whisper
Keeping one's back to a wall or corner
Shaking uncontrollably
Flinching at noises
Gripping something so hard one's knuckles turn white
Stiff walking, the knees locking
Beads of sweat on the lip or forehead
Grabbing onto someone to feel protected
Eyes appearing damp and overly bright
Stuttering and mispronouncing words
Tremors in the voice
Jerky movements, squirming, cringing, and bumping into things
Licking the lips and gulping down water
Sprinting or running
Sweeping a shaky hand across the forehead to get rid of sweat
Gasping and expelling one's breath
Slapping a hand over the mouth to silence one's uncontrolled whimpering
Pleading with or talking to oneself

INTERNAL SENSATIONS:
Shakiness in the limbs (causing increased clumsiness)
A racing heartbeat that causes pains in the chest
The sensation of one's hair lifting on the arms and nape of the neck

Dizziness and weakness in the legs and knees
A loosening of the bladder
Holding one's breath, or gulping down breaths to stay quiet
A stomach that feels rock hard
Hypersensitivity to touch and sound

MENTAL REACTIONS:
Wanting to flee or hide due to a sense of impending doom
The sensation of things moving too quickly to process
Images of what-could-be flashing through the mind
Flawed reasoning
Jumping to a course of action without thinking things through
A skewed sense of time
Mistrusting one's own judgment (when it comes to safety and security)

ACUTE OR LONG-TERM RESPONSES FOR THIS EMOTION:
Uncontrollable trembling
Fainting
Exhaustion or insomnia
The heart giving out
Panic attacks, phobias, or depression
Substance abuse
Withdrawing from others
Tics (a repetitive grimace, a head twitch, talking to oneself, etc.)
Resistance to pain from rushing adrenaline

SIGNS THAT THIS EMOTION IS BEING SUPPRESSED:
Denying fear through diversion or changing topics
Turning away from the cause of the fear
Attempting to keep one's voice light
A watery smile that's forced into place
Masking fear with a reactive emotion (anger or frustration) or showing false bravado
Overindulgence in a habit (nail biting, lip biting, scratching the skin raw, etc.)
Telling jokes in a voice that cracks

MAY ESCALATE TO: Anger, Terror, Paranoia, Dread

MAY DE-ESCALATE TO: Agitation, Overwhelmed, Wariness, Relief

ASSOCIATED POWER VERBS: Cast, creep, cry, flee, flutter, force, freeze, gasp, gouge, grab, gulp, hiss, jar, jump, overcome, panic, paralyze, pierce, quiver, rush, seize, shake, shriek, shrink, startle, strike, swivel, throb, torment, tremble, unleash, vibrate

WRITER'S TIP: Prime readers for an emotional experience by describing the mood of a scene as your character enters it. If your character is antsy, the reader will be too.

RECOMMENDED RESOURCES

If you would like to try some further reading, we recommend starting with these books.

The Emotion Thesaurus: A Writer's Guide to Character Emotion helps writers create emotional responses for characters that are personalized and evocative. This handy tool is a writer's best friend, helping them navigate the difficult terrain of showing character emotion. (Angela Ackerman and Becca Puglisi)

The Emotional Craft of Fiction: How to Write the Story Beneath the Surface explores how to use the character's inner experiences to take readers on an emotional journey of their own. (Donald Maass)

The Conflict Thesaurus: A Writer's Guide to Obstacles, Adversaries, and Inner Struggles (Volumes 1 and 2) is a primer on utilizing conflict to build tension and high stakes, challenge characters as they traverse their arcs, and keep readers emotionally invested from beginning to end. (Angela Ackerman and Becca Puglisi)

Scene and Structure teaches authors to build a framework for their novel that relies on cause and effect to serve the story action, prolongs the main character's struggle, and "worries" readers into following the story to the very end. (Jack M. Bickham)

ADD WRITERS HELPING WRITERS®
TO YOUR TOOLKIT!

Over a decade of articles are waiting to help you grow your writing skills, navigate publishing and marketing, and assist you on your career path. Sign up for blog updates to get expert craft advice from resident writing coaches delivered weekly to your inbox, stay informed about forthcoming books, and discover unique resources. You can also access even more practical writing tips by signing up for our Master Storytelling Newsletter (https://writershelpingwriters. net/subscribe-to-our-newsletter/).

PRAISE FOR...

THE EMOTION THESAURUS

"One of the challenges a fiction writer faces, especially when prolific,
is coming up with fresh ways to describe emotions. This handy compendium fills
that need. It is both a reference and a brainstorming tool, and one of the resources
I'll be turning to most often as I write my own books."
~ **James Scott Bell, best-selling author of** *Deceived* **and** *Plot & Structure*

THE POSITIVE AND NEGATIVE TRAIT THESAURUSES

"In these brilliantly conceived, superbly organized and astonishingly
thorough volumes, Angela Ackerman and Becca Puglisi have created an invaluable
resource for writers and storytellers. Whether you are searching for new and unique ways
to add and define characters, or brainstorming methods for revealing those characters
without resorting to clichés, it is hard to imagine two more powerful tools for
adding depth and dimension to your screenplays, novels or plays."
~ **Michael Hauge, Hollywood script consultant and author of**
Writing Screenplays That Sell

THE URBAN AND RURAL SETTING THESAURUSES

"The one thing I always appreciate about Ackerman and Puglisi's Thesauri series is how
comprehensive they are. They never stop at just the obvious, and they always over-deliver. Their
Setting Thesauri are no different, offering not just the obvious notes of the various settings
they've covered but going into easy-to-miss details like smells and tastes. They even offer to
jumpstart the brainstorming with categories on potential sources of conflict."
~ **K.M. Weiland, best-selling author of**
Creating Character Arcs **and** *Structuring Your Novel*

THE EMOTIONAL WOUND THESAURUS

"This is far more than a brilliant, thorough, insightful, and unique thesaurus. This is the best primer on story—and what *really* hooks and holds readers—that I have ever read."
~ Lisa Cron, TEDx Speaker and best-selling author of
Wired for Story **and** *Story Genius*

THE OCCUPATION THESAURUS

"Each and every thesaurus these authors produce is spectacular. *The Occupation Thesaurus* is no different. Full of inspiration, teachings, and knowledge that are guaranteed to take your writing to the next level, it's a must. You need this book on your craft shelf."
~Sacha Black, best-selling author of fantasy and the *Better Writing* **series**

THE CONFLICT THESAURUS, VOLUMES 1 & 2

"If characters drive the story, then conflict operates as the engine to every tale. Keeping this tenet in mind, writing experts Angela Ackerman and Becca Puglisi return with their most ambitious, hefty thesaurus yet, examining conflict in multiple dimensions and on multiple levels. Every writer should keep this volume handy as they work."
~ Ekta R. Garg, editor and author of *The Truth About Elves*

Curious about our books? Download samples of all the volumes in our special
Show-Don't-Tell Pro Pack, available at Writers Helping Writers®.
(https://writershelpingwriters.net/
writers-helping-writers-descriptive-thesaurus-sampler-2/)

EVERYTHING YOU NEED TO CREATE
IN ONE PLACE

Ready for a game-changer?

In today's crowded market, only exceptional fiction gets noticed. So the authors of this book created One Stop for Writers—a go-to web app that will activate your imagination and provide the story support you need to create stronger, fresher stories. It contains:

- The largest show-don't-tell descriptive database available anywhere
- A hyper-intelligent Character Builder tool
- Custom Character Arc Blueprints
- Story Maps, Scene Maps, and Timeline tools
- Idea generators
- Templates, worksheets, tip sheets, and checklists that demystify a variety of storytelling elements
- Craft tutorials and terminology glossaries
- The Storyteller's Roadmap, a step-by-step system for planning, writing, and revising a story or novel

If you've been searching for a resource to shorten the learning curve and help you create authentic characters who are part of well-structured, engaging plots … well, One Stop for Writers will change the way you create fiction. No more staring at the screen, wondering what to write. No more wishing you had an expert to help you navigate story craft. Get ready to write stronger fiction faster.

Visit One Stop for Writers (https://onestopforwriters.com/) and test-drive our 2-week FREE TRIAL. If you choose to subscribe, use the **ONESTOPFORWRITERS** code for a one-time discount of 25% off any plan.

See you at One Stop!

ABOUT THE AUTHORS

Angela Ackerman and **Becca Puglisi** are story coaches, international speakers, and co-authors of *The Emotion Thesaurus: A Writer's Guide to Character Expression* and its many sequels. Commonly called "the Gold Standard of writing guides," these best-selling books are sourced by universities, recommended by agents and editors, and are used by novelists, screenwriters, and psychologists around the world. To date, their series has sold over 1.2 million copies.

Long-time writing partners, Angela (a Canadian) and Becca (an American) first met in an online critique group, and after reading a few of each other's stories, quickly became each other's biggest fan. They began collaborating on books in 2012, and through a mutual passion for helping writers, co-founded Writers Helping Writers, a popular description and how-to hub, and One Stop for Writers, an innovative creativity portal for one-of-a-kind tools that give writers exactly what they need to craft unbelievably rich stories and characters.

Made in United States
Troutdale, OR
08/11/2024

21932628R00120